The Language of Power

Writing About Women
Feminist Literary Studies

General Editor

Esther Labovitz
Pace University

Advisory Board

Marie Collins
Rutgers-Newark University

Doris Guilloton
New York University

Lila Hanft
Case Western Reserve University

Mark Hussey
Pace University

Helane Levine-Keating
Pace University

Heather Rosario-Sievert
City University of New York

Vol. 19

PETER LANG
New York • Washington, D.C./Baltimore
Bern • Frankfurt am Main • Berlin • Vienna • Paris

Roberta Rosenberg

The Language of Power

Women and Literature, 1945 to the Present

PETER LANG
New York • Washington, D.C./Baltimore
Bern • Frankfurt am Main • Berlin • Vienna • Paris

Library of Congress Cataloging-in-Publication Data

Rosenberg, Roberta.
The language of power: women and literature, 1945 to the present/
Roberta Rosenberg.
p. cm. — (Writing about women; vol. 19)
Includes bibliographical references and index.
1. Literature—Women authors—History and criticism. 2. Literature, Modern—
20th century—History and criticism. 3. Women and literature.
4. Feminism and literature. I. Title. II. Series.
PN471.R67   808.8'99287'09045—dc20   95-1690
ISBN 0-8204-2799-3
ISSN 1053-7937

Die Deutsche Bibliothek-CIP-Einheitsaufnahme

Rosenberg, Roberta:
The language of power: women and literature, 1945 to the present/
Roberta Rosenberg.
– New York; Washington, D.C./Baltimore; Bern;
Frankfurt am Main; Berlin; Vienna; Paris: Lang.
(Writing about women; Vol. 19)
ISBN 0-8204-2799-3
NE: GT

The paper in this book meets the guidelines for permanence and durability
of the Committee on Production Guidelines for Book Longevity
of the Council of Library Resources.

© 1996 Peter Lang Publishing, Inc., New York

All rights reserved.
Reprint or reproduction, even partially, in all forms such as microfilm,
xerography, microfiche, microcard, and offset strictly prohibited.

Printed in the United States of America.

Table of Contents

Acknowledgements vii

Preface by Professor Catharine Stimpson xi

Introduction 1

Chapter One   Law, Equality and Women's Work 19

Chapter Two   Sex, Marriage and the Family 61

Chapter Three   Women and Spirituality: A Journey From Nothingness to New Naming 123

Chapter Four   Multicultural Voices: The Intersection of Race, Class and Ethnicity 183

Chapter Five   Power and the Female Contemporary Literary Tradition 235

Works Cited 253

Index 269

Acknowledgements

"Against Coupling," SELECTED POEMS by Fleur Adcock. Copyright (c) 1983 by permission of Oxford University Press.

Excerpts from "Roosters" from THE COMPLETE POEMS 1927-1979 by Elizabeth Bishop. Copyright (c) 1979, 1983 by Alice Helen Methfessel. Reprinted by permission of Farrar, Straus & Giroux, Inc.

Excerpts from "BLACKS" by Gwendolyn Brooks, (c) 1991 by Third World Press, Chicago. All rights reserved.

"Our Tongue was Nahuatl," copyright (c) 1995 by Ana Castillo. From MY FATHER WAS A TOLTEC, published by W. W. Norton, New York in 1995; first published by West End Press in 1988. Reprinted by permission of Susan Bergholz Literary Services, New York.

Excerpts from EMPLUMADA (1981) by Lorna Dee Cervantes. Reprinted with the permission of the University of Pittsburgh Press.

"Refugee Ship" by Lorna Dee Cervantes is reprinted with permission from the publisher of A DECADE OF HISPANIC LITERATURE (Houston: Arte Publico Press—University of Houston, 1982.

Excerpt from "Latin Women Pray," by Judith Ortiz Cofer from TRIPLE CROWN (1987), (c) Bilingual Press, Arizona State University, Tempe, AZ.

Excerpts from H.D. COLLECTED POEMS. 1912-1944. Copyright (c) 1982. The Estate of Hilda Doolittle. Reprinted with permission of New Directions Publishing Company.

Excerpt from I AM A BLACK WOMAN published by Wm. Morrow & Co., 1970, by permission of the author.

Excerpts from BLACK FEELING, BLACK TALK/ BLACK JUDGEMENT by Nikki Giovanni. Copyright (c) 1979. Reprinted with permission from William Morrow & Company, New York. All rights reserved.

Susan Griffin. LIKE THE IRIS OF AN EYE. Harper & Row, 1976. O.P.

From the Book SHE HAD SOME HORSES by Joy Harjo. Copyright (c) 1983 by Joy Harjo. Used by permission of the publisher, Thunder's Mouth Press.

Joy Harjo, excerpt from IN MAD LOVE & WAR (c) 1990 Wesleyan University Press by permission of University Press of New England.

"Pro Femina," copyright (c) 1965 by Carolyn Kizer. From KNOCK UPON SILENCE by Carolyn Kizer. Used by permission of Doubleday, a division of Bantam Doubleday Dell Publishing Group, Inc.

Grateful acknowledgement is given to New Directions Publishing Corporation for permission to quote from the following copyrighted works of Denise Levertov.

BREATHING THE WATER (Copyright (c) 1984, 1985, 1986, 1987 by Denise Levertov)

CANDLES IN BABYLON (Copyright (c) 1978, 1979, 1980, 1981, 1982 by Denise Levertov)

COLLECTED EARLY POEMS, 1940-1960 (Copyright (c) 1957, 1958, 1959, 1961, 1979 by Denise Levertov)

POEMS, 1960-1967 (Copyright (c) 1958, 1959, 1960, 1961, 1962, 1963, 1964, 1965, 1966, by Denise Levertov)

POEMS 1968-1972 (Copyright (c) 1965, 1966, 1967, 1968, 1970, 1971 by Denise Levertov Goodman. Copyright (c) 1971, 1972, 1987 by Denise Levertov)

"Eve" in COLLECTED POEMS by Dorothy Livesay. Reprinted with permission of the author.

Excerpt from "Memories of West Street and Lepke" from SELECTED POEMS by Robert Lowell. Copyright (c) 1976 by Robert Lowell. Reprinted by permission of Farrar, Straus & Giroux, Inc.

Excerpted from "THE TOKEN WOMAN" from LIVING IN THE OPEN by Marge Piercy. New York: Alfred A. Knopf, Inc. Copyright (c) 1974, 1976 by Marge Piercy and Middlemarsh Inc. Used by permission of the Wallace Literary Agency, Inc.

Excerpt from "WELLFLEET SABBATH" From AVAILABLE LIGHT by Marge Piercy. New York: Random House, Inc.

Acknowledgements

11 words from "MARY'S SONG" from ARIEL by SYLVIA PLATH. Copyright (c) 1963 by Ted Hughes. Copyright Renewed. Reprinted by permission of HarperCollins Publishers, Inc. and Faber & Faber, London.

37 words from "NICK AND THE CANDLESTICK" from THE COLLECTED POEMS OF SYLVIA PLATH. Copyright (c) 1966 by Ted Hughes. Copyright renewed. Reprinted by permission of HarperCollins Publishers, Inc. and Faber & Faber, London.

58 words from "DADDY" from ARIEL by Sylvia Plath. Copyright (c) 1963 by Ted Hughes. Copyright Renewed. Reprinted by permission of HarperCollins Publishers, Inc. and Faber & Faber, London.

"Kore in Hades" in SELECTED POEMS by Kathleen Raine. Copyright (c) 1988. Reprinted with permission of the author.

"The Birth of Venus" in THE COLLECTED POEMS: MURIEL RUKEYSER (1978). Copyright Muriel Rukeyser.

"Who in One Lifetime" in A MURIEL RUKEYSER READER, W. W. Norton, New York, 1994, (c) William L. Rukeyser.

"The Poem as Mask" in OUT OF SILENCE, TriQuarterly Books, Evanston Il., 1992, (c) William L. Rukeyser.

Excerpt from WE A BAddDD PEOPLE. Copyright (c) Sonia Sanchez, Reprinted with permission of the author, 1995.

Excerpt from HOMECOMING by Sonia Sanchez. Copyright (c) Broadside Press, 1969.

Excerpt from "O the chimneys" from O THE CHIMNEYS by Nelly Sachs, Copyright (c) 1967 by Farrar, Straus & Giroux, Inc. Reprinted by permission of Farrar, Straus & Giroux, Inc.

Excerpts from THE COMPLETE POEMS by Anne Sexton. Compilation copyright (c) 1981 by Linda Gray Sexton and Loring Conant, Jr. executors of the will of Anne Sexton. Reprinted by permission of Houghton Mifflin Co. All rights reserved.

STEVIE SMITH: COLLECTED POEMS OF STEVIE SMITH. Copyright (c) 1972 by Stevie Smith. Reprinted by permission of New Directions Publishing Company.

"Chinatown" in PICTURE BRIDE by Cathy Song. Copyright (c) 1983 Reprinted with permission of Yale University Press.

Anne Stevenson, excerpt from "The Suburb," REVERSALS (c) 1964 by Anne Stevenson Elvin, Wesleyan University reprinted by permission of the University Press of New England.

"Star Quilt" from STAR QUILT (c) 1984 by Roberta Hill Whiteman. Reprinted by permission of Holy Cow! Press (Duluth, Mn).

"The Centaur" by May Swenson. (c) 1956 and renewed 1984. Used with permission of The Literary Estate of May Swenson.

Excerpts from "For My People" and "Since 1916" in THIS IS MY CENTURY: NEW AND COLLECTED POEMS (1989) by Margaret Walker. Reprinted with permission from the University of Georgia Press.

"Eve to Her Daughters" in COLLECTED POEMS, 1942-1970 by Judith Wright. Reprinted with permission of Angus & Robertson Pub., London.

Preface

Professor Catharine Stimpson
Rutgers University

From the beginning, women in America have written. The first published poet in America was a woman, Anne Bradstreet, born in England in 1612, who died in Colonial America in 1672. The first black published poet in America was a woman, Phillis Wheatley, born in Africa around 1753, brought to Colonial America as a slave, who died in 1784, by then legally free but desperately poor and ill. The first best-selling novel in America was by a woman, Susanna Haswell Rowson, born in England in 1762, who published *Charlotte Temple: A Tale of Truth*, a story of seduction and betrayal, in 1791.

During the nineteenth century, women, both black and white, built on this legacy. Many, like Harriet Beecher Stowe, were hard-working professional authors and journalists. Some, like Emily Dickinson, were aflame with individual genius. In 1891, a scholar, tracing the "Woman in Literature" in America, wrote approvingly that American women had "during the last forty years, supplied to our literature an element of great and genuine value; and that while their productions have of course varied in power and richness they have steadily gained in art."[1] Aiding and abetting this expansion were the efforts, once so radical, to give women a better education. The first institution of higher education for women, Mount Holyoke College in Massachusetts, was established in 1837. In the first half of the twentieth century, the traditions of writing women, many of whom could now benefit from a decent education, grew and proliferated. No genre, no style, and few subjects were alien. One of the greatest of subjects was women's lives and the meanings of being a woman.

Yet, no matter how brilliant and diligent writing women were, they met with opposition—in part because they were women who claimed the right to write, to speak in public, to aspire to cultural power and authority. If they were minority women, the opposition was even fiercer and more ignorant. Women's literature itself records this opposition. Famously, Bradstreet, in her poem "The Prologue," declares bluntly, "I am obnoxious to each carping tongue/Who says my hand a needle better fits." Wheatley, with piercing but controlled irony, writes that some view her "sable race with scornful eye."

In brief, writing women lived, at best, with a mixed message about gender from the larger social order. They could write, but they shouldn't. If they did write, it wasn't very good. If it was good, it was because it seemed like a man's writing. Writing women, of course, were not alone in getting a mixed message about gender. Women were told that they were Americans, worthy of life, liberty, and the pursuit of happiness, especially if they were white women. Yet, women did not have basic civil rights and liberties. Women did not get the vote until 1920, 144 years after the signing of the Declaration of Independence. Women were told that they were responsible for the well-being of their children. Yet, women very often lacked the domestic tranquillity and economic security necessary for bringing up children. Either men could or would not supply this tranquillity and security, or women's own incomes were pitiful.

Throughout the nineteenth and twentieth centuries, these and other contradictions in women's lives have become intolerable. When this has happened, a movement for women's rights has emerged from the messes and structures of history. Women's writing has predicted, encouraged, defined, questioned, and remembered this development. In the 1960s, such a movement re-emerged in the United States and other countries. It is still with us, although modern feminism, having broken into various activities, is less feminism than feminisms.

The marvelous subject of Roberta Rosenberg's useful, lively and provocative study is women's writings after 1945 and their relationship to the society that also generated contemporary feminisms. Although most of her authors are from the United States, she also looks at other literatures in English. She focusses on five crucial themes: work; marriage, sex and family; spirituality; the polyvocality of women, the differences among them, primarily those of race, class and ethnicity; and literary theory, ideas about reading, writing, and texts.

Rosenberg then shows the treatment of these themes changing over the post-war decades. In the 1960s and the 1970s, writers were angry, legitimately so. Their work exposed the difficulties of women's lives, the hypocrisies of patriarchal sex and marriage, the reasons for women's anger. This literature, also a quest for a better and different life, prized autonomy, freedom, and equality. During the 1970s, women writers realized how hard the struggle for autonomy, freedom, and equality was; how enormous the differences were, not only between men and women, but among women. Nor was the public work force a blissful replacement for the domestic work space. If women of the 1950s were to embody the myth of the "super homemaker," women of the 1970s were to embody the myth of the "professional superwoman." Disillusioned, their literature often dramatized bitter sex wars, conflicts between men and women, and women-centered worlds, set away from the sex wars. These dramas of women-centered worlds showed a renewed interest in the central figure of the mother. Then, in the 1980s and 1990s, literature began to imagine the possibility of a rapprochement between the sexes, a redeemed heterosexuality that could permit other sexualities to flourish too.

One of the magnificent themes of literature is that of the quest, the search, the serious journey. Since 1945, writing women have themselves embarked upon a quest. They are travelling though linguistic space in order to describe and imagine the perilous and exciting journeys of our age. These journeys have passed, not only through geographical space, but through sexual, psychological, social and political space. The monsters along the way are us, our fears and needs, our structures of domination and submission, our destructive roles. Such journeys are not yet over; the end is not yet in sight. Therefore, the stories of writing women today are not yet finished. Women, however, are writing them. Roberta Rosenberg's account proves to us all how powerful their literary quest is and how rich their stories are.

Note

1. Helen Gray Cone, "Woman in Literature," *Woman's Work in America,* ed. Annie Nathan Meyer. New York: Henry Holt, 1891, p. 122.

Introduction

> These are the tranquillized FIFTIES and I am forty. Ought I to regret my seedtime?
> Robert Lowell, "Memories of West Street & Lepke"[1](1957)

> The Problem lay buried, unspoken, for many years in the minds of American women. It was a strange stirring, a sense of dissatisfaction, a yearning that women suffered in the middle of the twentieth century ... she was afraid to ask even of herself the silent question—"Is this all?"
> Betty Friedan, *The Feminine Mystique* (1963)[2]

> The personal as political ... has permitted at least some women to recognize that their personal unhappiness has political or social roots and that the best way to ease it may not be to take another Valium.
> Elizabeth Fox-Genovese, *Feminism Without Illusions*[3] (1991)

Although Robert Lowell believed the fifties to be a period of tranquillity, and thousands of television viewers were instructed that "Father Knows Best," the years immediately following World War II were neither as tranquil nor as quiescent as the popular imagination may remember. The decades after the war saw an unprecedented transformation in the ways women viewed themselves, their society, and their ability for self-expression in both literature and life. If any seeds were sown after the war, they were the seeds of rebellion.

The Forties and Fifties: Sowing the Seeds of Discontent

From the first tentative questioning of social, religious, political and aesthetic values and norms in the late forties and early fifties to the radical re-visioning of patriarchal (male-dominated) society in the seventies and eighties, women writers have described, analyzed and evaluated their worlds and given voice and literary representation to what Betty Friedan in *The Feminine Mystique* called the "problem which has no name" (Friedan 1963, 11).

Women in the fifties *seemed* more accepting and complacent about their roles in the given social order than their sixties and seventies sisters, many of whom judged patriarchal society and found it wanting; however, since World War II, there has been a concerted re-examination of established ethical and social norms. Feminism did not, like Athena, spring full-grown from the head of Betty Friedan in her 1963 treatise, but rather was an outgrowth of a society which had been slowly changing since the mid-nineteenth century women's movements. The late forties and fifties were not, as Lowell and others have suggested, uniformly "tranquillized," but rather represent a time of frustration and subtle ferment brought about by the displacement of traditional social, political, religious and sexual values.

If the fifties were ostensibly docile, it was probably in the widespread distribution of tranquilizers to middle-class women who could not "adjust" to their male-defined duties. However, as Elizabeth Fox-Genovese notes, women in the sixties no longer wanted Valium and a host of other sedatives; they would become tranquil, but not before they became free.

Although post-war experts tried to pressure women and men into an ideology of "adjustment" which reinforced traditional norms, female writers from many nations and in many languages, including Simone de Beauvoir in *The Second Sex* (1949) were no longer willing to accept women's inferior status to men in the family, the society, the church or the arts. When de Beauvoir called the traditional woman "an eternal child,"[4] she redefined what it meant to be "mature" and "adjusted" for the rest of the century. She criticized the dependent woman as traditional wife and mother—the "other" to men (de Beauvoir 1952, xix). Instead of praising feminine docility and accommodation, de Beauvoir found that these "virtues" produced a powerless, intemperate adult, unable to assume responsibility for herself or others—hardly a definition of "mature" in any sense of the word.

Furthermore, in 1949, de Beauvoir made the connection between race, class and gender when she compared male-dominated, traditional women to "workers, black slaves, colonial natives [who] like grown-up children ... accept without argument the verities and the laws laid down for them by other men (de Beauvoir 1952, 665). American and British writers who read de Beauvoir's treatise in its first English translation in 1952 were also becoming aware of their connection to other marginalized and oppressed peoples, just as Doris Lessing saw, in 1952, the similarities between disenfranchised black Rhodesian natives and white housewives.

Despite popular opinion to the contrary, the forties and fifties represented an awakening for feminine self-identity. May Sarton proclaimed a need for feminine action in her 1948 poem, "My Sisters, O, My Sisters" when she wrote that women will never find their greatness, will never find their true identity until they equal the power of men.[5] During the seemingly passive fifties, Muriel Rukeyser envisioned a social apocalypse in the form of a goddess of "human love" who would overthrow the male god of war; this "girl," as Rukeyser prophesied her, was "born in a tidal wave of the father's overthrow,/the old rule killed and its mutilated sex." Rukeyser saw the goddess as an antidote to the devastation of World War II, riding "shoreward, from death to us as we are at this moment on/the crisp delightful Botticellian wave."[6]

The Personal as Political: Bringing the "War" Home in the Sixties

Fifties discontent was given voice and authority in the sixties, a time of socio-political upheaval and power redistribution. If there is one constant in this tumultuous decade, it is the persistent questioning of the status quo and the critique of "patriarchal" power. During this period, imaginative writers, activists and average citizens realized that their national and personal problems—nuclear war, the polluted environment, domestic violence—were symptomatic of a larger social illness.

Furthermore, many female activists who had wished to create a more just society after World War II realized that their malaise was as much personal as public. "Adjusting" to their situation, therefore, would not be a sign of maturity, but of cowardice, as Doris Lessing's young Martha Quest learns. There was something about the way people interacted in families and society which kept the environment—physically and spiritually—repressed, unhealthy and anxious.

Although initially women might blame themselves and seek "self-help" books and chemical tranquilizers, many women, according to historian Elizabeth Fox-Genovese, needed to reject patriarchal "good" advice.[7] Instead, these women needed to acknowledge that they, alone, could not solve their gender-related frustrations. Carol Hanisch, who in the late 1960s would be among the first people to use the feminist phrase "the personal is the political," suggested that there should be no psychotherapy, no analyst's couch for unhappy women: "Women are messed over not messed up!" she argued. "We need to change the objective conditions, not adjust to them. Therapy is adjusting to your bad personal alternative."[8]

Thus, by announcing that "the personal is political," post-war feminists interpreted their personal powerlessness as a consequence of inequalities in the larger world. A struggle for personal equality and justice was not a private affair, but a public battle waged with other women—their sisters—against a patriarchal hierarchy intent on maintaining power. These women, would insist on bringing the "war" home into the personal arena—family, workplace, bedroom, church and literature—spheres of life usually thought of as "neutral" and, therefore, immune to political action.

This politicizing of private life, indicative of post-modern culture as a whole, can be seen clearly in Adrienne Rich's attack on patriarchal society as "the power of the fathers: a familial-social, ideological, political system in which men—by force, direct pressure, or through ritual, tradition, law, and language, customs, etiquette, education, and the division of labor, determine what part women shall or shall not play, and in which the female is everywhere subsumed under the male."[9] From this critique of the "personal as the political" comes a new understanding of "gender" which will function as a major metaphor in women's lives and literature for the rest of the twentieth century.

An understanding of the differences between "gender" and "sex," however, is a prerequisite for comprehending the social and literary issues of the period. One's "gender" is distinct from one's "sex" because sex is a biologically determined fact of nature while gender is a "culturally and socially shaped cluster of expectations, attributes and behaviors *assigned* to that category of human being by the society into which the child was born."[10]

When the post-war world began to question all institutional norms, it naturally focused on one obvious manifestation of power—the ability to define human identity and potential on the basis of gender and to impose roles which limit or circumscribe individual autonomy. De Beauvoir and others, however, rejected the concept of "woman" as a divinely designated weak "other" or irrational child and, instead, viewed gender as a metaphor for an entire host of other unequal and deleterious norms which created master/slave hierarchies within the larger world.

The tyranny of gender became a metaphor for many constraints which the powerful impose on the weak and disempowered; therefore, inequitable gender relations became a symbol of a larger Western moral corruption characterized by the abuse of power. An analysis of the ways in which women have been traditionally "subsumed" under the male would provide an understanding of how oppression and repression are maintained in a theoretically "free" modern world. Social scientists as well as imaginative writers would begin to provide "crucial insights into the ways women's experience has been shaped in relation to men's and how sexual hierarchy and unequal distributions of power have become established."[11]

This connection between gender and power, however, was not original to the post-war period. In 1929, Virginia Woolf dissected the nature of patriarchal power held by what she termed "the professors." In her landmark book *A Room of One's Own*, Woolf described the "angry patriarchs"[12] of English society and wondered why men, who held all the money and influence, were so hostile towards seemingly impotent women. Yet, after reflecting on this "absurd" anger, Woolf concluded that it was the "attendant sprite of power" (Woolf, 34). Linking class and gender oppression, Woolf argued that the rich needed to conquer the poor in order to justify their superior position. She then made an analogy to gender relations: "Hence the enormous importance to a patriarch who has to conquer, who has to rule, of feeling that great numbers of people, half the human race indeed, are by nature inferior to himself. It must indeed be one of the chief sources of his power" (Woolf, 35). Her analysis of gender and class struggle convinced Woolf that relations between women as men were "inscrutable" (Woolf, 24) and problematic. However, in 1929, she held out little hope for improvement.

Female writers in the sixties, however, saw this same perplexing "inscrutability," but they sought political solutions in their literature. This topic would provide the substance for innumerable novels, plays, poems and essays; a description of power relations would also lead to one of the most fundamental questions in contemporary literature and life: how does one maintain freedom in a society which often, through physical coercion or, more effectively, subtle psychological pressure, tries to force ostensibly autonomous people into a prescribed hierarchy of values that they did not themselves consent to or create?

During the sixties, poets like Adrienne Rich would begin to "dive into the wreck" of patriarchal culture in order to understand its power and undertow while critics like Kate Millett in *Sexual Politics* (1970) argued that patriarchal gender roles were "perhaps even more a habit of mind and a way of life than a political system."[13] Many female writers equated the power struggles in personal life with other civil rights movements in order to create a feminist literature "committed to uncovering what is all around us and to revealing the power relations that constitute the creatures we become. 'The personal is the political' is the credo of this critical practice"[14]

One goal of the post-war era of women writers and theorists in all disciplines, therefore, would be to write the story of modern woman's dilemma and to present her as a symbol for all disenfranchised peoples; their goal was ambitious since they desired to confront the nature of patriarchal power in order to demystify it. They wanted to analyze how hierarchies function, who sanctions them and how they could be revised or overthrown. Their idealistic goal would be to imagine in literature a personal freedom which would complement and strengthen difference while maintaining equality—an autonomy within diversity. In order to accomplish this vision, it would be necessary to personalize and politicize sexuality and power as well as all the arenas of private life: marriage, family, race, religion, work and art.

In her book, *Writing A Woman's Life*, Carolyn Heilbrun describes this process in terms of "power and control."[15] Heilbrun contends that artistically as well as politically "women have been deprived of the narratives, or the texts, plots, or examples, by which they might assume power over—take control of—their own lives." The acquisition of "*public* power and control," therefore, became one of the fundamental goals of the women's movement in both literature and life (Heilbrun 1988, 17-8).

This politicizing of the personal also helped to expand the scope of "serious" literary topics to include subjects previously thought trivial, the stuff of domestic novels—childbirth; relations between mothers and children; friendships between women; sexual and social relationships between women and men. Literary depictions of women and their pursuit of equitable personal relations became metaphors for any individual's search for freedom within a closed, preordained society. The feminist quest, therefore, was a woman's version of the Odyssey, but the modern epic was in a woman's voice and frame of reference. Gender constraints provided the obstacles to human development which the Greeks had assigned to fate and mortality; and as contemporary patriarchy replaced the classical immutable gods, women's literature found its subject and focus.

At first, however, some critics complained that the new women's literature refused to address the traditional "important" subjects of all "high" art. Many female authors, therefore, had to defend themselves against critics who felt they had undermined the importance of their literature by dwelling on women's "trivial" experiences instead of the "big" issues found in heroic classical literature. For instance, Doris Lessing argued in the "Introduction" to her landmark novel, *The Golden Notebook* (1962) that "at last I understood that the way over, or through this dilemma [about proper important subject], the unease at writing 'petty personal problems' was to recognize that nothing is personal, in the sense that it is uniquely one's own. Writing about oneself, one is writing about others since your problems, pains, pleasures, emotions—and your extraordinary and revolutionary ideas—can't be yours alone."[16]

By viewing women's struggle with patriarchal society as another example of the confrontation between "the individual conscience and its relationship with the collective," Lessing could write a big book with a "small personal voice."[17] Her heroines learn that their dilemmas are not the problems of failed adjustment experienced by atypical, neurotic women, but rather that their quest for freedom is symbolic of all disempowered people in a collective and conformist culture. In collapsing the public and private, the personal and political, Lessing hoped, in *The Golden Notebook*, to "break through the personal, the subjective, making the personal general" and, therefore, of macrocosmic importance—a fitting subject for "high" art (GN, xiii).

The "personal as political," therefore, provides an heroic structure to the literature of female personal struggle; it equates one woman's desire for freedom with the traditional hero's goal to liberate his nation from tyranny. As women wrote fiction, poetry, essays and plays in the second half of the twentieth century, therefore, they questioned the patriarchal nature of public discourse and envisioned a world free of inequitable power. Their new era would be a world of (1) equal laws and opportunity in the workplace and public life; (2) freedom from prescribed gender roles in sexuality, marriage and the family; (3) spirituality and religion unimpeded or circumscribed by an anthropomorphic "male" God; (4) acceptance for all peoples regardless of race, class or ethnicity and (5) equal access to all artistic creations, both within and outside of the academy.

Exiting the Patriarchal Home in the Seventies

The utopian quest described above, however, was not always attainable by the real women or literary heroines who sought it. Literature in the seventies was replete with both hope and disillusionment as women who aspired to greater autonomy confronted unyielding gender realities. Female characters in the literature of the forties and fifties despaired at home, while sixties women took to the streets and the courts in order to find political solutions to their personal problems. Ironically, in the seventies and eighties, when legal and public equality seemed attainable, many women in literature and life still questioned the extent of their liberation. Although laws and public attitudes towards women had theoretically changed in the late sixties and early seventies, women remained tied to husbands and old patriarchal norms. Frustrated by slow progress and patriarchal resistance, feminist activists and writers imagined a "woman-centered analysis" and a new creative space for women.

Obstacles to a more egalitarian society in the seventies and eighties, furthermore, can be explained in terms of the disparity between what social scientists Ellen Boneparth and Emily Stoper define as "role equity" and "role change."[18] As mentioned previously, gender roles dictate patterns of behavior which the society assigns to individuals based on biology instead of merit. Laws can change official government policy and provide access to jobs, housing and education; yet "role change," a transformation of personal attitudes about women and men, may remain unaffected. This distinction is of central importance in analyzing women's frustrations in the seventies: "equity issues rest on basic economic, social, and political values. In contrast, change ... involves the redefinition of sex roles in some areas, the elimination of sex roles in others. Most importantly, it changes the roles of men as well as women" (Boneparth and Stoper, 17).

Feminists who fought for role equity in the sixties and early seventies, to some degree, attained it; however, when they returned home in the early seventies, they found their personal gender roles unchanged because men and women's attitudes had not been transformed as well. It was, at this point, that women, as well as literary heroines, began to ask whether a "liberated patriarchy" was an oxymoron, a contradiction in terms.

The "personal as political" in the seventies, therefore, took on a different meaning. "Political" no longer meant the courts or public activism, but divided into two trajectories. One pointed to the new "woman-centered" reality of Alice Walker, Adrienne Rich and a host of other female writers who sought a world defined in terms of feminine values and voice. Walker's "womanism"[19] and Rich's "lesbian continuum"[20] helped to define a safe haven for women's consciousness and creativity. The other trajectory, however, is less optimistic and more separatist, characterized by Sandra Gilbert and Susan Gubar as "sex wars"[21]—a battle for hegemony or control between men and women. Gilbert and Gubar explain that these "sex wars" set the stage for a violent and troubled contemporary literature. It is, in fact, this cultural environment which makes Andrea Dworkin's thesis possible—that male/female sexual relations are always hostile to women.[22]

If there is a "cease-fire" to this sexual antagonism, however, it is evident in the literature and philosophy from the mid-eighties to the nineties as many artists, theorists and activists of both genders began to seek a rapprochement between the sexes. Margaret Atwood, Jane Flax, Doris Lessing, Terry McMillan, Elaine Showalter, Fay Weldon are just a few of the contemporary writers who view the predicament of all people—real or imagined—as prisoners of gender. And yet, this new communal effort is just beginning as this book is written. The decade of the nineties will test the compassion, patience and fortitude of all people interested in human equality.

The Language of Power: Women and Literature: 1945 to the Present

Each chapter in this book will analyze a prevalent theme in the literature written by women from 1945 to the present. Although a survey of literature written by men would have been an excellent complement, the constraints of space have limited the discussion to female-authored texts only. This book could not hope to be even a comprehensive study of all female authors writing after World War II. Instead, five literary themes are analyzed in literature and social history and several representative texts are provided in order to give the reader a sense of the important issues discussed in women's literature of the period. Women's attitudes towards work; marriage, sex, and the family; spirituality; race and ethnicity; and literary theory changed dramatically during the latter half of the twentieth century, and it is the goal of this book to explain and illustrate this transformation from the late forties through the nineties. If there is one central idea which unites this diverse literature, it is the knowledge that unequal power relations permeate and color all aspects of women's lives, politically, socially, culturally and artistically.

Chapter One, "Law, Equality and Women's Work," explores the societal factors which bring about changes in the public workplace and women's professions. As more women work outside the home and have fewer children, literature imaginatively portrays female characters confronting all the dangers, tensions and triumphs of working women. Contemporary literature represents these women as they attempt to maintain their balance in a world of shifting loyalties and new commitments. No longer "safe" in the separate sphere of the home, women begin to develop the resources to participate in public life and, yet, maintain their ties to the home. Some writers optimistically explore the new opportunities for self-determination and economic enfranchisement. However, many authors acknowledge the price that must be paid in personal terms.

Although female characters experience problems similar in kind to those encountered by successful male characters, they often face additional dilemmas because the patriarchal social order will not or can not accommodate itself easily to a female presence. In addition, the almost obsessive quest for "meaningful work" in the fifties and sixties is tempered by the experiences of women in the literature of the seventies and eighties. "Meaningful" to whom they ask in the late eighties? In addition, the loneliness of success is a pervasive theme in the literature of the period as female characters appreciate but react ambivalently to their newly won economic empowerment.

Chapter Two, "Sex, Marriage and the Family," explores familial and sexual relations as they are transformed by modern life. Divorce, single-parenting, birth control and liberated gender norms all contribute to a redefinition of sex, marriage and the family in literature and life. Increasingly freed from patriarchal definitions of a male-centered nuclear family, female literary characters create their own norms and gender arrangements. However, many contemporary writers find both excitement and anxiety in the opportunities which arise from this freedom.

Frustrated and constrained by the oppressive homogeneity of the fifties suburbs or the racism and sexism of white America, white and black female characters in the sixties seek the liberty to experiment sexually and socially in a variety of nontraditional relationships. The elation over sexual emancipation and increased autonomy, however, is tempered in the seventies and eighties by a need for a new communalism, a maternity no longer defined by masculine property rights and heterosexual marriage; some female authors reject masculinity altogether in favor of a woman-centered reality distinct from patriarchal society.

Motherhood as a literal and metaphoric heroism, the ultimate bond between women and their children, therefore, becomes one of the central themes in women's writing during the contemporary period. However, this newly emancipated woman who rejected patriarchal familial norms and oppressive gender roles is sometimes isolated and self-critical, even as she prides herself on her willingness to experiment and create her own destiny.

Chapter Three, "Women and Spirituality: A Journey" explores the changing female attitudes towards the established Judeo-Christian tradition and the "fatherhood" of the divine. Whether their vision is "orthodox" in its orientation—holding to an established set of traditional Western religious rules and observances—or "heterodox"—departing from a specific church doctrine in order to formulate a personal theological alternative, post-war women confront the power issues which they insist are found in the spiritual as well as secular life.

Women writers discuss the changing conceptions of God, faith, guilt and redemption as their characters question the male-centered conceptions of the divine. Devout *and* atheistic contemporary authors alike portray a female character who is caught within the strictures of a repressive or moribund Judeo-Christian tradition and follow her revolt from or revision of her spirituality. Sometimes this rebellion leads to a rejection of organized religion altogether; othertimes, women characters seek an alternative which transcends traditional hierarchies and embraces a woman-centered spirituality or the worship of the goddess.

Heretics, mystics, questers of all faiths and orthodoxies inhabit women's literature in the last half of the twentieth century. Some are empowered by their newly acquired freedom while others see the specter of chaos, in a "de-centered" world without the stabilizing presence of God, the father. What characterizes this "theopolitical" debate about feminine spirituality, however, is the knowledge of choice and self-empowerment; no longer forced to practice the religion of their fathers, contemporary women are free to recreate, revise or maintain their traditional faiths.

Chapter Four, **"Multicultural Voices: The Intersection of Race, Class, Ethnicity and Gender,"** is both a critique of and a complement to white, middle-class women's imaginative literature. Although women may share similar experiences of oppression, it becomes evident quite early in the feminist movement that women of color, the poor and ethnically diverse women encounter unique problems in patriarchal society. White, female authors can empathize about shared hardships, but women from multicultural backgrounds must also speak for themselves. The nature of racial and class oppression and its power to distort and dehumanize are important themes in this contemporary literature.

Multicultural contemporary literature is also an optimistic new force because it seeks community in diversity within an often fragmented, post-modern world. Paula Gunn Allen, Alice Walker, Maxine Hong Kingston, Tillie Olsen and other multicultural writers provide new voices in literature, voices long silenced by racial prejudice, poverty and ethnic bigotry. "Speaking for themselves," therefore, becomes not only an artistic act of faith, but another example of political activism. Traditions long ignored or denigrated are finally, in the latter half of the twentieth century, given voice, substance and artistic empowerment during this period. And readers from all backgrounds are introduced, possibly for the first time, to a rich variety of new perspectives and aesthetic visions.

The Conclusion, **"Power and the Contemporary Female Literary Tradition,"** is an assessment of women's post-war aesthetic theory and its impact on literature and feminist thought. As women enter the previously male bastions of education, publishing and literary scholarship, they seek not only to change the demographics of art, but also its perspective. They question the "universality" of a Western, male literature previously considered "neutral" in its orientation. Scholars in actual universities and female characters in literature confront a patriarchal view of art which insists on its apolitical nature while it maintains the hierarchies of the Western, male literary tradition. This chapter, therefore, summarizes some of the most controversial questions in feminist literary theory and art today. What should female and male students learn and why? Who gets to choose? Who makes art? How are women and men represented in this art? What is the relationship between a misogynist male literary tradition and actual violence against women? Is there a female aesthetic and can it be traced in literature written by women? What is the relationship between art and life, art and social equality and political action? *Who* really decides and by what criteria? Although there are no easy answers to these complicated questions, many female writers, in fiction and essays, passionately debate the issues.

Women's contemporary literature has undergone some dramatic changes since World War II. Even in the seemingly tranquil fifties, there was a general dissatisfaction and frustration with the status quo and patriarchal society as women sought control over their lives. During the sixties, many female activists and imaginative writers believed that this personal freedom would be achieved through changes in the public world. The term, "the personal is political," therefore, became a statement of individual and communal faith that female activism would bring about autonomy.

However, after laws were passed and policies changed, many feminists and female authors saw the traditional gender roles intact, and the old attitudes unaltered. During the sixties, women wanted equal opportunity and were prepared to fight for it in the streets and in print. During the seventies, however, women authors viewed this equality with greater skepticism. Instead of being more like men, women saw feminine qualities as different and worth retaining. For this reason, a "woman-centered analysis," which encouraged women to cultivate their differences from men, was created in literature and life.

The literature of the eighties and nineties is a mixture of fifties' frustration, sixties' anger and faith, and seventies' celebration and skepticism. A new interpretation of gender which transcends power relationships is now being explored by female and male imaginative writers who seek common aesthetic ground. The literature of the last decade of the twentieth century is often diverse and multi-faceted in its perspectives and visions as it seeks a balance between personal autonomy and communal values. If there is any constant in this literature, it is the belief that the quest for personal fulfillment is not a trivial or narrow goal, but is rather, an important political step for all people in contemporary society—the personal is political in art as well as life.

Notes

1. Robert Lowell, "Memories of West Street and Lepke," in *Selected Poems* (New York: Farrar, Straus and Giroux, 1976), 91-2.

2. Betty Friedan, *The Feminine Mystique* (New York: Dell Books, 1963), 11; hereafter cited in text.

3. Elizabeth Fox-Genovese, *Feminism Without Illusions: A Critique of Individualism* (Chapel Hill: University of North Carolina Press, 1992), 249; hereafter cited in text.

4. Simone de Beauvoir, *The Second Sex*. 1953. Trans. and ed. H. M. Parshley (New York: Bantam, 1951), 665; hereafter cited in the text.

5. May Sarton, "My Sisters, O, My Sisters," in *Collected Poems: 1930-1973* (New York: W.W. Norton, 1974), 77.

6. Muriel Rukeyser, "The Birth of Venus," in *The Collected Poems: Muriel Rukeyser* (New York: McGraw-Hill, 1978), 417-8.

7. For an historical discussion of the medical "advice" offered to women throughout the ages, see Barbara Ehrenreich & Deirdre English's *For Her Own Good: 150 Years of the Experts' Advice To Women* (New York: Anchor Books, 1979).

8. Carol Hanisch, "The Personal Is Political," in *The Radical Therapist*, ed. Jerome Agel (New York: Ballantine Books, 1971, 153.

9. Adrienne Rich, *Of Woman Born: Motherhood As Experience and Institution* (New York: Bantam Books, 1976), 57; hereafter cited in the text.

10. Hester Eisenstein, *Contemporary Feminist Thought* (Boston: G.K. Hall, 1983) 7; hereafter cited in text.

11. Jill Conway, et al. *Learning About Women: Gender Politics & Power* (Ann Arbor: University of Michigan Press, 1987), xxiii); hereafter cited in text.

12. Virginia Woolf, *A Room of One's Own* (New York: Harcourt Brace Jovanovich, 1929) 33-34; hereafter cited in the text.

13. Kate Millett, *Sexual Politics* (Garden City: Doubleday, 1970), 63; hereafter cited in text.

14. Mary Dietz, "Context Is All: Feminism and Theories of Citizenship," in *Learning About Women: Gender Politics & Power*, ed. Jill Conway et all (Ann Arbor: University of Michigan Press), 1; hereafter cited in text.

15. Carolyn Heilbrun, *Writing a Woman's Life* (New York: W. W. Norton and Company, 17; hereafter cited in the text.

16. Doris Lessing, *The Golden Notebook* (New York: New American Library, 1962), xiii; hereafter cited in text as *GN*.

17. Doris Lessing, *A Small Personal Voice* (New York: Random House, 1974.

18. Ellen Boneparth and Emily Stoper, "Introduction: A Framework for Policy Analysis," in *Women, Power and Policy: Toward the Year 2000*, second ed (New York: Pergamon, 1988), 17; hereafter cited in text.

19. Alice Walker, *In Search of Our Mothers' Gardens* (New York: Harcourt Brace Jovanovich, 1983), xi; hereafter cited in the text as *In Search*.

20. Adrienne Rich, "Compulsory Heterosexuality and Lesbian Existence," in *The Signs Reader*, ed. Emily and Elizabeth Abel (Chicago: University of Chicago Press, 1983) 156; hereafter cited in text.

21. Sandra Gilbert and Susan Gubar, "Sex Wars—Not the 'Fun' Kind," *New York Times Book Review*, 23 December 1987, 23; hereafter cited in text.

22. Andrea Dworkin's equates heterosexual intercourse with warfare, the violation and domination of the weak (women) by the strong (men). For more information, see her book *Intercourse* (New York: Macmillan, 1987); hereafter cited in the text.

Chapter One

Law, Equality and Women's Work

> They were forced to spend their days in work which produced great fatigue—not because it was physically killing, but because it was monotonous, endless, required no mental concentration, gave no hope of advancement or recognition, was sometimes senseless and was controlled by the needs of others or the tempo of machines.
> (Friedan 1963, 295)

In her analysis of women and "the problem that has no name," in *The Feminine Mystique* (1963), Betty Friedan compared the housewife in suburbia to the World War Two concentration camp prisoner and asked the reader: is the suburbanite's home "a comfortable concentration camp?" Although the comparison seems now as it did then, a bit overstated, and applicable only to white, middle-class women, Friedan felt that both the concentration camp victim and the suburban housewife suffered from a lack of meaningful work, an essential ingredient of identity and humanity. Both the prisoner and the housewife, according to Friedan, shared the demoralizing fate of people required to do "endless, monotonous, unrewarding" work which lead to "a slow death of mind and spirit" (Friedan 1963, 296).

Friedan's controversial comparison in 1963 was one of the best publicized comments on women and work after the war; however, it was certainly not the first in either contemporary literature or essays.[1] The controversy about the nature of women's work continues to be a matter of impassioned private and political debate. Although a climate of acceptance has replaced the hostility towards professional women found in post-war texts like Ferdinand Lundberg and Marynia F. Farnham's *Modern Woman: The Lost Sex*,[2] (1947) female and male authors have prophesied doom as well as nirvana for the society that allows women to seek equal opportunities in the workplace.

In order to understand the implications of working women in both literature and life, it is important to realize that after World War II the percentage of working women *never* declined; although fifties women did have a record number of children, they also entered the workplace in increasing numbers. According to the U.S. Census Bureau, 24% of women were in the workforce in 1940; 27% in 1950; and 32% in 1960.[3] In addition, the number of women over thirty-five in the workforce had expanded dramatically from 8.5 million in 1947 to nearly 13 million in 1956 (Kaledin, 64). The conception, therefore, of an entirely indolent, passive housewife population, cloistered in docile domesticity in the fifties was more illusion than fact. Although the professional woman was beginning to emerge in the fifties as a new role for the housewife, access to this option *was* limited and frustration was high.

The Forties and Fifties: Confusing Versions of the Good Life

In the literature of the fifties, there was widespread confusion about women's "proper" and, therefore, moral or ethical place in the world of work. After the war, domesticity and housework were viewed as natural and "normal" occupations for women, even though 32%, near one-third, of the female population worked outside the home by the end of the decade. Ambivalence among housewives over conflicting role models, exhaustion on the part of female workers who were trying to live in both the man's public and woman's private spheres led to a general malaise. "What is the right way for women to be?" housewives and working women asked by the end of the decade. Some of the answers, as well as the frustrations, were given voice in the literature of the period.

The "mixed messages" given women in the fifties are apparent in Adrienne Rich's description of her own life. Immediately after graduating from college and publishing her first book of poetry in 1951, she married and had three children before she was thirty. When she looked back at this decision in her essay, "When We Dead Awaken," she admitted that there was nothing overt in the environment to warn me: these were the fifties ... middle-class women were making careers of domestic perfection ... the family was in its glory. Life was extremely private; women were isolated from each other by the loyalties of marriage. I have a sense that women didn't talk to each other much in the fifties. ... If there were doubts, if there were periods of null depression or active despairing, these could only mean that I was ungrateful, insatiable, perhaps a monster.[4]

Feminine frustration is portrayed in Rich's 1951 poem "Aunt Jennifer's Tigers" in which a repressed "Aunt Jennifer" sublimates her rage in the needlework pictures of prideful, fearless tigers who march across a screen, oblivious to male presences.[5] Her rebellious art, however, is ironically executed by hands which are encircled by marriage bands. The Aunt's seemingly pretty needlework is, therefore, a tangible expression of the silent rage which characterized some literary women during the fifties—a reticence which would turn many female authors into "monsters" of frustration.

In "Snapshots of a Daughter-in-Law" (1958-60), Rich describes another repressed woman.[6] Aunt Jennifer's tigers have, by the end of the decade, evolved into angry women whose minds have festered in what was thought to be matrimonial bliss but instead was rage, fantasy and anger. Rich dramatizes the woman's rage as she describes a fifties housewife who attempts to do housework and write poetry at the same time. Her life becomes a loaded weapon instead of a work of art.

The major distinction between Aunt Jennifer and the woman in "Snapshots," however, is that the latter woman may possess the potential for change, the possibility of redemptive work as salvation, even if she is delayed in her metamorphosis. In the poem, the final image of flight from a cage provides an opportunity for the woman to escape the circles which have caught Aunt Jennifer and others. The new active woman will be motion, the antithesis of stasis. Rich envisions her chasing the air currents like a helicopter or a boy—the image of liberated flight.

Despite the optimism at the end of "Snapshots," Rich does not believe that freeing the woman from indolence will happen easily or without pain. She acknowledges that few women will desire to place themselves in the vanguard of any new freedom movement. The punishments for offending women will be swift and severe. The woman's evolution from domestic docility to meaningful work is described in military metaphors usually reserved for public conflicts and war. The right to work, therefore, will be a political challenge to the status quo, not an isolated private decision by an individual woman. Even in the fifties, Rich sees the battle lines as clearly drawn.

Many other writers in the fifties describe similar struggles on the part of women who often, in despair, seek meaningful work in a hostile world. In Tillie Olsen's "Tell Me a Riddle," Eva, an old and dying woman who has been married for forty-seven years looks back in anger at her difficult life and relationship with her husband and children. She, like Aunt Jennifer, resents the endless domestic work which gives her little time to read or acquire a sense of herself as a separate human being. Her indignation, however, can find no release, cannot metamorphose into the swift beauty of Rich's helicopter woman. Instead, Eva's anger is described as an "old scar tissue ruptured" or "wounds festered anew" and finally as a "bitter as gall" cancer which finally defeats her.[7]

Although ostensibly a devoted, conscientious housewife and mother, Eva has amassed a lifetime of anger towards her husband and children who stood as impediments to her own creativity. She, like Aunt Jennifer, felt the terrors of ceaseless domesticity, "from those years she had had to manage, old humiliations and terrors rose up, lived again, and forced her to relive them. The children's needings; that grocer's face or this merchant's wife she had had to beg credit from when credit was a disgrace" (Tell, 67). When her husband asks her to give up their house and move to an adult community ironically called, "the haven," she finally stands her ground and defies him: "She would not exchange her solitude for anything. **Never again to be forced to move to the rhythms of others**" (Tell, 68).

The battle over the house, therefore, is actually a political struggle for independence between the once obsequious Eva and her domineering husband. It is fought like a war, with the male and female children taking sides. However, in 1961 when this story was first published, Tillie Olsen could imagine no "peaceful" truce to this struggle except the death of the mother from cancer.

There is no more hope for peaceful settlement between Eva and her husband than there is a peaceful resolution to the confrontation between nuclear superpowers in the fifties—another battle for control mentioned in the story. When Vivi's daughter returns home from school, she asks her mother about a consent form which was supposed to be signed and returned to school that day. "Didn't you even ask Daddy? Then tell **me** which plan and I'll check it: evacuate or stay in the city or wait for you to come and take me away" (Tell, 87). The symbolic importance of the "disaster plan" can be understood when one sees it as just another example of an insoluble problem of domination between warring factions. Instead of peaceful resolution, countries imagine nuclear annihilation and draw up evacuation plans and erect fall-out shelters. As Eva dies of cancer, she reflects on the outcome of another war with personal effects— World War Two: "*Slaveships deathtrains clubs enough The bell Summon what enables 78,000 in one minute (whisper of a scream) 78,000 human beings we'll destroy ourselves*" (Tell, 108-09). Compromise in either the public or private worlds does not seem a ready possibility in Eva's world of the fifties. Her life has been one of self-abnegative work with little opportunity for creative endeavor.

Another literary work which portrays the confusion about woman's roles and work in the fifties, and offers little concrete resolution is Sylvia Plath's *The Bell Jar* (1963). Esther Greenwood, the highly successful and aggressive main character in the novel is on her way to fulfilling her dreams for a career. She describes herself at the beginning of the novel as the fifties version of a female Horatio Alger: "Look what can happen in this country, they'd say. A girl lives in some out-of-the-way town for nineteen years, so poor she can't afford a magazine, and then she gets a scholarship to college and wins a prize here and a prize there and ends up steering New York like her own private car."[8] However, this feminine version of the "rags to riches" story does not follow the male prototype. Esther, who is as conflicted about success and career as the fifties itself, admits early in the book that she "wasn't steering anything, not even myself" (*BJ* 2).

Esther's personality is in conflict between what she believes the society wants her to be—a domesticated, passive wife and mother—and her own aspirations for success and career. Her preoccupation with "twins," the subject of her senior thesis, is symbolic of her dilemma because Esther herself is a divided self—philosophically "twinned." She has fantasies of prominence as a writer, but she also wants a man to come and save her from the demands of the world. She is not willing to give up plans for a successful literary career and become, as her mother urges her, a truly valuable English major—one who knows shorthand.

Although the English major with shorthand may be the ideal career for the educated fifties girl, Esther admits that she "hated the idea of serving men in any way. I wanted to dictate my own thrilling letters" (*BJ*, 62) Had she had the courage to choose career over marriage and children, Esther might have survived and become Jay Cee, her role model and editor at the magazine where Esther worked for the summer. However, Esther remains caught between two worlds, one of static domesticity, personified by her mother and the other of active professionalism.

Esther's problem, she decides in true fifties fashion, is that she is "neurotic" because cannot choose one "adult" alternative. She wants both career and family and cannot imagine a world which would sanction such a compromise. "I saw my life branching out before me like the green fig tree in the story," she complains. "One fig was a husband and a happy home and children, and another fig was a famous poet and another fig was a brilliant professor, and another fig was Ee Gee, the amazing editor" (*BJ*, 62). Yet despite this extraordinary promise of nourishment, Esther believes that she must select only one and, therefore, reject the others. "I saw myself sitting in the crotch of this fig tree, starving to death, just because I couldn't make up my mind which of the figs I would choose" (*BJ*, 63). In her refusal or inability to select one path, Esther, like other literary figures in the fifties, endangers her entire existence. She must choose or die—compromises do not seem possible.

Ironically, Esther perpetuates the same rigid gender-role stereotyping which victimizes her. She views the smart, caring editor Jay Cee, as physically comical and dowdy. Esther describes Jay Cee as someone who looks "terrible, but very wise" (*BJ*, 32) Despite the fact that Esther fantasizes that Jay Cee is her mother, she, nonetheless, makes the editor the butt of her jokes. Later in the novel, she describes another powerful professional woman as a "a stumpy old Classical scholar with a cropped Dutch cut" (*BJ*, 180). Esther has unconsciously assimilated the stereotypes which perpetuate rigid gender roles— either a loving, seductive wife or an ugly, unlovable or "unnatural" professional woman. And for this reason, Esther sits in the crotch of the fig tree and starves. There do not seem to be adequate models for a young aspiring writer who feels she is "like a racehorse in a world without racetracks" (BJ, 62).

Although domesticity and mindless housework seem "a dreary and wasted life for a girl with fifteen years of straight A's" (BJ, 68), Esther cannot envision a feasible alternative. She views her inevitable future as wife and mother as a political condition much "like being brainwashed . . . numb as a slave in some private, totalitarian state" (*BJ*, 69). Like Eva in "Tell Me A Riddle," Esther sees the political dimension to her personal dilemma, but she can find no solution. Instead, she decides to accept the fifties designation of career women and herself as neurotic: "If neurotic is wanting two mutually exclusive things at one and the same time, then I'm neurotic as hell." (*BJ*, 76). The two Esthers are fifties "twins" trapped under the bell jar: "If I looked in the mirror," she confesses, "it would be like watching somebody else, in a book or a play. But the person in the mirror was paralyzed and too stupid to do a thing" (*BJ*, 121). When Esther searches for a world of meaningful work separate from the home, she finds only frustration.

Martha Quest, the young heroine of Doris Lessing's *Children of Violence* series, is another ambivalent girl caught in a world of conflicting values. Although this novel is set in the years immediately preceding World War II, Martha's world is similar to the fifties environments created by Rich and Plath. In *Martha Quest* (1952) the fifteen-year-old girl who has grown up in the countryside of Rhodesia is in the process of learning to reject her mother's mindless housework. Martha feels a "positive contempt" for traditional women's work, the "dull staple of their lives—servants, children, cooking."[9]

Yet, Martha's reaction is not just an example of intergenerational conflict because the practice of domesticity is prevalent among her own generation as well. Martha attends a meeting of intellectual men who gather, with their wives, to discuss the important social and political issues of the day. When the babies begin to cry and the young mothers abandon the conversation, Martha resolutely promises herself that she will never sacrifice her intellect to others' needs.

Yet Martha's aggression is always tinged with passivity; when presented with a world of opportunities, she often retreats, afraid to take the challenge she swears she desires. Like Esther, she is a character caught in a spider's web of contradictory desires. One example of this confusion is found in Martha's decision not to take the university matric examination which would have opened up scholarship opportunities to her while simultaneously providing an escape from the family's isolated colonial farm life. Does she wish to spite her mother who has bragged for years about the university scholarships her talented daughter will surely win? Or, does Martha fear the very success which will make her an aggressive, independent professional woman?

Martha has the idealism, but lacks the requisite role models, skills and discipline necessary for self-determination. Instead, she daydreams in fairy tale fashion that "some rich and unknown relation would come forward with a hundred pounds, and say, 'Here, Martha Quest, you deserve this, this is to set you free'" (*MQ*, 166). She also fantasizes about a myriad of other careers, all unrelated to her skills or abilities. After writing several articles and poems and receiving rejection notices, a prematurely disillusioned Martha returns to the mating game at the Sports Club. As her professional options evaporate along with her "escape into glorious freedom and untrammelled individuality" (*MQ*, 212), Martha relinquishes her sovereignty and marries Douglas in March of 1939, just as the narrator of the novel informs the reader that Hitler has seized Bohemia and Moravia.

Martha Quest and Europe theoretically know right from wrong and should be able to follow a rational course of action. However, both women and nations succumb to the irrational forces of war and dictators. Martha, a young, modern twentieth century woman who has felt "obliged to repudiate the shackled women of the past" (*MQ,* 8) acquiesces to a thralldom identical to her mother's despite the advantages and alternatives offered her. Simultaneously, Europe is being seduced by the dictators, losing its freedom and giving itself up to war, having learned little from World War I. Thus, the political ramifications of Martha's aborted "quest" are evident. Her inability or unwillingness to find meaningful direction or work persuades her that the "infinite security" of the dictator/husband is preferable to a life on one's own. Almost immediately, even before the wedding to Douglas, however, she will learn, as will Europe, the high price paid for political or sexual appeasement.

Yet Martha's dilemma and her willing sacrifice of personal autonomy are comprehensible when one surveys the vast number of outcast or frustrated working women who inhabit the literature of the fifties and early sixties. Even women who are successful in their professions are often portrayed, by both female and male authors, as missing some essential humanity. Across the Atlantic and thousands of miles away from Martha and Rhodesia, Carson McCullers weaves a humorous and satirical tale entitled, "Madame Zilensky and the King of Poland," (1951) about a male music professor and his renowned colleague, Madame Zilensky. However, the mysterious Madame Zilensky who arrives at the college with three vague sons and no husband, constantly loses her possessions, including all of the family's clothes. She seems only concerned about a missing metronome, and ignores her new house and children.

In addition, none of the boys look like their mother, although they all resemble each other. There is a disconnection surrounding Madame Zilensky which the narrator, correctly or incorrectly, blames on her self-absorption in work. In fact, he describes Madame Zilensky as a "sick patient."[10] Madame Zilensky has "day and night . . . drudged and struggled and thrown her soul into her work . . . [with] not much of her left over for anything else. Being human, she suffered from this lack and did what she could to make up for it" (MZ, 109). According to the narrator, Madame Zilensky's strategy for filling an empty life is to create great lies about important places and people she has encountered on her travels: "Through the lies, she lived vicariously. The lies doubled the little of her existence that was left over from work and augmented the little rag end of her personal life" (MZ,109).

Flannery O'Connor also portrays the personal sacrifices made by successful working women in many of the short stories she writes in the fifties. Although her purpose in creating these hard-working but souless women is to demonstrate the need for Christian redemption,[11] O'Connor's portraits of ambitious, working women conform to negative fifties prototypes. Mrs. McIntyre in "The Displaced Person" is one example of the independent, self-sufficient and yet heartless women who run their own lives without the benefit of a male—husband or God.

Mrs. McIntyre's work ethic is the driving force in her life, the reason she married a seventy-five year old judge when she was thirty. Coldly materialistic, she feels little pity for Mr. Guizac, the Polish World War II "displaced person" she hires to work on her farm. In fact, she smugly repeats her deceased husband's favorite aphorism, "one fellow's misery is the other fellow's gain"[12] as a rationale for exploiting both white and black farm workers. In a burst of sacrilegious fervor, Mrs. McIntyre declares that Mr. Guizac is her "salvation" because "he has to work! He wants to work!"(DP, 270).

For O'Connor, Mrs. McIntyre represents the materialistic contemporary woman who has learned to live on her own in the modern, souless post-war world. Self-centered and ambitious, she depends on no one, not her current workers or three husbands, all of whom prove worthless in the end. Despite her independence, however, Mrs. McIntyre is hardly an admirable character. When her jealous field hands decide to murder the displaced person, Mrs. McIntyre fails to warn him. Thus, Mr. Guizac is destroyed by a heartless, material world which betrays the helpless. The energetic, clever and inexhaustible Mrs. McIntyre, however, does not survive the betrayal either, but instead develops a "nervous affliction" (DP, 299) which renders her paralyzed and blind, symbols of her inert soul.

Although O'Connor also presents male versions of the Mrs. McIntyre prototype in other stories, her focus on industrious women who trade spirituality for material success is prevalent in her work and, therefore, reinforces fifties stereotypes about dangerously ambitious women who sacrifice their humanity in order to become workers in the world. Despite O'Connor's self-acknowledged literary purpose[13] to awaken the reader to a need for religion in a godless world, it is important to note that she often uses "unnatural" characters who are predominately female to further theological mission.

Negative or ambivalent attitudes towards working women in the fifties, however, were more numerous among white authors than among African-American writers. As bell hooks notes in her important book *Ain't I A Woman: Black Women and Feminism* (1981), "most black women have not had the opportunity to indulge in the parasitic dependence upon the male that is expected of females and encouraged in [white] patriarchal society. The institution of slavery forced black women to surrender any prior dependence on the male figure and obliged them to struggle for their individual survival. . . . Few black women have had a choice as to whether or not they will become workers."[14] Since work both within and outside of the home was a given for many women of color, literature in the forties and fifties did not often portray black female workers as either unnatural or conflicted. Women in African-American literature work hard, often without the direction of men; as hooks remarks, "participation of black women in the work force has not led to the formation of a feminist consciousness" (Hooks, 82) because black women do not equate jobs with freedom; for better or worse (usually the latter), black women have always worked.

Gwendolyn Brooks' poem "Bronzeville Woman in a Red Hat" (1960) presents a positive picture of the black maid who has retained her warmth and compassion despite the dehumanizing conditions under which she works. The fearful, racist, white Mrs. Miles who hires the "Bronzeville Woman" is initially afraid of the black woman's strength and vitality. When the woman first walked through the Miles door, she is described as "A lion, really. Poised/To pounce. A puma. A panther."[15] Yet, the Bronzeville woman is hardly the predator Mrs. Miles imagines. Ironically, it is Mrs. Miles, herself, who is the parasite, feeding off of the tragic lives of the poor women she hires to clean her home.

Although Mrs. Miles does not see the goodness in the Bronzeville Woman, her "creamy child" runs to the maid, not his mother, when he cuts his finger. From his maid he receives compassion not available from the aloof mother who resents the child's preference. Although the mother tries to pry her son from "the cannibal wilderness/Dirt, dark," he continues to cling to the Bronzeville woman, "Conscious of kindness, easy creature bond./Love had been handy and rapid to respond" (BW, 369-70). Working and loving are not mutually exclusive traits for black women, and the Bronzeville Woman is just one example of a balance which seems unattainable for white female characters in the fifties.

The strength and humanity of the working black woman are also portrayed in Brooks' poem "Queen of the Blues" as the independent Mame finds that she must rely on herself. She sings to her audience, "show me a man/What will love me/Till I die./Can't find no such a man/No matter how hard/You try."[16] She has worked hard for her lover or "daddy" and "scrubbed hard in them white folks'/Kitchens/Till my knees was rusty," but she has found no one on whom she can depend. Brooks, however, does not see her as mean-spirited or emasculating, but rather as a "queen" and asks, "Why don't they [men] tip their hats to a queen"(QB, 58-9).

Lorraine Hansberry portrays the frustrations of women's career aspirations in her Pulitzer Award winning play, *A Raisin in the Sun* (1959) which takes its title from the Langston Hughes' poem: "What happens to a dream deferred?/Does it dry up like a raisin in the sun/Or, does it explode?"[17] Lena Younger and her daughter Beneatha dream of emancipating and empowering work and success in 1959. When Lena gives her son money to set aside for his sister Beneatha's medical school education, he spends it on a failing business, leaving Beneatha without the means of continuing her education. She eventually marries the Nigerian Joseph Asagay and moves to Africa without completing the schooling she needs. However, the characters maintain their dignity as they attempt to transcend both the racism and sexism in their culture; their economic hopes are "dreams deferred" until the late sixties when there is an "explosion" of rage at the lack of professional opportunities for both black women and men.

If it were possible to summarize the nature of women and work in the fifties, it would be to stress both the "dream" and its "deferral." When women did work, it was often the mindless, soul numbing, unending housework described by Olsen, Plath, and others. For those characters who sought careers, frustration, community ostracism and even death were the results. And as Adrienne Rich notes in her "Snapshots for a Daughter-in-law," there were not many women who would apply for that particular fate.

Quite often, women with careers were portrayed as "odd," and destined for ruin, as in the character of Miss Amelia who runs a distillery and the town's only general store in Carson McCuller's well known short story, "The Ballad of the Sad Cafe" (1951). Women in literature desired work which was not exhausting either physically or spiritually and yet they rarely attained it.

The alternative to this despair or anger, however, was the comic handling of working women seen in Betty Macdonald's popular *The Egg and I* (1945) and Shirley Jackson's *Life Among the Savages* (1953) and *Raising Demons* (1957). Both writers provide humorous vignettes of housework or "women's work" which trivialize the problems and thus the frustrations as well. What is particularly interesting to note is that Shirley Jackson, like Sylvia Plath, ambivalently represents the conflicted fifties woman who regards women's lack of autonomy with both amusement *and* genuine horror. It is, after all, Jackson who wrote the famous short story "The Lottery" (1948) about scapegoating and the power of repressive societies to inflict death on nonconforming individuals and women. The children who stone to death the aggressive Mrs. Hutchinson are only somewhat more malevolent "savages"[18] than the children in Jackson's humorous stories. It is also Jackson who writes of the schizophrenic, but highly gifted Natalie Waite[19] in *Hangsaman* (1951) and her "adjustment" to the society which views her as peculiar. Like Plath, Jackson has two faces—one accommodating, the "good girl" who wishes to please and comply and the other—deeply distrustful, angry and resentful of a society which crushes nonconformity and initiative.

Critic Elizabeth Janeway analyzes the conflicted women of this period who are dependent on men but also enraged "at their situation and, at the same time, their acceptance of their lot."[20] She notes, however, that women's "rebellion is private" because "the area outside the conventional role is bleak. Those who do not accept it must expect to experience varying forms of disaster" (Janeway 1979, 353). It is not until the early sixties and the advent of the civil rights movement, that women realize the ineffectiveness of "private rebellions"; women who seek careers as doctors, lawyers, businesswomen will have to transform the workplace and their own psyches before they can find their way out of the house.

The Sixties and Seventies: Role Equity vs. Role Change

By 1960, 35% of all women were employed, comprising one-third of the entire labor force.[21] In addition, women were going to college in larger numbers than ever before (36% of all undergraduates in the fifties), and thus, there were many women who had the education required for the professions unavailable to Eva and Martha Quest (Hartmann, 49). Yet, there were few laws which protected working women from sex discrimination. Newspapers contained employment advertisements classified by sex, and, most importantly, women who felt themselves the object of prejudice had no legal recourse, even if they did have the courage to defy the system.

The early sixties, however, saw dramatic changes in women's work because of a series of revolutionary laws which would give women and other oppressed groups equal protection in the workplace. The Equal Pay Act of 1963 provided for equal pay for equal work; thus, female and male clerical workers, teachers or doctors could not be paid different salaries for similar jobs. In addition, the civil rights movement helped professional women attain equality through Title VII of the Civil Rights Act of 1964 which prohibited discrimination based on sex as well as race, color, religion or national origin. In 1967, Executive

Order 11375 extended affirmative action to women and in 1972 Title IX of the Educational Amendments Act threatened to cut off federal funding from educational institutions which discriminated on the basis of sex.

These federal laws changed not only the legal environment, but also did much to transform public opinion about working women. During the sixties, new organizations like the National Organization for Women (1966) and Women's Equity Action League (1968) began to lobby for a variety of women's social issues including job equality. The powerlessness experienced by women working in the fifties was lessened by these governmental actions.

However, it is important not to strike a too self-congratulatory note at this point because although "role equity" and women's legal rights had improved, actual "role change" had not (Boneparth and Stoper, 17). The distinction between these two terms is crucial to an understanding of the era because the disparity between "equity" and "change" will be reflected in not only women's lives, but in their literature as well. A gender "role" for both men and women prescribes "a pattern of behavior individuals adopt in response to social expectations (Boneparth and Stoper, 17). This behavior dictates not only personal or private behaviors, but instructs men and women in every aspect of their public and private lives. Sociologists Ellen Boneparth and Emily Stoper make an important distinction, however, when they differentiate sixties legislation which created "role equity" from actual "role change." The difference between the two "explains the relatively easy acceptance of some women's policies and the massive resistance to others. Equity fits with the American political tradition of fairness and equality before the law; equity issues rest on basic economic, social, and political values. In contrast change challenges traditional sex role ideology. It involves the redefinition of sex roles in some areas, the elimination of sex roles in others. Most importantly, it changes the roles of men as well as women" (Boneparth and Stoper, 17).

For this reason, new laws guaranteeing women's equality in the workplaces of the United States, Europe and other nations were more easily accepted than real change in attitudes towards women themselves. The laws made it possible to sue one's boss or the corporation which discriminated; however, legislation would do little to change the boss' patriarchal notions about women, or women's guilt for "abandoning" their traditional roles. The optimistic, aggressive activism of the sixties modified the legal environment dramatically. However, in the late sixties and early seventies, it became increasingly evident that a real transformation of the patriarchal social order would require more than an act of Congress or an international referendum. Sixties literature reflects this awareness—both the hope and disillusionment of women as they learn the difference between role equity and change. It would be necessary to change not only public laws, but women's and men's personal attitudes about themselves in order to achieve true equal opportunity.

One vehicle for this transformation of attitudes was an institution which developed in the sixties called the "consciousness raising group" where a number of women got together in order to discuss their personal problems and offer each other support and advice. Much has been written about the "C-R" group by social scientists and novelists because it served as a catalyst for private and public change. The historian Susan Hartmann describes the C-R group as "crucial to the development of feminism" (63) because it sanctioned and legitimized the frustration and discontent that fifties women felt. Women in groups were not told they were maladjusted, unwomanly, neurotic or immature. In addition, the connection with other women provided a commonality not available previously. The group became the embodiment of the personal as political: "what appear to be personal problems are often common to all women and are shaped by social institutions ... [and] susceptible to political solutions" (Hartmann, 63-4).

The sixties consciousness-raising group provided not only the substance but also the structure for several important novels which were published in the sixties, seventies and eighties. These literary works were written about "groups" of women with different backgrounds, intellectual abilities and ambitions who suffer the personal and public effects of patriarchal society. Often the novels concentrate on the efforts of the women to free themselves from societal constraints in order to establish themselves in careers or marriages (more often unhappy marriages). Although Mary McCarthy's *The Group* (1963), is set in the thirties and forties, other contemporary novels chart the course of women's personal fortunes from the repression of the fifties to the apparent "freedom" of the sixties, seventies or eighties. Most importantly however, these books portray the disparities between role equity and role change mentioned above. It is this difference between the illusion and the reality of individual autonomy, which is the subject of books as diverse as Mary McCarthy's *The Group* (1963), Doris Lessing's *The Golden Notebook* (1962), Marilyn French's *The Women's Room* (1977), Rona Jafee's *Class Reunion* (1979), Gloria Naylor's *The Women of Brewster Place* (1982), Alice Adam's *Superior Women* (1984) and Margaret Atwood's *Cat's Eye* (1989).

Many of the characters in these novels are theoretically free to seek an education and meaningful work. Yet, they often remain trapped within a circumscribed pattern of gender related behavior, which is as often self-imposed as societally dictated. Although women are guaranteed equitable treatment in the workplace, they must learn how to free themselves from the gender roles which cannot be legislated away. Some succeed and others do not, but what remains a constant in these novels is the battle each woman must fight in order to maintain her autonomy against social conformity.

In *The Group*,[22] Mary McCarthy analyzes eight Vassar graduates during the thirties and forties who, despite their education and social standing, make little of their newly acquired advantages. Libby MacAusland, the intellectual, becomes a literary agent while another chooses to be a veterinarian. These privileged women, however, symbolize the problems encountered by seemingly emancipated women in the modern world. Kay Strong, whose wedding begins the book and whose death at twenty-nine concludes the novel, is representative of the confusion and frustration of "free" women who are liberated in fact but not in reality. After being committed to a mental hospital by her husband, Kay is released but prefers to stay. The pressures of dealing with conflicting desires and norms prove too much for her and many of the other women in the novel.

The "free women"(GN, 3) who inhabit Doris Lessing's world of *The Golden Notebook* (1962) in the summer of 1957 also face the perplexing disparities between role equity and role change. They live alone, are educated and "free" to pursue their careers in any way they deem possible, yet they remain mired in indecision, afraid to act in decisive ways which would provide them with meaningful work.

Although Anna is a published writer and Molly has successfully worked in a number of different occupations, both women are unsure of how to proceed in life. Anna says of her present condition, "Free women.... They still define us in terms of relationships with men, even the best of them." Molly, answers cynically, "Well, *we* do, don't we? ... it's awfully hard not to" (GN, 4). When Molly tells Anna that she believes they are both "a completely new type of woman," Anna tersely replies "There's nothing new under the sun" (GN, 4). Molly and Anna are learning that the "freedom" to develop their own public and professional lives has its own frustrations; Molly admits to herself that she has squandered her abilities without developing a career and, therefore, considers herself a professional failure. She urges her friend Anna to write another book, possibly as a way of justifying the choices that both unconventional women have made in their lives. Learning from her own mistakes, Molly warns Anna not to squander her potential: "I keep telling you ... I'll never forgive you if you throw that talent away. I mean it. I've done it, and I can't stand watching you—I've messed with painting and dancing and acting and scribbling, and now ... you're so talented, Anna. *Why*? I simply don't understand" (GN, 6).

Anna has no answer to her friend's question. The powerful career and its attendant success, so initially important to newly freed women, seem to have lost their attractiveness for Molly and Anna. Lessing's "free women" can, if they wish, emulate the successful men of England like Molly's former husband Richard. Yet both women find Richard's existence as stultifying and meaningless as traditional housework. In an argument about the career of their son, Tommy, Molly attacks Richard and says, "I don't want Tommy to be a businessman. You are hardly an advertisement for the life. Anyone can be a businessman, why, you've often said so to me. Oh come off it Richard, how often have you dropped in to see me and sat there saying how empty and stupid your life is?" (GN, 22).

Tommy, who represents the new generation, is a foil for his mother and her ideologies; his attitudes towards work mirror her own. He has the entire social order at his disposal, could go to college or work in industry, but chooses to sit in his room and brood. Like his mother, Tommy knows what he doesn't want, but not what he desires. He says to his mother and Anna, "I'd rather be a failure, like you, than succeed and all that sort of thing. But I'm not saying I'm choosing failure, does one? I know what I don't want, but not what I do want." (GN, 37). If Tommy, Anna and Molly all suffer from a "paralysis of the will" (GN, 262) brought on (according to Richard) by having "too many choices" (GN, 270), then the alternative is a reversion to earlier domination, a solution fraught with its own problems. Anna's ideal work is symbolized by an art which does not compartmentalize life, but instead envisions it as a cohesive and unified whole of human experience bound in a Golden Notebook. However, she, temporarily gives up her quest at the end of the novel and opts for a life of activism, advising people in a marriage clinic, joining the Labour Party and teaching a class for juvenile delinquents. Her choice is no more satisfactory than her friend Molly's who will marry a progressive businessman. Anna has "integrated" herself into British life, but she has not found the meaningful existence through work which she believed her freedom would offer her. Critic Patricia Spacks views Molly and Anna's dilemma as symptomatic of "free" careerist women in twentieth century literature in general: "In the twentieth century, social possibilities are greater, and the image of the 'free woman'—often promiscuous, often intellectual, priding herself on being emotionally undemanding but often seen nonetheless as 'castrating'—has been established in fiction by men and women authors alike."[23] Ironically, it is women's presumed liberty, according to Spacks, which makes Anna, "an appropriate object for [male] casual lust ... Her 'freedom' thus becomes a means for her victimization" (Spacks, 309).

Marilyn French in *The Women's Room* (1977) also analyzes the ironic dilemmas experienced by "free" women in contemporary society. It is not just a matter of passing non-discriminatory laws and providing women with the pill. Role change must be effected as well as role equity. As in *The Golden Notebook*, role change is a good deal more problematic than equity. In fact, equity or as the Americans called it in the sixties, "women's liberation," provided new problems for women while eliminating old frustrations.

In order to portray how working women were affected by liberal attitudes towards careers in the sixties, French presents the story of Mira and her friends as they make their individual ways through stifling fifties marriages to equal professional opportunities in the sixties and early seventies. Theoretically, for the aggressive, non-conforming and ambitious woman, it should be a hopeful and optimistic ascent. However, Mira, the main character and narrator of the story, sees both the excitement and sacrifices required. By the novels's end, neither Mira nor the reader is sure that the inevitable journey out of the bedroom and kitchen and into the classroom and boardroom was worth the struggle.

Offered a job in Africa, Mira is confronted with the working woman's new archetypal choice—to follow her lover or her career—a dilemma which has still not been resolved or eliminated in contemporary women's literature. Mira's mutually exclusive choices are similar to those of Esther or Molly's—husband or career, book or baby; the utopian vision of an enfranchised, unified existence sought in *The Golden Notebook* encounters the obstacles created by a society with unyielding gender roles. Unlike women in the past, however, Mira decides not to follow Ben to Africa and become a secretary or the mother of his children. "She loved Ben . . . But now (after forty years) she wanted to do her own work, she wanted to pursue this stuff, this scholarship that she loved so much."[24] Later she finds that Ben has married, had several children and is living the fifties existence in the sixties—little has changed despite the civil rights marches and laws.

More importantly, however, Mira's hard-won career as a college teacher has not proved to be worth the personal sacrifice.

There seem to be few good opportunities for a forty-year-old English professor, and thus she takes a position in a community college in Maine where she is alternately excited, depressed, but always lonely. She has exchanged the oppression of the patriarchal system for the tedium of academe, neither of which provide the happiness she seeks. Her quest for a life replete with meaningful work has not been achieved, and the reader is left to wonder if this is, as Mira and others suggest, a woman's fate given the prevailing social order into which she is born.

Anne Sexton, the Pulitzer Prize winning poet, also speculates about the ambiguities of women's fate in several of her poems published in the sixties. In "Housewife" (1962), Sexton sees "some" women as almost biologically connected to their homes, "Some women marry houses./It's another kind of skin . . . The walls are permanent and pink./See how she sits on her knees all day,/faithfully washing herself down."[25] Of these women's ability to alter the course of their lives, to get up off their knees and abandon the house, Sexton sees little hope: "A woman *is* her mother./That's the main thing" (H, 77).

However, by 1966 Sexton imagines a freedom in an androgynous state found in a Christian heaven. It is within this new asexuality that women can reject the house and its demeaning work in order to live on a higher plane of existence. In "Consorting with Angels,"(1966) the speaker complains, "I am tired of being a woman,/tired of the spoons and the pots/tired of my mouth and my breasts . . . tired of the gender of things."[26] Yet, she dreams of a new city where "no two [are] made in the same species," a city of sexless individuals "each one like a poem obeying itself,/performing God's functions" (CA, 111). The speaker desires to live in that city, merging with both Adam and Eve until she is "not a woman anymore,/not one thing or the other" (CA, 112). It is in this holy androgynous state which has transformed her into "all one skin like a fish," that she is able to be "no more a woman/than Christ was a man" (CA, 112). It is at this point that she can do the work she was intended to do, but first she must escape the gendered fate of life on earth.

Although there is a great deal of ambivalence about the prospects for women's success in the existing social order, many American writers in the sixties and early seventies were hopeful. In their poetry and fiction they praised the ennobling power of significant work and urged women to seek means of attaining it. In "Pro Femina" (1963), Carolyn Kizer states that, "While men have politely debated free will, we have howled for it,/Howl still, pacing the centuries, tragic heroines."[27]

Kizer wants these women who imitate Madame Defarge, Jane Austen and Saint Joan to find meaningful aggressive activity and empowering careers; however, at the same time, she cautions women to work in their own ways not trying "to be ugly by aping the ways of the men" (p. 42). Kizer looks forward to a woman's perspective which rejects men's "Swearing, sucking cigars and scorching the bedspread." Forget the fraternity of men, she advises the aspiring writer. The resourceful female writer should find her own way, rejecting the traditional "expectation of glory: *she writes like a man!*" (pp. 48-9). Kizer, like Lessing, uses the expression "free women" to describe those women who, emancipated from patriarchal prototypes can create, accomplish and succeed in a new world. However, she stresses that women must succeed *on their own terms*, providing both a new vision and voice.

Marge Piercy's poem "To Be of Use" (1973) is also a testimonial to the ennobling power of women's work. "The people I love the best," she writes, "jump into work head first/without dallying in the shallows/and swim off with sure strokes almost out of sight." Her images, like Rich's in "Snapshots of a Daughter-in-Law" praise activity, not traditionally associated with the feminine: "I love people who harness themselves, an ox to a heavy cart./who pull like water buffalo, with massive patience,/who strain in the mud and the muck to move things forward,/who do what has to be done, again and again."

Piercy, like Kizer, seems to be confident of the road ahead—both want to get moving as quickly as possible with the fewest delays. Piercy describes this ideal work as a perfect blend of the practical and the artistic, the beauty and utility found in a Greek amphora or a Hopi vase. Rejecting indolence and, instead, singing the praises of meaningful work, Piercy makes the comparison between a person and a pitcher: "The pitcher cries for water to carry/and a person for work that is real."[28]

Some women writers who deplore the mindless activity of the housewife and praise the professional woman know that sexism and demeaning work are plentiful in public as well as private life. Judy Grahn describes "Ella, in a square apron, along Highway 80" in *The Work of the Common Woman* (1970) as a "copperheaded waitress;/tired and sharp-worded"[29] who has had to arm herself with word as well as gun against the men who insult and humiliate her. Ella is self-protective and dangerous, "a rattlesnake" who has paid a high price for her autonomy in this dehumanizing world. Work, in and of itself, therefore, is no panacea for the woman; a political solution or transformation of the nature of the social order is required first.

Black authors in the sixties, likewise, praise the self-reliant, independent working woman, but they, too, do not view work itself as the feminist salvation posited by many white, homebound, middle-class authors. The opinions of Maya Angelou, Gloria Naylor, Alice Walker and others would be closer to Judy Grahn's than Kizer or Piercy. Work, both within and outside the home, is necessary for independence and survival, but it is also often soul-numbing and demeaning within the pervasively racist and sexist society in which it takes place.

In *I Know Why The Caged Bird Sings*, (1969) Maya Angelou's portrayal of her grandmother, Momma, provides an example of this complex attitude towards hard work and independence. Momma, as Angelou tells the reader of this autobiography, is the strongest, most self-reliant and courageous woman or black person in Stamps, Arkansas. She owns the only store serving both black and whites, and has the resources to lend the white dentist money during the depression. Yet, it is also this professional and autonomous Momma who must call spoiled, racist white girls "Miz" when they enter her store and is forced to hide her son Willie in a barrel when white "boys" go out on a lynching party at night. In addition, Momma's constant activity, discipline and industry have exacted a toll. Her stoical life has made it difficult for her to express her feelings in any outward way: "Her world was bordered on all sides with work, duty, religion and 'her place.' I don't think she ever knew that a deep-brooding love hung over everything she touched."[30]

The importance of financial autonomy, however, is not lost on the rebellious, but proud Maya who later in the autobiography recounts her personal victory as the first black streetcar conductor in San Francisco. Here, at last, is a profession which is also a symbol of freedom. When she is told that blacks cannot apply for the position, she becomes determined to get it in any way possible. With a mind "locked like the jaws of an enraged bulldog," Maya promises herself: "I WOULD HAVE THE JOB. I WOULD BE A CONDUCTORETTE AND SLING A FULL MONEY CHANGER FROM MY BELT. I WOULD" (Caged, 225, 227).

Ironically, her final success makes her more, not less vulnerable because it gives Maya a visibility which makes her a target for the "tripartite crossfire of masculine prejudice, white illogical hate and Black lack of power" (Caged, 231). Becoming the powerful conductorette, therefore, will not solve Maya's more fundamental problem—how to acquire freedom and autonomy in a society predicated upon the impotence of women and blacks. Personal advancement without societal transformation will make her private victories insubstantial. Public and private worlds are dependent on each other—no matter how courageous and ambitious the woman, one's personal life is dependent on public politics.

Looking with a critical eye at the "advances" fought for and won in the sixties, Kiswana Browne, a young, African-American woman in Gloria Naylor's *The Women of Brewster Place* (1980) sees the paradoxes as well as the potential created by equal opportunity for black women and men. In an argument with her middle-class mother, who has benefitted from civil rights legislation and now lives in the black affluent suburb of Linden Hills, Kiswana rejects her rightful inheritance—good education and high powered jobs—for a life in the impoverished ghetto called Brewster Place. Her perplexed mother tries to persuade her daughter to return to school, and move back to Linden Hills. "If you hadn't dropped out of college and had to resort to these dead-end clerical jobs,"[31] her mother argues, you would now be in a well-paying career with all its fringe benefits and power.

Kiswana, however, views her mother's quest for success and status as both snobbish and racist. "How can you—a black woman—sit there and tell me that what we fought for during the Movement wasn't important just because some people sold out" (*W*, 84). This concept of "selling out" in order to move up the career ladder into a power position is a shift in sensibility from the earlier white, middle-class, feminist attitudes towards work and career. In the fifties, opportunities were few. With new legislation and equal opportunity in the sixties and seventies, the choices were available to some ambitious and determined women. Yet, quite early, before Betty Friedan, herself, would announce the "Second Stage"[32] of feminist thought, African-American writers were already speculating about the "costs" of success. What price power, when power had to be interpreted as domination over less fortunate individuals—a basic precept of patriarchal society.

The confrontation between Kiswana and her mother represents the struggle between the first stage of women and men who benefitted from the Civil Rights Act of 1964 and the next generation which reaped both the rewards and the liabilities of their parents' success.[33] Kiswana and her seventies generation—black and white—want to be powerful women, but they need to redefine what it means to be empowered. Unlike her rebellious daughter, Kiswana's mother can only envision working *within* the system, not against it, and instructs her daughter to "get an important job where you can have some influence. You don't have to sell out" (*W*, 84). Kiswana's mother reminds her daughter that "when all the smoke had cleared [in the sixties and seventies], you found yourself with a fistful of new federal laws and a country still full of obstacles for black people to fight their way over—just because they're black. There was no revolution" (*W*, 84). A similar argument could be made for gender equality.

Once black and white women *could* participate in the workplace of the late seventies and eighties, many began to wonder if they wanted to join the existing order. "Selling out," becoming "white" or an androgyne—a female version of the corporate male—became an extremely important theme in the literature of women and work. And it is with their tripartite perspective of race, gender and class, that African-American female writers pointed to the pitfalls of success. In each case, the successful individual might have to betray her race, class or sex in order to acquire power. The question in the seventies became not whether women *could* succeed but whether the struggle would be worth it once they did.

Some women's literature of the seventies and eighties began to speculate about possible solutions to this dilemma over "man's work." In fact, the development of what Frances Bartkowski terms the "feminist utopia"[34] is just one response. Several novels including Monique Wittig's *Les Guerilleres* (1969), Joanna Russ' *The Female Man* (1975), E. M. Broner's *A Weave of Women* (1978), Suzy McKee Charnas' *Motherlines* (1978), and Ursula Le Guin's *The Eye of the Heron* (1983) imagine utopian worlds where either/or confrontations between the strong and weak do not exist. In *Woman on the Edge of Time* (1976), Marge Piercy creates Connie Ramos, a thirty-seven year old Chicana woman, who lives in modern New York but is in touch with a non-violent, cooperative society in the year 2137.[35]

Through her relationship with one of its emissaries, Luciente, Connie is introduced to a new order of work which does not pit people against each other, does not require that the successful betray their weaker sisters and brothers. Having heard the political message for equal rights in the sixties and seventies, Connie has tried to work for social change, but has become increasingly disillusioned by the inevitable outcome of her activity: "I was young and naive and it was supposed to be a War on Poverty . . . But it was just the same political machine . . . We ended up right back where we were. They gave some paying jobs to so-called neighborhood leaders. All those meetings. I ended up with nothing but feeling sore and ripped off." Luciente's utopian experience provides Connie with an alternative to this bleak view of activism. "You lose until you win," Luciente replies, "that's a saying those who changed our world left us. Poor people *did* get together" (WET, 154).

Joanna Russ's *The Female Man* (1975) also provides a glimpse at a world in which meaningful women's work and society are possible, but Whileaway is utopian because it has excluded men and their patriarchal ways. Whileaway represents a utopian society ten centuries in the future in which men have not existed for 800 years. Women marry each other and produce female children who are raised communally after being separated from their biological mothers at the age of four or five. Early female education is based on practical, independent work: "how to run machines, how to get along without machines, law, transportation, physical theory."[36] Most importantly, Whileaway girls must find some suitable and important life activity—they cannot wait for a prince charming who has been extinct for 800 years: "Whileawayans work all the time. They work. And they work. *And they work*" (FM, 54),

Russ juxtaposes this healthy Whileawayean industry with the neurotic world of Laura who is indolent and frustrated. When the Whileawayan Janet Evanson asks Laura if she is happy in her existence, Laura does not take responsibility for her own life, but rather, blames her problems on her working mother, a librarian, whose ambitions are, according to fifties Freudian theory, just another example of "penis envy" which has "deformed" Laura (FM, 65).

The angry and repressed Laura refers to men as "the man," (FM, 66) an expression with connotations which suggest power relationships of gender, race and class. "Working for The Man" will never be a satisfactory experience, according to Laura, because it is fraught with divided loyalties and insoluble dilemmas: "Whenever I act like a human being, they say . . . of course you're brilliant. They say: of course you'll get a Ph.D., and then sacrifice it to have babies. They say: if you don't you're the one who'll have two jobs and you can make a go of it if you're exceptional, which very few women are, *and if you find a very understanding man*. As long as you don't make more money than he does" (FM, 66).

However, the idyllic world of Whileaway does not really seem a possibility for contemporary "earth" women. At the book's conclusion, the narrator asks her "little book" to "bob a curtsey at the shrines of Friedan, Millett, Greer, Firestone, and all the rest"[37] and to "live merrily, . . . even if I can't and we can't." (FM, 213). Joanna's Russ' imaginative flight into Whileaway provides the blueprint but not the practical program for attaining the dream. The life of natural energy, undirected or circumscribed by others, does not seem possible in Joanna Russ' world of 1975. Even when women can attain the position they deserve, success requires a fortitude and endurance most non-superwomen types do not possess.

The Eighties and Nineties: The Redefinition of Success

Writers of realistic essays and fiction in the eighties and nineties share the same complex, ironical vision found in earlier women's writing. However, one of the most important revisions in attitudes towards work, women and society can be found in Betty Friedan's *The Second Stage* (1981), a sequel to her 1963 *The Feminine Mystique*.

After nearly twenty years of struggling for equal rights, antidiscrimination legislation in the workplace and school, Friedan characterizes the "first stage" of feminism as "full participation, power and voice in the mainstream, inside the party, the political process, the professions, the business world" (Friedan 1981, 13). Although she believes that the original goals have been met and women have garnered public power in society, she senses "the exhilaration of 'superwomen' giving way to a tiredness, a certain brittle disappointment, a disillusionment with 'assertiveness training' and the rewards of power" (Friedan 1981, 7).

In her book, Friedan quotes one of the many representative women who has found success and position in work, but remains as unsatisfied as her housewife counterparts in the fifties. Of her management position, one female executive explains, "It was exciting at first, breaking in where women never were before. Now it's just a job. But it's the devastating loneliness that's the worst.... Maybe I should have a kid, even without a father. At least then I'd have a family. There has to be some better way to live" (Friedan 1981, 7).

In portraying the dissatisfaction of contemporary professional women, Friedan is not suggesting that women return to the kitchen; however, she does outline the priorities for a second stage of feminist thought which would go beyond the equality of workplace legislation to a new sense of personal and political egalitarianism: "What are the limits and true potential of women's power? ... I believe that the personal is both more and less political than our own rhetoric ever implied. I believe that we have to break through our own *feminist* mystique now to come to terms with the new reality of our personal and political experience and to move into the second stage" (Friedan 1981, 13).

Despite their obvious differences, Friedan, Piercy, Russ and other imaginative writers all concentrate their attention on improving the status quo by transforming the present social structure into a more humane, family-centered order. Friedan's second stage would "come to terms with the family," by involving both men and women in a movement which would "transcend the battle for equal power in institutions." Most importantly, however, in the second stage, new communal values like those found in Whileaway would "restructure institutions and transform the nature of power itself" (Friedan 1981, 13). In the early eighties, Friedan wants women to reject "obsolete power games and irrelevant sexual battles that never can be won, or that we will lose by winning" (Friedan 1981, 14) and instead take a hard look at modern "success."

In *The Second Stage*, Friedan asks directly what many fiction writers, poets and dramatists have imaginatively represented in literature: "D[o] we want equal access to the same system or the power to change it? Can you change the system only by becoming a part of it? Once you are in it, does it change you instead?" (Friedan 1981, 17). The last question, "does it change you instead," is a particularly relevant one in women's literature in the late seventies and eighties because many writers present the powerful, well-educated woman as no more satisfied in the patriarchal workplace than the housewife who was entrapped in the "feminine mystique" of twenty years ago.

In the second stage of feminist thought and within the literature of the eighties, writers will continue to question whether a professional career defines liberation: "We've broken through to get these jobs women never had before," Friedan concedes. But professional accomplishment cannot be a feminist panacea. "What do you do about life, children, men, loneliness, companionship, the need to have a real home—things no one thought about when we were so obsessed with liberating ourselves" (Friedan 1981, 48). Much of the literature of the eighties and nineties reflects both Friedan's angst and hope as well as her commitment to a world which transcends traditional gender roles and power struggles.

Women and Work in the Eighties: The Redefinition of Success

The ambitious woman who has attained "success" in traditional terms often still remains anxious about her accomplishments in eighties literature. Although some might argue that women who have "made it" by traditional male standards of success are no longer powerless, some women disagree: "The simple solution of gaining more power in the context of existing power structures has been rejected by many feminists as perpetuating patterns of oppression. Much feminist thought, therefore, has gone into seeking ways to restructure power relations, in both public and private spheres, so that they are more democratic, participatory, and just" (Boneparth and Stoper, 18).

Although Boneparth and Stoper's opinions are primarily based upon their research in the social sciences, their description of feminist vs. patriarchal attitudes towards power and work is reflected in literature as well. They believe that "the woman's movement has come to distinguish between power *over* and power *for*. The feminist critique of power has been directed at ways of reducing the power of one group *over* another" (Boneparth and Stoper, 19).

Since 1980, many imaginative writers have also critiqued both the potential and pitfalls of this revolutionary attitude towards power. One early manifestation of this preoccupation is found in the literary analysis of "token women," those successful women who have been given higher status through career advancement, but who often forget the people and inequitable conditions they have left behind. Marge Piercy's poem "The Token Woman" (1976) provides a scathing indictment of such an individual who has accepted "power over," but does not seek "power for," to use Boneparth and Stoper's terminology. "The token woman," Piercy comments, "stands in the Square of the Immaculate/Exception blessing pigeons from a blue Pedestal." Despite her "exceptional" power, the token woman provides no aid to the more unfortunate; her power is used only for her own needs, "The token woman falls like a melon seed/on the cement: why has she no star shaped yellow flowers?"[38]

Ultimately, this seemingly special woman sows no seeds, blazes no trails, rectifies no injustices:

> Another woman can never join her,
> help her, sister her, tickle her
> but only replace her to become her
> unless we make common cause,
> unless she grows out, one finger of a hand,
> the entering wedge, the runner
> from the bed of rampant peppermint
> as it invades the neat clipped turf
> of the putting green (TW, 71-2).

Piercy's poem is a call to all "token women" to "put out runners" to other women and thus "invade" the neatly "clipped" patriarchal workplace. Feminine communalism and net-working, begun in the political sixties, but cast aside in the careerist seventies, are emphasized in Piercy's poem and other literary texts. The unappealing alternative to power sharing and mutual concern among newly empowered professional women is the artificial "token woman," a female who "comes luxuriously stuffed with goosedown/able to double as sleeping/or punching bag" according to Piercy (TW, 71).

Probably one of the most positive models for "working" women is found in Susan Griffin's poem, "I Like to Think of Harriet Tubman" (1976). Although Tubman's "work" was the rescuing of slaves in nineteenth century America, she is the archetypal nurturer, a woman who "had no use for the law/when the law was wrong." She is a woman who "lived to redress her grievances,/and she lived in swamps/and wore the clothes of a man/bringing hundreds of fugitives from/slavery, and was never caught,/and led an army,/and won a battle."[39]

A symbol of the new worker who frees herself, but does not forget those still enslaved, Tubman is also a warning that men need "to take us seriously" for as Griffin argues "there is always a time to make right/what is wrong,/there is always a time/for retribution/and that time/is beginning" (HT, 12). If Adrienne Rich speaks of a loaded gun, in the fifties, it is Susan Griffith who seems willing to use it in the late seventies.

The paradoxes and dilemmas confronting newly enfranchised professional women are the subject of books as diverse as Margaret Drabble's *The Realm of Gold* (1975) and *The Middle Ground* (1980), Barbara Gordon's *I'm Dancing as Fast As I Can* (1979), Anne Tyler's *Dinner at the Homesick Restaurant*, Margaret Atwood's *Bodily Harm* (1982), Gail Godwin's *The Odd Woman* (1976) and *A Mother and Two Daughters* (1982), Judith's Rossner's *August* (1983), Susan Cheever's *Looking for Work* (1985), and Mary Gordon's *Men and Angels*.[40] Once female characters have acquired some power and command in the public world, they need to decide how to use it wisely within or outside of the traditional social structure. The importance of informed action, therefore, becomes a central topic for women in literature and life.

In her Pulitzer Prize winning novel *Foreign Affairs* (1984), Alison Lurie presents a moving portrayal of Vinnie Miner, a fifty-four year old female professor of folklore and children's literature whose career has been more successful than her life. The "Old Song," which opens Chapter One of the novel, serves as an epigraph for Vinnie's isolated and austere existence: "As I walked by myself/And talked to myself,/Myself said unto me,/Look to thyself, Take care of thyself,/For nobody cares for thee."[41] Although Vinnie is a well-known professor of children's literature at an Ivy League college in the East, she is accompanied by an imaginary dog named "Fido" or, "self-pity" (*FA*, 1) as Vinnie names him.

This self-pity emanates from Vinnie's own sense that she is worthless, expendable to others even though her professional work is well-known enough to be discussed in prestigious magazines like the *Atlantic*. Despite the fact that she lives in a culture "where energy and egotism are rewarded" (*FA*, 4), Vinnie feels unappreciated and alone.

Underneath the tough, eccentric exterior, therefore, Vinnie is a vulnerable woman who understands that the human connections which make life meaningful have eluded her. She is especially wounded by professional attacks on her competence as a scholar and researcher because, as she herself admits, "those who have no significant identity outside their careers—

no spouse, no lover, no parents, no children—do take things hard" (*FA*, 10-11).

Despite her seeming desire for connection, however, Vinnie has a well developed fear of intimacy and has calculated a life which avoids the personal. Once given to sexual fantasies, Vinnie has, of late substituted a "feminist fantasy" in which she is the "recipient of various prizes and honorary degrees" (*FA*, 170). Thus, the well-guarded Vinnie is not receptive to a retired engineer she meets on a plane trip to England. The intellectual, ambitious woman who has so carefully avoided the personal and passionate side of her nature, has always side-stepped the "terrible danger" of becoming "wholly, entangled, caught" (*FA*, 367) in another person's life. And, thus she learns too late that she has missed her opportunity for intimacy.

Vinnie, however, does not desire a permanent transformation. Instead, she retreats back into the persona of V.A. Miner, returns to her unfettered but isolated academic life and convinces herself that "it's not her nature, not her fate to be loved, to live with anyone, her fate is to be always single, unloved, alone—"(*FA*, 424). At the end of the novel, Vinnie has become reacquainted with the imaginary dog Fido or self-pity, her permanent traveling companion through life. She "keeps up her spirits" by attempting to convince herself of her professional importance: "I'm not a bit sorry for myself. I'm a well-known scholar; I have lots of friends on both sides of the Atlantic . . . finished an important book on playground rhymes" (*FA*, 425). Despite her bravado, however, no one—neither the main character nor the reader—is convinced by Vinnie's self-congratulatory pronouncements.

In *Cat's Eye* (1989), Margaret Atwood offers another portrait of the perceptive, intelligent but conflicted professional woman. What separates this novel from its predecessors, however, is not the subject—the fortunes and misfortunes of a professional artist as she analyzes her position and potential in life—but rather the conclusions that the narrator draws about the nature and importance of work and accomplishment. Elaine Risley, a moderately successful Canadian painter on the brink of her first gallery retrospective, is a haunted, incomplete, often depressed woman. Twice married, alternately discriminated against and seduced as a young art student, Elaine has been abused by the patriarchal institutions (including marriage) she has passed through from the forties to the seventies. Therefore, Elaine could, like her predecessors, blame society and men for her suffering.

Yet Elaine regards gender and its betrayals as an additional layer in the mystery that women and men call time and memory. Her inability to trust can partially be explained in terms of her personal experience as a woman at the hands of a misogynist society which prevented women from studying and working; however, her discomfort with her success, her reluctance to connect with others, her ambivalence about power and its handservant—ideology, her skepticism about the nature of reality and fantasy, are also dictated by forces which influence all contemporary women and men.

Elaine looks back through the prism of time to the forties when she was a young girl and finds that all the forces which operated on her at eight or nine, are still present at fifty. And since "nothing goes away,"[42] the inequities of past gender experiences return to torment the free, successful adult who has, presumably, "outgrown" the past. Although Atwood does not use the social science terms "role equity" vs. "role change," she might agree that "role equity" is more easily achieved than a "role change" which would free women and men from past preconceptions. In fact, it may be impossible for Elaine Risley and others who had their "formative" years in the forties and fifties, to effect a role transformation.

For it is in the forties that Elaine learns about girls' rules from her sadistic eight year old friend, Cordelia:

> I see that there's a whole world of girls and their doings that has been unknown to me, and that I can be part of it without making any effort at all. I don't have to keep up with anyone, run as fast, aim as well, make loud explosive noises, decode messages, due on cue. I don't have to think about whether I've done these things well, as well as a boy. . . . Partly this is a relief (CE, 57).

Even in adulthood when Elaine is an autonomous, successful painter and Cordelia is a former resident of a mental institution, Elaine feels that the experiences with Cordelia in the forties have caused her to "lose power" (CE, 113). When Anna, a feminist journalist asks the adult Elaine, "Could you maybe say something about your generation of artists—your generation of woman artists—and their aspirations and goals," Elaine retorts, "What generation is that?" When Anna suggests that Elaine is a child of the seventies, Elaine corrects her: "The seventies isn't my generation . . . The forties . . . That was when I grew up" (CE, 93).

Elaine's hostility or distrust of Anna and her feminist principles extends to the women's movement in general. Although she envies these women's "conviction . . . optimism . . . carelessness . . . fearlessness about men, their camaraderie," Elaine also confesses her fear of her own gender: "women collect grievances, hold grudges and change shape. They pass hard, legitimate judgments, unlike the purblind guesses of men, fogged with romanticism and ignorance and bias and wish. Women know too much, they can neither be deceived nor trusted. I can understand why men are afraid of them, as they are frequently accused of being" (CE, 399).

Ironically, Elaine, who has directly benefitted from feminist activism in the workplace, surreptitiously avoids women and their organizations. Although she agrees with the radical feminist belief that men "are violent, wage wars, commit murders . . . do less work and make more money . . . shove the housework off on women," she finds "sisterhood a difficult concept" whereas "brotherhood is not" (CE, 360-61).

A victim of a post-war society which has denigrated women's art and mindlessly devised "BOYS" and "GIRLS" entrances at school, Elaine should welcome gender equality. However, she cannot; she imagines "Cordelia" waiting to catch her in some imperfection, some failure. Against this oppression, male, patriarchal dominance seems faint-hearted, a pale shadow. When a woman at a sixties consciousness-raising group announces that "what is wrong with us [women] the way we are is men," it does not seem to apply to Elaine's torment. Or, does it?

Cordelia, the chief antagonist in this novel, possibly embodies a thwarted, ineffectual goodness which festers and evolves into a twisted, aggressive sadism in little girls without adequate outlet for their energies. For Cordelia and her sisters whose "formative" lives were shaped in the forties, there are few escapes, and thus, their exertion of "will" metamorphoses into willfulness directed against peers who are even weaker than themselves. Those who cannot escape, attempt to imprison others—a theme that Atwood discusses dramatically in a previous novel, *The Handmaid's Tale* (1985).

Despite the advances in equal opportunity which make women and men equals in the workplace, Elaine remains trapped within her childhood experience, interpreting the present and the future through a "series of liquid transparencies" (CE, 3) called personal history. It is for this reason that she is uneasy about her success, undecided about where to go in middle age. She is tentative about her fame, noting that "alongside my real life I have a career, which may not qualify as exactly real" (CE, 15). Paradoxically, however, the adult Elaine describes herself repeatedly as "lost," (CE, 14) even as she acknowledges that her fame has brought her "a public face . . . I have made something of myself, something or other, after all" (CE, 20). However, in the next instance, the fearful nine-year-old resurfaces and subverts any self-esteem the adult artist has garnered.

In one of the final scenes, Elaine returns to a place of former disempowerment, the public school she attended with Cordelia. She sees the obvious architectural reforms of egalitarian education and momentarily feels relieved. The old "boys" and "girls" doors are gone, although the play areas are still segregated. However, the ghosts of the past are not as easily renovated as school doors. Political reforms can only modify physical, public reality; spiritual transformation is harder to effect. As Elaine stands in the school yard, she feels the persistence of memory push against her "like opening the door against a snowstorm" (CE, 420). The successful, professional woman who is free to express her ideas in art, to marry and divorce anyone she pleases, to educate her own daughters to be accountants and doctors, still shivers in the dark and pleads: "Get me out of this, Cordelia. I'm locked in. I don't want to be nine years old forever" (CE, 421).

Despite her economic and social liberation, Elaine is still a prisoner of her traditional upbringing and its gender norms. Modern feminist writers like Nancy Chodorow in *The Reproduction of Mothering* (1978) and Carol Gilligan in *In A Different Voice* (1982) provide an understanding of the nature of "formative" gender ideologies which "lock" both boys and girls into rigid patterns of behavior and account for some of the frustration that women and men experience in contemporary life and work. In addition, Elaine's problems are indicative of general post-war malaise and a world filled with many choices but few guidelines for moral and ethical behavior.

Conclusion

Images of working women from 1945 to the present have changed dramatically in many respects from the days in which professional fulfillment was implausible or impossible to the present view of the career woman successfully negotiating her way through the world. Although the "problem" which had no name in the fifties has been named and defined, the literature of the late eighties and nineties suggests that old problems have been replaced by new ones. Many women writers look with both skepticism and amused bewilderment as the fifties myth of the super homemaker evolves into the myth of the professional superwoman. Public success does not seem as satisfying from the inside as frustrated and disenfranchised housewives first imagined.

Although no longer thwarted by sexually discriminatory laws and workplace practices, women have, nevertheless, not achieved all the freedoms that were sought during the idealistic sixties. During the last three decades of the twentieth-century, women writers have revealed the difficulty of adapting to role change, despite far-reaching social reforms and role equity. The women and men in the literature of the past two decades face new problems, ones which, because they originate in the psyche and not the courts are not easily eliminated; although writers still view the personal as the political, they concede that revolutionizing the political world does not simultaneously improve the personal sphere. Although there is no desire to return to the stifling domesticity of the fifties, there seems to be an acknowledgement on the part of some contemporary women writers that public success brings with it both power and frustration. Betty Friedan emphasizes the potential rather than the pitfalls of this new social stage when she characterizes it as an opportunity to "create new standards at home and at work that permit a more human and complete life not only for [women] ... but also for men" (Friedan 1981, 55).

In her book, *Writing Beyond the Ending* (1985), literary critic Rachel Blau Du Plessis also calls for new aesthetic standards for women which would reflect their changed position both at home and in the workplace: "Once upon a time, the end, the rightful end of women in novels was social—successful courtship, marriage—or judgmental of her sexual and social failure—death,"[43] Du Plessis argues in her book. Nineteenth-century women would achieve success and prestige through the work of others—their husbands—or not at all. The traditional romance plot, therefore, which repressed the main character and "valorize[d] heterosexuality" limited the ability of women to imagine conclusions for themselves which were uniquely their own. Death became the punishment for those women who looked for alternative endings in literature or life, for women who rejected "the 'social script' or plot designed to contain her legally, economically, and sexually" (Du Plessis, 15). Until the twentieth century, Du Plessis argues, "any plot of self-realization [for women] was at the service of the marriage plot" and needed to end with this resolution. Modern literature would, therefore, have to rewrite the endings of women's literature to reflect their new opportunities for self-actualization in the workplace and at home. How this would be done is still to be seen as women authors learn to "write beyond the [traditional] literary endings" and transform both their lives and their literature.

Notes

1 See Eugenia Kaledin's chapter on "Work" in *American Women in the 1950's: Mothers and More* (Boston: Twayne, 1984); Rosalyn Baxandall, Linda Gordon, and Susan Reverby, eds. *America's Working Women: A Documentary History, 1600-present* (New York: Harcourt, Brace, Jovanovich, 1974).

2 See Ferdinand Lundberg and Marynia F. Farnham's *Modern Woman: The Lost Sex* (New York: Harper & Row, 1947). Lundberg and Farnham attack feminists and professional women as "neurotic" individuals who "turn their backs on the feminine life" (303) and who are therefore responsible for juvenile delinquency and alcoholism among children as well as a host of other social ills.

3 Eugenia Kaledin, *Mothers and More: American Women in the 1950's* (Boston: G.K. Hall, 1986), 63; hereafter cited in the text.

4 Adrienne Rich, "When We Dead Awaken: Writing as Re-Vision," in *On Lies, Secrets, and Silence: Selected Prose 1966-1978* (New York: W.W. Norton, 1979), 42; hereafter cited in text. For a good introduction to critical thought on Adrienne Rich see *Reading Adrienne Rich: Reviews and Re-Visions, 1951-81*, edited by Jane Roberta Cooper (Ann Arbor: University of Michigan Press, 1984).

5 Adrienne Rich, "Aunt Jennifer's Tigers" in *The Fact of a Doorframe: Poems Selected and New: 1950-84* (New York: W.W. Norton, 1984), 4.

6 Adrienne Rich, "Snapshots of a Daughter-in-law" in *The Fact of a Doorframe: Poems Selected and New: 1950-84* (New York: W. W. Norton, 1984), 36.

7 Tillie Olsen, "Tell Me a Riddle," in *Tell Me A Riddle* (New York: Delacorte Press, 1961), 67; hereafter cited in text as "Tell."

8 Sylvia Plath, *The Bell Jar* (New York: Bantam, 1971), 2; hereafter cited in text as *BJ*. Plath was driven by a need to succeed and a fear of success. Her conflicted attitudes are evident in her collected writings: *Letters Home: Correspondence 1950-63*, ed. Aurelia Plath (New York: 1975) and *The Journals of Sylvia Plath*, edited by Ted Hughes and Frances McCullough (New York: Dial Press, 1982).

9 Doris Lessing, *Martha Quest* (New York: New American Library, 1952),2; hereafter cited in text as *MQ*. *Martha Quest* is the first in a five volume series entitled, *Children of Violence*, which follows Martha through a series of experiences. The other novels in chronological order are: *A*

Proper Marriage, A Ripple from the Storm, Landlocked and *The Four-Gated City* (1952-69).

10 Carson McCullers, "Madame Zilensky and the King of Poland," in *The Ballad of the Sad Cafe and other Stories* (New York: Bantam, 1951, 109; hereafter cited in text as "MZ."

11 For a fuller discussion of Flannery O'Connor's work, see Chapter Three.

12 Flannery O'Connor, "The Displaced Person," in *Three by Flannery O'Connor* (New York: New American Library, 1970), 275; hereafter cited in text as "DP."

13 See O'Connor's essay, "Catholic Novelists and Their Readers," in *Mystery and Manners*, ed. Sally and Robert Fitzgerald (New York: Farrar, Straus & Giroux, 1962), 169-90.

14 bell hooks, *Ain't I A Woman: Black Women and Feminism* (Boston: South End Press, 1981), 82; hereafter cited in text.

15 Gwendolyn Brooks, "Bronzeville Woman in a Red Hat" in *Blacks* (Chicago: Third World Press, 1991), 367; hereafter cited in text as "BW."

16 Gwendolyn Brooks, "Queen of the Blues," in *Blacks* (Chicago: Third World Press, 1991), 58-9; hereafter cited in text as "QB."

17 Lorraine Hansberry, *A Raisin in the Sun* (New York: Random House, 1959), np.

18 Shirley Jackson, "The Lottery," in *The Magic of Shirley Jackson* (New York: Farrar, Straus & Giroux, 1966), 137-46.

19 Shirley Jackson, *Hangsman* (New York: Farrar, Straus & Giroux, 1951).

20 Elizabeth Janeway, "Women's Literature," in *Harvard Guide to Contemporary American Writing*, ed. Daniel Hoffman (Cambridge: Harvard University Press, 1979), 353; hereafter cited in text.

21 Susan M. Hartmann, *From Margin to Mainstream: American Women and Politics Since 1960* (New York: Alfred A. Knopf, 1981), 49; hereafter cited in text. For excellent, detailed graphs and charts on the impact of working women from 1800-1980, see Nancy Woloch's *Women and the American Experience* (New York: Alfred A. Knopf, 1984) pgs. 541-48.

22 Mary McCarthy, *The Group* (New York: New American Library, 1965).

23 Patricia Spacks, *The Female Imagination* (New York: Alfred A. Knopf, 1975), 308; hereafter cited in text.

24 Marilyn French, *The Women's Room* (New York: Ballantine Books, 1977),490; hereafter cited in text as *WR*.

25 Anne Sexton, "Housewife," in *The Complete Poems: Anne Sexton* (Boston: Houghton, Mifflin, 1981), 77; hereafter cited in text.

26 Anne Sexton, "Consorting with Angels," in *The Complete Poems: Anne Sexton* (Boston: Houghton, Mifflin, 1981), 111; hereafter cited in text as "CA."

27 Carolyn Kizer, "Pro Femina," in *Knock Upon Silence* (Seattle: University of Washington Press, 1963), 42; hereafter cited in text as "P."

28 Marge Piercy, "To Be of Use," in *Circles on the Water: Selected Poems of Marge Piercy* (New York: Alfred A. Knopf, 1982), 106; hereafter cited in text as "T."

29 Judy Grahn, "II. Ella," in *The Work of a Common Woman* (New York: St. Martin's Press, 1978), 63.

30 Maya Angelou, *I Know Why The Caged Bird Sings* (New York: Bantam, 1970), 47; hereafter cited as *Bird*. Angelou has published a number of sequels to this first autobiography including *Gather Together in My Name* (1974), *Singin' and Swingin' and Gettin' Merry Like Christmas* (1976).

31 Gloria Naylor, *The Women of Brewster Place* (New York: Penguin Books, 1980), 83; hereafter cited as *W*. Also see Naylor's novel *Linden Hills* which deals with the evolution of the black, middle-class.

32 Betty Friedan, *The Second Stage* (New York: Summit Books, 1981); hereafter cited in text.

33 See Bell Hooks' discussion of black woman and work in "Continued Devaluation of Black Womanhood," in *Ain't I A Woman: Black Women and Feminism*, pgs. 51-86.

34 For an in-depth analysis of the genre, see Frances Bartkowski's *Feminist Utopias* (Lincoln: University of Nebraska Press, 1989), 5; hereafter cited in text.

35 Marge Piercy, *Woman on the Edge of Time* (New York: Fawcett Crest, 1976), 154; hereafter cited in text as *WET*. There are many studies of feminist science fiction including *The Feminine Eye: Science Fiction and the Women Who Write It*, ed. Tom Staicar (New York: Ungar, 1982); *Future Females: A Critical Anthology*, Marlene S. Barr ed. (Bowling Green: Bowling Green State University Popular Press, 1981); and Natalie M. Rosinsky's *Feminist Futures—Contemporary Woman's Speculative Fiction* (UMI Research Press, 1984).

36 Joanna Russ, *The Female Man* (Boston: Beacon Press, 1975), 50; hereafter cited in text as *FM*.

37 The narrator is referring to some of the primary feminist essayists in the sixties and seventies including Betty Friedan's *The Feminist Mystique* (1963); Germane Greer's *The Female Eunuch* (1970); Shulamith Firestone, *The Dialectic of Sex: The Case for Feminist Revolution* (1970).

38 Marge Piercy, "The Token Woman," in *Living in the Open: Selected Poems of Marge Piercy* (New York: Alfred A. Knopf, 1977), 71-2; hereafter cited in text as "TW." For a non-fiction account of tokenism, see Suzanne Gordon's essay, "The New Corporate Feminism," in *The Nation*, February 5, 1983, 129.

39 Susan Griffin, "I Like to Think of Harriet Tubman," in *Like the Iris of an Eye* (New York: Harper & Row, 1976), 12; hereafter cited in text as "HT."

40 The subject of women, work and contemporary literature is an enormous one, surely worthy of a book of its own. My selection of a few examples should suggest some representative works only. A sub-genre on this topic includes non-fiction essays and interviews with women writers. See Janet Sternburg, ed. *The Writer on Her Work* (New York: W. W. Norton, 1980); Peggy W. Prenshaw, ed. *Women Writers of the Contemporary South* (Jackson: University Press of Mississippi, 1984); Claudia Tate, ed., *Black Women Writers at Work* (New York: Continuum Publishing Company, 1983).

41 Allison Lurie, *Foreign Affairs* (New York: Avon Books, 1984), 1; hereafter cited in text as "FA."

42 Margaret Atwood, *Cat's Eye* (New York: Doubleday & Co., 1989), 3; hereafter cited in text as "CE." Atwood also analyzes the professional woman in several other novels including *The Handmaid's Tale* (1985), *The Edible Woman* (1969), and *Lady Oracle* (1976) among others.

43 Rachel Blau Du Plessis, *Writing Beyond the Ending* (Bloomington: Indiana University Press, 1985), 1; hereafter cited in the text.

Chapter Two

Sex, Marriage and the Family

> It is the project of twentieth-century women writers to solve the contradiction between love and quest and to replace the alternate endings in marriage and death that are their cultural legacy from the nineteenth-century life and letters by offering a *different set of choices*.
> (Du Plessis, *Writing Beyond the Ending*, 4).

In her short story "Winter Night," (1946) Kay Boyle refers to the social chaos and familial disconnection caused by World War II as "a time of apprehension" in which "nobody stayed anywhere very long any more."[1] The main character in the story, a little girl named Felicia, is reassured, however, by her working mother that "when the fathers came back, all this would be miraculously changed" (WN, 352). Everyone and everything would revert to their traditional patterns and they "would live in a house again, a small one, with fir trees on either side of the short brick walk, and Father would drive up every night from the station just after darkness set in" (WN, 352). Felicia equates this promise with the return of order and light in her life and fervently prays for the resumption of prewar domesticity and the nuclear family. Little do Felicia and her mother realize that, in many respects, life after the war would never be quite the same again.

As Boyle's short story opens, however, both daughter and mother are in a "waiting" pattern, apprehensive about the present and future and nostalgic about the past. Felicia awaits her mother's return from the office, only to be told by an indifferent servant—referred to in the story as "the voice" (WN, 353)—that her mother will not be home for dinner. Instead, the lonely girl's dinner companion will once again be a surrogate "sitting parent." Accustomed to the anonymity of servants and "sitting parents," Felicia expects a silent dinner and an impersonal recitation of a fairy tale before bed.

Felicia's surrogate parent has an entirely different scenario in mind, however. She decides to tell the young American girl about a far worse sort of familial disconnection, the horror of the World War Two concentration camps in which husbands are separated from wives and mothers are dragged off for extermination while their children are left behind to be cared for by compassionate souls like the sitting parent who herself was a surrogate mother to an unfortunate camp girl. And, although Felicia is far better off than her European counterpart, all children suffer the isolation and fragmentation caused by the war. It is for this reason that Felicia, as well as the entire post-war world, look to the return of their fathers and the little house and garden after 1945: the resumption of peaceful alliances after many years of sacrifice.

Boyle's story, therefore, provides an excellent background to the conditions affecting families during and immediately following World War Two. After many years of separation, American and European families sought both stability and order after chaos and discontinuity. The fathers' return after the war heralded the end of "apprehension" and fear and the beginning of fulfillment and love. Women and men wanted to forget the despair and fragmentation symbolized by Boyle's "family life" in and out of concentration camps. In order to accomplish this, "experts" and ordinary citizens alike suggested that women like Felicia's mother exchange their jobs in the office for a life of domestic tranquility. The rewards for a woman's willing suspension of autonomy were explicit: the "fathers" would return and reassert their power and stabilizing influence and love, healing the war's wounds.

The strong desire for post-war "normalcy" also necessitated a return to traditional gender roles; Felicia's mother and other post-war women, were asked to adapt and conform to rigid and sometimes anachronistic definitions of femininity and masculinity as the price for a democratic heterosexuality which would defeat the forces of communism or authoritarianism. In his speech to the graduating class of Smith College in the mid-fifties, Adlai Stevenson asked the young women to devote themselves to their future husbands as one way to "defeat totalitarian, authoritarian ideas."[2] Stevenson believed that Western marriage and motherhood were "another instance of the emergence of individual freedom in our Western society" (Stevenson, 116) which could fight the cold war "in the living-room with a baby in your lap or in the kitchen with a can opener in your hand" (Stevenson, 114).

Ferdinand Lundberg and Marynia Farnham's immensely popular treatise, *Modern Woman: The Lost Sex* (1946) provided the necessary theory to support a return to rigid, judgmental and punitive gender roles. They saw only two "healthy" roles for women—wife and mother—and defined the "drive for equalization" between the sexes as a "collective suicide."[3] Lundberg and Farnham compared the feminists to Soviet collectivists, an anathema in the early days of the Cold War. "As the rivals of men, women must, and insensibly do, develop the characteristics of aggression, dominance, independence and power" which would inevitably lead to personal neurosis and collapse of democracy (Lundberg and Farnham, 236). In a positive explosion of post-war paranoia, Lundberg and Farnham equated "women's sexual freedom" with alcoholism, sexual frigidity, divorce, a rising crime rate, atheism, romanticism, juvenile delinquency, migrations of displaced persons, and war. In their chapter entitled "Ways to a Happier End," the authors suggested that women must be attracted back to the home with the help of "a governmental supervisory agency devoted to serving women who live as women—that is, women as mothers" (Lundberg and Farnham, 360). Although Lundberg and Farnham rejected Hitler's wartime "female solution" which was to order women back home, they did hope that women could be convinced or coerced into assuming their "rightful" roles in the home.

The reaction to both subtle pressure or overt coercion—a type of sexual McCarthyism—was predictable. Although the fifties was a time of high marriage and birth rates, enforced domesticity produced anxiety and resistance as women in literature and essays questioned the restrictive sex role ideologies. The tension brought about by this untenable situation finally exploded in the rhetoric and activism of the sixties which defied "patriarchal" or male-dominated society.

The peace and tranquility imagined by the lonely and immature Felicia in the late forties, therefore, failed to materialize when the "fathers came marching home" or in any decade thereafter. Instead, the decades following the war saw an unparalleled questioning of traditional sexual norms and the patriarchal family. The female literary response to this situation was immediate as women authors attempted to adapt and transform sexuality, marriage and the family. Not surprisingly, it is the history of this revolution in both sexuality and family life which provides one of the central themes in twentieth century women's literature.

The Fifties: The Struggle for New Gender Definitions

Although the birth rates in the fifties reached an all-time peak in 1957 of 25.3 per thousand women and the average marriage age of women was twenty (nineteen in 1951)[4], all was not domestic bliss in the late forties and fifties. Morris Dickstein views the fifties as a schizophrenic age, "a great period for home and family, for getting and spending, for cultivating one's garden," but also "an Age of Anxiety . . . a quiet despair, whose symbols are the Bomb and the still vivid death camps and a fear of Armageddon."[5]

Political, social and sexual fear of competition, in fact, seemed to be a common denominator of the decade. In addition to an obsessive preoccupation with Communism, male veterans were equally suspicious about the newly acquired independence women developed during the war. As Nancy Woloch notes in her book *Women and The American Experience*, "domestic ideology [in the fifties] incorporated the backlash against women and the fear of female competition that had followed the war" (Woloch, 496). In order to mitigate both sexual and political anxiety in the post-war era, the above mentioned "sexual McCarthyism" joined forces with Freudian principles in the late forties and fifties to create the cult of a sexually passive "womanly woman" who would be the standard bearer for a sanctified democratic domesticity.[6]

The equation of feminine passivity, patriarchal marriage and the triumph of "Western democracy," would return to haunt those who instilled it in fifties women. Many repressed women who, throughout the forties and fifties "sought to be good" and, therefore, passive would metamorphose into angry, rebellious sixties women who would question the basis of the patriarchy itself.

In her 1945 short story, "Sex Education," Dorothy Canfield dramatizes the dangers of raising sexually ignorant, repressed little girls in a complex modern society. The narrator of the tale is an older woman who remembers being told three stories by her Aunt Minnie, involving a minister and the cornfield.[7] The first time Aunt Minnie tells the story, she warns the narrator about the inherent dangers in flouting restrictions and going out alone; children should stay on the narrow path and out of the cornfield, "*especially you girls,*" she admonishes. "It's no place for a decent girl. You could easy get so far from the house nobody could hear you if you hollered. There are plenty of men in this town that wouldn't like anything better than—"(Sex, 231).

When her Aunt retells the story to a group of the narrator's married friends years later, the emphasis has changed considerably. Now, Aunt Minnie reveals both her attraction to the minister and ignorance about her youthful feelings. She explains her initial lack of self-awareness as the result of early gender role training: "that was the way they brought young [female] people up in those days, scaring them out of their wits" (Sex, 236). She knows now that "T'would do girls good to know that they are just like everybody else—human nature *and* sex, all mixed up together." (Sex, 237, 240).

The knowledge that women are "human nature *and* sex," reason and passion, however, would not be acknowledged in the forties when this story was published or in the fifties, even after the 1953 Kinsey report published some very startling statistics and facts about female sexuality in its report entitled *Sexual Behavior in the Human Female*.[8] Instead, post-war women were expected to sublimate or repress their sexuality in order to make themselves into good mothers and wives. This repression was, in fact, given social and medical validation by the adoption of Freudian principles in Helene Deutsch's *The Psychology of*

Woman—A Psychoanalytical Interpretation (1944). In *The Feminine Mystique*, Betty Friedan cites the misinterpretation and misuse of Freudian principles in the fifties as a major contributor to the destructive "feminine mystique": "Instead of destroying the old prejudices that restricted women's lives, social science in America merely gave them new authority" (Friedan 1963, 116-7)

Although many women heeded the experts' advice, many writers voiced frustration over missed opportunities for sexual and emotional expression. In fact, this topic became a persistent theme in the literature of fifties writers like May Swenson. In her poem "The Centaur" (1956) a ten-year-old girl abandons herself to the woods instead of Aunt Minnie's cornfields in order to become a "centaur," a Greek mythological creature, half man and half horse. The little girl fashions the horse out of a willow tree and rides it through the woods. United with the sensuous, sexually provocative horse, the child acknowledges that she is both "the horse and the rider,/and the leather I slapped to his rump/spanked my own behind . . . my thighs hugging his ribs."[9]

Despite her sensual reverie, however, the young girl had to return home to her anxious, controlling mother. As if in anticipation of the older woman's remarks, the young girl "smoothed" her skirt when she entered the room with the "clean linoleum" floors. To her mother's question *"Where have you been?* the young irrepressible girl answers *"Been riding."* When her mother notices that her skirt is stretched "awry," she asks *"What's that in your pocket?"* to which the girl answers, *"Just my knife."* The conversation ends, however, on a symbolic note, as the mother subtly warns her daughter about the dangers of riding with "centaurs"—*"Go tie back your hair,* said my mother,/and *Why is your mouth all green?"* (Centaur, 238-39. The daughter's imagination, however, cannot be "tied back" as easily as her hair. Her mouth, verdant with nature, is a silent reproach to the woman whose fear would keep her daughter indoors and away from horses, sexuality and life. Furthermore, in this poem, Swenson juxtaposes the housewife and her clean floors with the sexually free, androgynous girl and the green earthiness of the world. The tension and antagonism between a domesticated mother and her sexually liberated daughter will be played out more dramatically in the sixties and thereafter. In 1956, however, Swenson's young girl sublimates her individuality in fantasy, a strategy which will not prove satisfactory to generations of young women who follow her.

Another woman whose life is constricted by social expectations and sexual taboos is that of Ginny in Grace Paley's short story "An Interest in Life" (1959). After being deserted by an insensitive husband whose parting Christmas gift was a broom, Ginny blames not the irresponsible husband, but herself for the abandonment: "I don't have to thank anything but my own foolishness for four children when I'm twenty-six years old, deserted, and poverty-struck," she confesses. "A man can't help it, but I could have behaved better."[10] The "behavior" about which Ginny is ashamed comes from her "passionate," and "wild" youth (Interest, 88). If the edifice crumbles, it is because the woman is not sufficiently steadfast and docile. Ginny's overtly sadistic husband is, thus, freed from culpability.

What is most interesting about the character of Ginny, however, is how completely she has incorporated the fifties norms about masculinity and femininity into her philosophy of life. Pregnant with a fourth child, she accepts her husband's abuse and abandonment by rationalizing that "men *must* do well in the world" while "a woman counts her children" in order to be happy (Interest, 94). When her husband threatens to leave her pregnant with three young children, she does not criticize or attack him but instead blames herself. Since her husband's happiness depends not on her or her children, he is, inexplicably, "justified" in searching for it elsewhere; Ginny feels this is, somehow, his due as a man and her lot as a woman.

Even as Ginny settles into an positive, mutually beneficial relationship with the lonely John Raftery, however, she continues to fantasize about her wayward husband; a woman of her decade, Ginny cannot imagine an egalitarian relationship, but prefers the fantasy of sexual acquiescence to a male aggressor. Although John Raftery represents a caring man who is willing to nurture her troubled son Girard, and treat her as a confidante, Ginny, nevertheless, prefers the sadistic, rakish husband. In fact, the story concludes ironically with a dream of reunion with the brutal husband as the two have unprotected sex on the kitchen's linoleum floor. Always the passive, suffering wife, Ginny is unable to break out of what Betty Friedan would call the Freudian "brainwashing" (Friedan 1963, 113) in order to imagine a less hurtful, humiliating relationship with a man.

It is this sado-masochistic world that Sylvia Plath recreates in her poem "Daddy" (1962). Although the poem is presumably written to her dead father, the universal implications about the nature of sexual or familial relationships are clear. The persona's father, who is alternately described as a "devil" or Hitler, has died and, thus, abandoned the young girl. Paradoxically, however, the poem's speaker does not celebrate her emancipation. Like Ginny in the Grace Paley short story who finds, strong, abusive men attractive, the narrator in "Daddy" longs for his return or a new incarnation of the tyrannical father in the form of a husband with "a Meinkampf look/And a love of the rack and the screw" to which this willing victim will say "I do, I do."[11] Her rationalization for this abusive relationship is clearly expressed in the famous lines, "Every woman adores a Fascist,/The boot in the face, the brute/Brute heart of a brute like you" (D, 223). The "love or the rack and the screw" has personal and sexual dimensions here, too, since sexuality and masochism are so closely related in Plath's mind.

If there is an important difference between Paley and Plath's characters, however, it is that the latter's voice is angry, enraged, even finally violent at the vampire "Daddy" whom she will defeat with "a stake in your fat black heart,"(D, 224). The passive Ginny awaits her itinerant husband's return like the second coming. Plath's rage is more associated with the anger of sixties and seventies writers like Erica Jong in *Fear of Flying* (1974) who quotes Plath's "Every woman adores a Fascist" as the title for the novel's second chapter.[12] And like Plath, Jong uses the quote to explode the myth of feminine docility inherent in popularized Freudian psychology.

Plath's equation of male aggression and Hitler will also be an important idea in the sixties, since Plath sees the political nature of personal relationships as being of central importance to feminist consciousness and literature. The "fascist" who is found in bedrooms and kitchens across the nation is not the proper punishment for a "wild" youth as Ginny suggests in the

Paley story but rather a sexual enemy who will be defeated in the activist sixties. Unlike the young girl in the Kaye Boyle story, women will, in the sixties, no longer be forlornly waiting for the "Father" or "Daddy" to come home and free them.

The equation of political and sexual tyranny, however, was certainly discussed prior to Plath by several essayists and novelists including Doris Lessing in *A Proper Marriage* (1952). In this book Martha Quest, who had married Douglas Knowell at the conclusion of *Martha Quest*, begins a tormented relationship with her new husband. Knowing immediately that the marriage is "a foolish mistake"[13] and that both marriage and sex instilled in her a "feeling of being caged and trapped" (PM, 28), Martha seeks a solution to her despair. Yet Martha has been trained in the culture of the "womanly woman" and has developed the "instinct to please" (PM, 26), a crucial characteristic of the "good girl." For this reason, she fatalistically immerses herself in romantic love: "love lay like a mirage through the golden gates of sex. If this was not true, then nothing was true, and the beliefs of a whole generation were illusory" (PM, 26).

Not to love Douglas would be unnatural, unfeminine, an insult to herself and her family. And yet, Martha, from the very beginning of the marriage, sees the political as well as the personal implications of her actions. Now she will be unable to criticize the colour bar in Rhodesia since such an action would be deemed unsuitable for the wife of a civil servant (PM, 32). She feels the "nets [of conformity] tightening around her (PM, 47), the very nets which would turn her into a replica of her own frustrated mother. Although Martha is told that when a girl is "properly married ... there is no greater happiness"(PM, 76), she finally must acknowledge that what is proper for others is unsuitable for her—sex, marriage and pregnancy all symbolize an annihilation of the self.

Martha's attitude towards pregnancy and children foreshadows the sixties antipathy to motherhood in such books as *Pronatalism: The Myth of Mom & Apple Pie* (1974) which will be discussed later in this chapter. Martha's revulsion towards sex and childbearing, however, cannot be blamed on her sexual frigidity or neurotic "penis envy." She doesn't fear intimacy but the irretrievable loss of autonomy as an inevitable consequence of marriage.

Despite her reservations, however, Martha can find no alternative path in the forties. When she looks to literature for prototypes, Martha only finds idealistic girls who get married and have babies, "perfectly happy to spend her whole life bringing up children with a tedious husband (PM, 206). Miserable and self-destructive, she concedes that, "either that's the truth or there is a completely new kind of woman in the world" which she, as yet, has not discovered (PM, 206). Against all propriety and traditional feminine instinct, Martha decides to abandon both her husband and baby daughter in order to pursue a new life elsewhere on the hope that "there must be, if not in literature, which evaded these problems, then in life, that woman who combined a warm accepting femininity and motherhood with being what Martha described vaguely but to her own satisfaction as 'a person.' She must look for her" (PM, 206).

This desperate cynicism towards marriage and the family are more widespread than Martha first imagined when she took her revolutionary step: "She was surprised that all the women of the set had come to her, one after another, in secret, to say that they admired her courage, and wished they could do the same" (PM, 335). For this reason, when Martha's repressive, malevolent mother arrives to warn Martha that "it was a woman's role to sacrifice herself, as she had done, for the sake of her children," (PM, 339) the advice goes unheeded.

Instead, Martha becomes a revolutionary in a personal as well as a political sense. She feels solidarity with the black Africans who also live in a repressive order run by white men. Martha, who makes her own declaration of independence from patriarchal sexuality, marriage and the family in pre-civil war Rhodesia, understands the connections among gender, class and racial oppression: "What did the state of self-displaying hysteria Douglas was in have in common with the shrill, maudlin self-pity of a leader in the *Zambesia News* when it was complaining that the outside world did not understand the sacrifices the white population made in developing the blacks? For there was a connection, she felt" (PM, 334).

The linkage which was apparent to Martha in the forties, however, was not as obvious to other women and men in the fifties. Although few female characters succeed in overthrowing or even modifying the traditional concept of sexuality and marriage as does Martha Quest in this novel, there is a pervasive questioning and quiet despair about women's inferior position in love or sexual relations as well as in the family.

One unexpected contributor to this theme is Eudora Welty who is more often associated with her tales praising tradition and community. Yet, in her short story entitled, "Circe," Welty retells the Greek tale of Odysseus and Circe found in Homer's *The Odyssey*. What is most surprising about the Welty "revision," however, is that it is told sympathetically from the woman's or goddess' point of view, a clear departure from Homer's male-centered epic. In Welty's version, the arrival of Odysseus and his men signals the end of Circe's work and invulnerability. When she gives a "welcome" to what she terms the "beautiful strangers," she acknowledges that "welcome [is] the most dangerous word in the world."[14] For the eternal goddess who wishes to maintain her "deathless privacy that heals everything" (Circe, 103), the intrusion of Odysseus and his men is fatal.

The sexual magnetism between Circe and Odysseus initiates a power struggle between the hero and the immortal goddess who "wanted his secret" (Circe, 105) because, as she admits, "before everything, I think of my power" (Circe, 103). At the conclusion of the story, she is left by Odysseus who is preoccupied only with his men and setting sail. Circe sees the greedy, ungrateful men as indicative of the entire gender. "Every since the morning Time came and sat on the world," she concedes, "men have been on the run as fast as they can go, with beauty flung over their shoulders" (Circe, 108).

The lack of true communication between lovers who are sexually but not spiritually connected, is left unresolved in the Welty story. Circe believes men to be "star gazers," (Circe, 102) who never appreciate the immediate beauty surrounding them, but are rather preoccupied with property and sexual conquest. Men in this world are as different from women as mortal from immortal, human from god—any temporary connection is ephemeral and often destructive to the privacy and power of women who willingly extend their hospitality to male "heroes."

The inability of men and women to find a meeting ground for love and union is also portrayed in Jean Stafford's short story, "Cops and Robbers" (1953) in her *Collected Stories* which won the Pulitzer Prize for Fiction in 1970. Outraged at his wife's presumed infidelity with an artist who is painting a family portrait of mother and child, Hugh Talmadge secretly takes his five year old daughter, Hannah, to the barber and has her hair cut. With the child's locks shorn, both the portrait and the presumed "affair" are both ruined. The father, who describes himself as "an old-fashioned man . . . the autocrat of this breakfast table"[15] is likened by his son to Hitler. The child's outraged mother has no rationale for her husband's behavior other than male malevolence: "Why do men do half the things they do? she asks a friend, "Why does Arthur treat you in public as if you were an enlisted man? . . . Why does Eliot brag to Frances that he's unfaithful? Because they're sadists, every last one of them. I am very anti-male today" (Cops, 424).

Stafford's portrayal of post-war marriage is as vicious and destructive a struggle for hegemony as any World War Two battle. Husbands are accused of exercising "gestapo" like control over frustrated and unfaithful wives and innocent children. Alcohol, madness and isolation provide the only subterfuges for those trapped in this family crucible. The insensitive and selfish mother can think of no one outside of herself while her suffering daughter stands unloved and uncomforted in the snow. Unlike Martha Quest, however, this mother cannot escape her situation by abandoning five children, but instead plans to "go to an analyst . . . if I am to continue this marriage until the children are reasonably grown" (Cops, 431).

Other female writers like Adrienne Rich offer few solutions to the ennui and despair they see as implicit in heterosexual relations in the forties and fifties. It would be nearly twenty-five years, in 1976, until Rich would write her concerted attack against marriage and motherhood as a patriarchal rather than fulfilling institution. In the fifties, however, in poems like "Living in Sin" (1955) Rich expresses the disillusionment of romance and sexual unions without providing a positive escape.

Although the couple in the poem have developed an exotic, bohemian life together, with exotic shawls upon the piano and wine and cheese dinners, their existence is empty. In the daylight of truth the woman commits the heresy of noticing the dusty reality and the dirt on the window panes. Unable to express her malaise, however, she dutifully sublimates her angst into housewifely action: she makes the bed and temporarily runs off the demons who haunt her life.[16]

Likewise, the characters in Iris Murdoch's *A Severed Head* (1961) acknowledge the emptiness of their married lives, but try to flee from its reality through adultery or intellectualism. In the novel, the narrator, Martin, describes himself and his marriage to Antonia as "perfectly happy and successful," despite the fact that he spends a great deal of time with his mistress Georgie.[17] Occasionally, the ironical Martin wonders whether he was "what Antonia wanted, or whether she didn't take me simply because she felt it was time to take somebody"; however, he resists such introspection and assures the reader that they are "formidably happy ... [a] handsome clever couple ... everyone's darlings" (SH, 16-7).

Ostensibly oblivious to the hypocrisy and emptiness of his little "arrangement," the coldly rational Martin explains that he "married Antonia in a church ... for social reasons," but considers nothing "sacred" in modern life: "I hold no religious beliefs whatever," he confesses to the reader. "Roughly, I cannot imagine any omnipotent sentient being sufficiently cruel to create the world we inhabit" (SH, 14). Although the cynical Martin does meet Honor Klein, a "severed head" who symbolizes a kind of primitive inanimate object which utters prophecies—a female personification of the Hebrew Ark of the Covenant—there seems little hope for happiness and love in any conventional sense. At the end of the novel, Honor tells him that their relationship has "nothing to do with happiness, nothing whatever." The best they can hope for in this world of reduced expectations is to "survive it" (SH, 248).

Although the characters in Rich's poetry and Murdoch, Lessing, Stafford and Welty's fiction undergo a similar disillusionment about their lives, only Martha sees the political, macrocosmic implications of her condition.

Most writers during the forties and fifties acknowledged their anxiety, but did not look beyond their personal problem to a political solution. It is Lessing, therefore, who provides a more radical minority viewpoint in her novel *Martha Quest* (1952)—hers is the emerging voice which reverberates in the sixties and seventies. No longer a silent sufferer or impotent intellectual, Martha Quest decides that revolutionary action is preferable to passive adjustment. Mr. Maynard, an admirer of Martha Quest and a spokesperson for the white Rhodesian patriarchy soon to be overthrown explains Martha's action as the logical outgrowth of her "true" parentage: "With the French Revolution for a father and the Russian Revolution for a mother, you can very well dispense with a family" (MQ, 345) he notes, to which Martha concurs that his pronouncement was "really a very intelligent remark" (MQ, 345).

Late Sixties to Mid-Eighties: Politicizing Sex and the Family

During the sixties and seventies, dramatic changes in social, legal and personal attitudes towards sexuality, marriage and the family account for what historian Nancy Woloch calls the "latest blast of the sexual revolution . . . The rules of the game had been shifting throughout the twentieth century," she notes, "but during the 1960's . . . the pace of change seemed to accelerate" (Woloch, 530). Among the changes she sees as most revolutionary were "a new enthusiasm for casual 'relationships,' uninhibitedness, open discussion, self-fulfillment and sexual free enterprise . . . among the unusually large cohort of youth and among adults finding a second youth in the sexual marketplace" (Woloch, 510). Books like Helen Gurley Brown's *Sex and the Single Girl* (1962), William Masters and Virginia Johnson's *Human Sexual Response* (1966) and Nena and George O'Neill's *Open Marriage: A New Life Style for Couples* (1972) call into question many of the traditional values associated with monogamous sexuality and patriarchal marriage.

Furthermore, in order to accomplish their egalitarian goals, civil rights and women's "liberation" groups during the decades politicized issues usually thought of as personal. Subjects which had been heretofore "taboo"—sexual stereotyping, child birth, sexual fulfillment, contraception, child care and abuse, homosexuality, sexual harassment, rape, pornography, adultery, and domestic violence—were now openly discussed in public forums as well as sixties "consciousness-raising" groups.

Liberalized attitudes towards contraception, abortion and divorce also made it more socially acceptable to live what would soon be called an "alternative life style." The Supreme Court gave its approval to contraception in Griswold vs. Connecticutl (1965), while the sale and distribution of birth control pills in the sixties made them widely available to many women. The first implementation of a "no-fault" divorce law based on "irreconcilable differences" instead of adultery made divorce less painful and more accessible. During the thirty years from 1950 to 1980, husband-wife households dropped from 80% to 60%, while divorce rates rose precipitously from 1960 to a high of one divorce for every marriage in 1975 (Wandersee, 131). This social change accounted for an entirely new class of single women and non-traditional living arrangements. In the fifties, the divorce rate stayed somewhat stable at fifteen per thousand married women aged fourteen to forty-four. By 1977, the rate had climbed to thirty-seven per thousand (Wandersee, 130), an increase of 250%; in 1960, 28% of women twenty to twenty-four were unmarried but by the end of the seventies, 50% of these women were single (Woloch, 530).

This "fluid" society which permitted casual sexuality and expanded definitions of marriage and family was, in some ways, a rejection of the traditional sexual norms supported by postwar Freudian and cold-war ideologies discussed previously. Many feminist writers in the sixties and seventies sought to reexamine patriarchal society's cardinal virtues: romantic love, heterosexuality and marriage. If these three "principles" of the establishment could be invalidated, then an entirely new social order—one which would allow an androgynous society free of sexual oppression—would be possible. Writers like Kate Millett, in *Sexual Politics* (1970), Shulamith Firestone, in *The Dialectic of Sex* (1970), Eva Figes, in *Patriarchal Attitudes* (1970), Ti-Grace Atkinson, in *Amazon Odyssey* (1974), Nancy Chodorow, in *The Reproduction of Mothering* (1974), Adrienne Rich in "Compulsory Heterosexuality and Lesbian Existence (1980) and *Of Woman*

Born: Motherhood as Institution and Experience (1976) as well as a host of other women essayists, psychologists and theorists sought to free women from restrictive gender roles and norms by exposing the hypocrisy and unequal power relations which held together what they termed "patriarchal" society.

In her radical analysis of sex, marriage and the family, Eva Figes argues in *Patriarchal Attitudes: Women in Society* (1970) that,

> in patriarchal society, male dominance must be maintained at all costs, because the person who dominates cannot conceive of any alternative but to be dominated in turn. And the sex act becomes symbolic of that situation—the man who lies on top of the woman is literally in the 'superior' position, and by doing so he controls the whole of the sex act.[18]

Figes sees the link between sexual passivity and political powerlessness and, therefore, interprets women's increasing aggressiveness in the sixties as indicative of their will to freedom. "When modern woman discovered the orgasm," she noted, "it was (combined with modern birth control) perhaps the biggest single nail in the coffin of male dominance" (Figes, 85). If women would give up the "good girl" docility which forced them into the traditionally prescribed roles of wife and mother, if they took responsibility for their own sexual and political lives, male hegemony would, Figes believed in 1970, end. Lesbian writers like Adrienne Rich also suggested similar aggressive strategies for emancipating women locked in a patriarchal world; however, Rich adopted a gynocentric, "woman-centered" world which would free itself of male domination through a separate society, based on the principles of "maternal thinking" and mutual concern rather than "masculine" competition and property rights.

Ti-Grace Atkinson and Shulamith Firestone critique the ideology of heterosexual "love," implying that "romance" along with heterosexuality force women to abdicate control over their own lives. Atkinson defines the "phenomenon of love" as "the psychological pivot in the persecution of women" and asks women, "if we were free, would we *need* love?"[19] Firestone even goes so far as to caution women against the "tyranny of the biological family"[20] which brainwashes women into believing they must devote themselves to marriage and children. Against the myth of romantic love, Firestone argues a new radical, separatist position: "Men were thinking, writing, and creating because women were pouring their energy into these men; women are not creating culture because they are preoccupied with love" (Firestone, 126).

In the late sixties and seventies, these iconoclastic ideas about sexuality, marriage and the family were imaginatively presented in the dilemmas and choices made by innumerable female literary characters as they sought freedom from restrictive gender roles. Although contemporary women's literature contains examples at variance with this perspective, many literary characters from the sixties onward share a general skepticism about masculinity and its social manifestation, patriarchy.

Often, these literary characters, like Rosamund in Margaret Drabble's *The Millstone*, eschew sexual intercourse altogether as another example of male domination. Female characters often find themselves in threatening worlds that seek to ensnare the unsuspecting free spirit. Alone, but not lonely, these women make the best out of a hostile world by either adopting a protective chastity or its radical opposite—an aggressive promiscuity characterized by Erica Jong's "zipless fuck" in her novel *Fear of Flying* (FF, 1).

Other female literary characters embrace maternity and motherhood, but remain equally skeptical about marriage and men; these women celebrate motherhood—actual or symbolic—in all of their interactions with the world. Yet the "woman-centered" world which they create is a world of women and children, usually daughters; men often figure as consorts or "studs"—unstable, irrational and insecure tyrants who vacillate between childish petulance and adult violence in order to accomplish their wills. Although there are many portraits drawn by women of loving, stable and well-balanced traditional heterosexual marriages, radical feminist thought as it is reflected in literature, seems wary of the nuclear family and the traditionally sanctioned patriarchal order. The women who make their way into the novels, plays and poems reflect that skepticism as they try to maintain their autonomy in a troubled world.[21]

Mary Allen, in her book, *The Necessary Blankness: Women in Major American Fiction of the Sixties* (1976), characterizes the image of women in sixties literature written by both women and men as permeated with sexual and familial disappointment and angst. Female characters in the works of Sylvia Plath, Joyce Carol Oates, John Updike and others are mired in hopeless marriages with "weakened and impotent male[s],"[22] an undesirable fate for sixties women who must develop a complementary "blankness" if they are to remain married. "What does a woman do when she is married to a schlemiel?" (Allen, 8) Allen cynically asks the reader.

If the woman seeks an outlet for her energies—either through work or childbirth—the results are equally disappointing. Allen contends that women are "doubly doomed in current fiction," because motherhood provides no creative outlet for a woman, but rather, during this period, "women are destined to fail in motherhood. A woman is damned if she has children and damned if she does not" (Allen, 181). This portrayal of sterile sexuality and destructive familial relations, a pervasive theme in sixties literature, is nowhere more evident than in the presentation of pregnancy and childbirth which Allen characterizes as "a disaster brought on by men, a violation of a woman's body and a way of manipulating her life (Allen, 181).

Although Allen's thesis about sex, marriage and the family in sixties literature may be extreme—more a reflection of the late seventies when she wrote the book than an objective rendering of the previous decade—her analyses of Sylvia Plath and Joyce Carol Oates are perceptive, especially when one compares these writers' views of pregnancy and motherhood with later writers in the late seventies who celebrate both experiences. In *The Bell Jar* (1963), Plath dramatizes Esther's first sexual experience with Buddy Willard as absurdly comic. Esther looks at Buddy's nakedness and can only think of a "turkey neck and turkey gizzards," which she concedes make her "depressed" (BJ, 55). If sexuality is not humorous, then it is dangerous, as is her relationship with the abusive, "woman-hater" (BJ, 87) Marco who reminds Esther of "a snake I'd teased in the Bronx Zoo" (BJ, 86).

The results of sexuality—pregnancy and motherhood—are equally inimical to Esther's sense of self. She nearly dies of a hemorrhage when she loses her virginity to a United Nations interpreter who tries to wheedle out of paying for her emergency hospital bill. Yet, by far the most frightening symbol in the novel is Dodo Conway, the young mother of six children who personifies all of Esther's fears of sexuality and motherhood. Dodo, her name no doubt symbolizing an animal on the verge of extinction, is a Barnard graduate who has devoted herself to pregnancy and children, "a woman not five feet tall, with a grotesque, protruding stomach . . . wheeling an old black baby carriage down the street" (BJ, 95).

Plath's views about children, however, were not consistently negative, however. In "Nick and the Candlestick" (1962) Plath writes a poem for her one-year-old son Nicholas who represents hope in a bleak world. The poem's speaker asks the baby, "O love, how did you get here?/O embryo/Remembering, even in sleep,/Your crossed position." The baby represents "love, love . . . the one/Solid the spaces lean on, envious," which provides her with momentary joy in the cold world. Nick is "the baby in the barn," the symbol of Christ's birth in Bethlehem. And yet, it was not long after this poem was written that Plath, herself, committed suicide. The baby could not defeat the "black bar airs" which "weld[ed] . . . like plums" to her soul.[23]

Joyce Carol Oates' sixties novels and short stories also reflect an antipathy and skepticism about sexuality and motherhood. One excellent example is found in *The Wheel of Love* (1970), winner of the National Book Award. In her story "Accomplished Desires," (1963) a young, ignorant girl named Dorie, has become infatuated with Mark Arber, a self-absorbed, professor of English and insensitive husband and father of three children. After a series of indignities, including the arrival of Dorie as a "boarder" in the Arber household and her subsequent abortion, Barbara—the long suffering poet/wife who has won a Pulitzer Prize—commits suicide. The suicide is not described as tragic, however, for it relieves Barbara of her miserable existence with the egomaniacal, alcoholic and adulterous Mark—a situation that even 10 years of psychoanalysis cannot improve. Before her death, the intuitive and gifted Barbara wonders,

"Did she hate these children, or did she hate herself? Did she hate Mark: Or, was her hysteria a form of love, or was it both love and hate together."[24]

Likewise, husband and children cannot defeat the forces of darkness which finally encompass Ginny, a young mother and wife in Oates' story, "The Children" (1968). Ginny, who is relieved to surrender her individuality and ambitions for a "sensible, attractive"[25] and suburban motherhood, finds herself inexplicably anxious and abusive towards her independent daughter Rachel. Finally, Ginny's despair at her own loss of control, provides the rationalization she needs to beat her daughter senseless. As she hits Rachel with a bloodied spoon she screams, "A bad girl! You're a bad girl!" (Children, 235). Not even her husband's intervention can mitigate her rage. Rather, when he attempts to stop the beating, she turns her anger upon him. Neither her husband, who is described as "a terrified man with glasses" (Children, 236) nor the stubborn Rachel merit their mother's violence and hatred. Yet, Joyce Carol Oates sees in the abysmal world of suburban marriage and motherhood, the breeding ground of madness and violence which she expands upon in her novels and short stories including *Expensive People* (1968), *Do With Me What You Will* (1973) and *The Goddess and Other Women* (1974).

Anne Stevenson's poem "The Suburb" (1964) also focuses on a similar although not violent female reaction to the eternally pregnant suburban housewife. For the woman in the poem, spring is not a time of renewal or rebirth, but rather it is a "no time" a moment when "leaves have come out looking/limp and wet like little green new born babies." The exhausted woman can spare no time for spring-time day dreaming or herself, "with so many in line to be /born or fed or made love to."[26] Birthing and making love are no longer special, life-fulfilling experiences; instead, they provide the details of the housewife's laundry list of duties. The suburban woman feels only bitterness at her fate, which is to be "hot and pregnant" each May. This realization is particularly bitter when she compares it to her former self "when I slept by myself—/the white bed by the dressing table, pious with cherry blossoms". (Suburb, 220). For those trapped by fate, there is no escape, and thus the woman allows herself to be erased by an unending succession of children. She is ensnared in a trap worthy of any Sophoclean hero or heroine.

Other treatments of the suburban housewife's dilemma are given a satirical or sardonic handling in humorous novels like Sue Kaufman's *Diary of a Mad Housewife* (1967). However, Kaufman's comedy could not mitigate the cynicism and skepticism about marriage, childbirth, and motherhood which were prevalent in both fiction and non-fiction during the period. In their popular anthology of essays entitled *Pronatalism: The Myth of Mom and Apple Pie* (1974) Ellen Peck and Judith Senderowitz openly attack the "myth" of maternal bliss and predict that once women are liberated, they may bypass motherhood completely and remain "childfree."[27] Yet, as has been suggested in Chapter One of this book, work and career did not provide the predicted panacea. Peck and Senderowitz' prophecy of large numbers of "childfree" women, never materializes.

Despite an open rebellion against patriarchy, a fear of sexuality, marriage and children does persist for the next two decades in contemporary literature. Novels, short stories and poetry written in the seventies, eighties and nineties continue to portray the chaos and anguish of husbands and wives, parents and children who live together in dysfunctional families. It is almost a given within this theme that the more the woman tries to improve her fate, the more entangled she becomes in the patriarchal web of relationships. Although independent, sexually aggressive women like Sasha in Alix Kates Shulman's *Memoirs of an Ex-Prom Queen* (1969), Isadora in Erica Jong's *Fear of Flying* (1974), Theresa Dunn in Judith Rossner's *Looking for Mr. Goodbar* (1975), or Lexi Steiner in Elizabeth Benedict's *Slow Dancing* (1985) try to "beat men at their own game" by becoming the seducer instead of the seduced, they ultimately fail to gain power in the "sex wars" so graphically portrayed in contemporary literature. At the outset of their adventures, Sasha, Isadora, Theresa and Lexi and others all believe that sexual aggressiveness and social freedom as women are synonymous; however, it is only after several misadventures and dangerous misalliances that they see their inexorable and intractable positions as women. Free love does not provide real emancipation, as all of the above battered heroines learn in these novels.

Although some women achieve autonomy and love within the traditional family structure, the condition is usually ephemeral. The "swinging singles" life of the sexually aggressive, unmarried woman explored in contemporary literature embodies the bravado of "living on the edge" found in beat generation novels like Jack Kerouac's *On the Road*. This "road" however is often empty and dangerous, not the most promising avenue to feminine mental or spiritual health. And yet, in retrospect, it seems almost necessary for women writers to place themselves in the active "masculine" role of sexual aggressor. By reversing roles with their male adversaries, women are able to imagine an alternative view of social relations which would prove more fulfilling than winning a particular skirmish in the sex wars.

Probably more than any other novel of the period, Erica Jong's *Fear of Flying* (1974) provides the prototypic sexual adventurism described above. In the book, Isadora searches for the "zipless fuck," a completely objective sexual encounter which will provide her with physical pleasure, but none of the demands or consequences of patriarchal marriage and motherhood. Isadora describes the celebrated experience as "a platonic ideal . . . it was necessary that you never get to know the man very well" (FF, 11-2). Anonymous and brief, the zipless fuck is also "absolutely pure. It is free of ulterior motives. There is no power game. The man is not 'taking' and the woman is not 'giving'" (FF, 14).

To Isadora, sexuality, love and marriage are all sinister concepts, instruments of male enslavement: "It didn't matter, you see, whether you had an IQ of 170 or an IQ of 70," she tells the reader, "you were brainwashed all the same. . . . Underneath it all, you longed to be annihilated by love, to be swept off your feet, to be filled up by a giant prick spouting sperm, soapsuds, silks and satins, and of course, money" (FF, 10). Her "zipless fuck," therefore, is a defense against getting involved, brainwashed and then "annihilated" by heterosexual love. What she learns initially from her newly emerging sexuality is what she first suspected—sexuality *is* power. When she seduces a man, she feels a "special kind of power over him—one that painting or writing [her profession] couldn't approach" (FF, 155). And yet, it is ultimately an empty victory without any long term benefit. "Sex," she confesses in the conclusion of the book "was no final solution" (FF, 254). Even before the advent of AIDS, Isadora recognizes that bedding all available men is dangerous, not only to her physical health, but to her mental well-being because, she notes, "if you reduce everything to that level of indifference, everything becomes meaningless. It's not existentialism, it's numbness" (FF, 258).

Isadora's promiscuity, however, protects her not only from intimacy, but also from maternity. Her antipathy towards the role of mother is based primarily on patriarchal motherhood, a condition which will be exploded in Adrienne Rich's book *Of Woman Born* (1976). In a utopian maternal world, Isadora would like to have a "wise and witty" daughter who could "grow up to be the woman I could never be. A very independent little girl with no scars on the brain or the psyche. With no toadying servility and no ingratiating seductiveness" (FF, 46). Since this ideal vision of motherhood is not available to her, Isadora opts for childlessness: "Somehow the idea of bearing *his* baby angers me. Let him bear his own baby! If I have a baby I want it to be all *mine*" (FF, 47).

Despite Isadora's perceptive articulation of women's dilemma, she can, in 1966, find no solution to her insoluble problem because "being a woman meant being harried, frustrated, and always angry. It meant being split into two irreconcilable halves" (FF, 157). The protective anonymity of both the "zipless fuck" and her marriage to Bennett provide no peace or solace for the hapless Isadora, and thus the book ends as it began, with the heroine in a state of flux and uncertainty.

Sasha, in Alix Shulman's *Memoirs of An Ex-Prom Queen* (1969), likewise, shares Isadora's cynicism about sexuality, marriage and children, even as she hops from one man's bed to another. Adultery, her own equivalent of the "zipless fuck," becomes a weapon she can use against her insensitive husband whose passion for her is just another example of the "joy of possession."[28] At the age of fifteen, Sasha learned that "love was a dangerous emotion. It was dynamite" (Memoirs, 63); Her defense against this domination is unabashed sexuality, adultery, even prostitution. She, like Isadora, will turn the tables on the victimizer in order to revenge herself and her sex. Her efforts, however, even as she engages in her philanderings seem more pathetic than brave, "Though I passed myself off as an adventuress," she confesses, "inside I knew I was really a coward" (Memoirs, 33).

Equally confusing and self-destructive is Theresa Dunn's chaotic world in Judith Rossner's *Looking for Mr. Goodbar* (1975). Theresa is also a conflicted character, a person with two selves—the nurturing school teacher who loves her students and the self-proclaimed "whore"[29] whose sex life consists of one night stands from a singles bar. Although she would like to become a individual who both thinks *and* feels, she remains a divided person until she is murdered, ironically, on New Year's Eve by a psychopath. An explanation for Theresa's paradoxical behavior, however, can be found in her reaction to sexuality and marriage as it is practiced in her world. Her married and often pregnant sisters have "real" (LMG, 138) lives, yet they seem desperately unhappy, "bound together by lovelessness" (LMG, 107), as her older sister Katharine describes it. Refusing to commit herself to any one man, Theresa finds safety in numbers—she sleeps with countless men and asks them to leave her bed almost immediately. However dangerous, sexuality will give her temporary autonomy until some other solution can be found.

It is not until Evelyn, a fellow teacher, asks her to join a women's conscious raising group that Theresa sees a way out of her meaningless life. It is Evelyn who links Theresa's individual problems to gender inequities when she suggests "that women thought they had their own unique problems, and that the problems were emotional, while in reality their problems were shared and political. Imposed on them by the culture" (LMG, 238). If women were to be truly free, they would need to join forces to combat social oppression and courageously construct a world in which a woman's identity was "deeper and more important than her relationship to a man" (LMG, 238). Theresa finds Evelyn's invitation to connect with other women, "frightening" (LMG, 237) because it suggests an end to the duplicity and anonymity which are part of her divided life. Because she cannot make the leap of faith, she returns to the bar where she meets a pathetic, tormented drifter, himself the abused child of five step fathers, who acts as her willing executioner.

The image of the sexually liberated, but emotionally repressed woman continues to be found in eighties literature, where the prototypic sixties adventuress remains virtually unaltered. Lexi and Nell, the main protagonists of Elizabeth Benedict's *Slow Dancing* (1985) are the better educated, more sophisticated and cynical, younger sisters of Isadora and Sasha. Yet, Lexi and Nell's fear of sexual involvement and marriage are nearly identical to that of their predecessors'. Lexi, a well-organized lawyer in California has more power and prestige than her earlier prototypes, but she uses her sexuality in a similar manner—as a protective device against intimacy in order to maintain her autonomy with men: "Sleeping with men you didn't care about was an acquired taste," the narrator remarks, and Lexi "had acquired it."[30] For this reason, Nell has a twenty-one day maximum for the duration of relationships (SD, 195), while Lexi believes that love lasts "about as long as a side of a forty-five" record (SD, 15). The best a woman can do in contemporary affairs is, therefore, a "slow dance."

The difference between Lexi, Nell and characters like Theresa Dunn, however, is that Lexi and Nell are cognizant of the inherent dangers of their choices and wish to do something about their potentially destructive behaviors. Lexi, who is sufficiently introspective enough to see her future as nothing more than "one of the great lays of someone else's past," admits to her friend, Nell, that she "doesn't want to be that woman anymore" (SD, 286). Likewise, Nell who has been writing "the definitive book in praise of single womanhood" becomes convinced that this state should be avoided, not praised because the women she meets are "all miserable" (SD, 10).

For these reasons, both Lexi and Nell decide to marry at the conclusion of the book, actions which will change not only their lives but their friendship as well. And yet, there is little enthusiasm for this revived traditional life; in fact, both women seem to view their decisions as a "sell-out" to the conservative political forces of Reagan and the religious right in which the novel takes place. When a male friend asks Nell if she will have children, she answers, "Yeah . . . I guess that's one of the possibilities for when you can't think of anything else to do these days. And think of how happy it would make Jerry Falwell . . . The possibility that you could give birth to a gun-toting Christian" (SD, 310). Her prospective marriage and family seem almost a political as well as a personal betrayal of values and principles.

Ann Beattie's novels—*Falling in Place* (1980) and *Love Always* (1985) as well as several short stories also portray the sexually liberated but paradoxically repressed lives of women who opt for alternatives to traditional family life in contemporary society. However, neither monogamy nor alternative living arrangements make for freedom, stability or happiness. In Beattie's story, "Tuesday Nights" (1977), the main character, a divorced mother, lives with a current boyfriend, Dan and her daughter Joanna, a child from her first marriage. None of the characters feels sexual animosity towards the other—the old patriarchal view of women as property is as obsolete in this world as is married fidelity and monogamy. When Joanna visits her biological father on Tuesday nights, she is confronted by an unending line of his "sleepies."[31] The narrator accepts this situation and does not make value judgments—she is openminded and thus free from the old traditional "thou shalts." This is hardly the world of Alix Shulman in which outraged husbands attempt to rape their wives as punishment for adultery.

Yet, despite this supposed freedom, there is an anxiety and unhappiness in Beattie's modern world which pervades the atmosphere. The main character's attempt to find self-direction and autonomy by isolating herself on Tuesday nights proves unsuccessful. At the end of the story, she and her latest lover are about to separate, probably as casually and aimlessly as they have lived together. While Beattie would surely not wish a return to the stifling fifties and sixties families, she views the fluid world of part-time lovers and "Disneyland dads" as depressing alternatives. The strangling web of relationships so prevalent in the fifties and sixties has been replaced by a world which lacks connectedness of any kind—too high a price, Beattie suggests, for autonomy.

The epigraph to Ellen Gilchrist's book of short stories, *Drunk with Love* (1986) might also apply to Beattie's work. Gilchrist quotes Albert Einstein's remark that "what has been overlooked [in the world] is the irrational, the inconsistent, the droll, even the insane, which nature, inexhaustibly operative, implants in an individual, seemingly for her own amusement."[32] While Beattie and Gilchrist dramatize contemporary life's shifting, inconsistent and ephemeral relationships, Gilchrist sees the sardonic humor within this world. Despite their differences, however, Gilchrist, like Beattie, criticizes the permissive (sometimes value-free) world in which sexual alliances have less permanence and seriousness than business partnerships. It is for this reason that Freddie Harwood in the title story, "Drunk with Love" wishes to kill himself when his girlfriend becomes pregnant with an ex-boyfriend's twins.

Freddie is hardly the old, patriarchal father, obsessed with continuing his seed through generations. His is the life of Berkeley, California in the eighties—non-judgmental, open sexual relations free of the trappings of the traditional nuclear family—about as different from Sasha's New York as one could get. Yet when Freddie becomes a "hero" by rescuing two Vietnamese children from a burning building during an earthquake, his old machismo, and along with it his paternal inclinations return. He grabs his elusive girlfriend and shouts at her with uncharacteristic ardor "You are going to marry me, goddammit. You can't play with somebody's affections like that. I'm a serious man and SERIOUS PEOPLE GET MARRIED" (DL, 11). However, heroism in this world seems as anachronistic as his marriage proposal which Nora Jane rejects: "I like you the most of anyone I've ever made love to or run around with. That's true and you know it. You're the best friend I've ever had. But I am not in love with you and that is also true" (DL, 13).

Meanwhile, the very pregnant Nora Jane temporarily falls into bed with Sandy, the actual father of the twins. Sandy, who exists as almost the personification of dysfunctionality in contemporary life, is a fitting partner for Nora Jane. Abandoned by his mother when he was a child, Sandy cannot maintain permanent relationships—sexual or otherwise—with anyone. Even as Nora Jane and he lie in bed together, Sandy reflects that "It [their love] was so fragile. It never stayed. It always deserted him. It always went away. It was here now. It would leave him alone" (DL, 23). If there is any sense of stability or rationality in this world, it comes quite humorously from the two fetuses—Tammili and Lydia—who rest in their mother's womb, listening to the outer human circus. Tamili, who has little patience for her mother's peripatetic ways, says to her sister "She's always changing. Up and down. Up and down." Her knowing sister Lydia cynically remarks, "Get used to it. We'll be there soon" (DL, 25). The reader can only surmise from this dialogue, that the world of Ellen Gilchrist is so hilariously skeptical, so jaded, that even fetuses are cynical.

The more pervasive view toward the state of male/female relations, however, is far less light-hearted. The idealistic hopes for a new conception of marriage in the early sixties, reflected in Denise Levertov's poem "About Marriage" (1962) quickly give way to less optimistic feelings in "The Ache of Marriage" (1964). In the earlier poem, Levertov warns her lover "don't lock me in wedlock, I want/marriage, an/encounter—/I told you about the/the green light of May."[33] Levertov envisions a perfect marriage as a place "in a green/airy space, not/locked in." In "The Ache of Marriage," however, the earlier mutual independence is transformed into an "ache." Earlier images of weightlessness and flight are contrasted with the "heavy" ache of thigh and tongue which ensnares the lovers: "We look for communion/and are turned away" she laments. The claustrophobia of marriage is symbolized by the "leviathan" which has swallowed the lovers who are "looking for joy, some joy/not to be known outside" of marriage.[34]

Late Seventies and Eighties: Motherhood and the Escape from the Patriarchal Family

Since marriage and heterosexuality may be seen as entrapments or anachronisms, many female contemporary writers view them with skepticism. In 1974, novelist, and essayist Rebecca West, wrote an analysis of modern women's literary response to marriage and the family entitled, "And they all lived unhappily ever after," identifying the major plot scenario between women and men in contemporary literature as "desertion."[35] She cynically noted that "mutual understanding has never been the strong point of the sexes" and that in contemporary literature, women and men's interactions have revolved around "deception of all sorts and degrees" (West, 779). In order to prove her thesis, West cited the women who people Doris Lessing's novels, many of whom have been discussed in this chapter. "It is a culminating disappointment," noted West, "that such a formidable woman [like Doris Lessing] who can carry about her such a heavy intellectual satchel ... cannot believe that women can hope for satisfactory sexual lives. That, indeed, she seems to regard as the most depressing feature of the modern world" (West, 779).

West did not explain why the major plot scenario of "desertion" or "they all lived unhappily every after" was so prevalent in contemporary writing. However, she finally concluded that the only explanation for the estrangement between women and men is that "men do not like women. But perhaps that last phrase should be written 'that men do not like.' It is possible that men are deficient in the capacity to love" (West, 779).

Many writers from the sixties onward concur with West's assessment of men and patriarchal society. The woman who seeks love in contemporary life would often not find it in the problematic relations between women and men, inside or outside of traditional marriage. Anne Sexton's poem, "For My Lover, Returning to His Wife," (1967) expresses the ironical relief that a mistress feels when her ephemeral lover returns home. Sexton contrasts the wife's stable, but unenviable position with that of the mistress' and finds the "loser's" position preferable. The wife is mired in marriage, a woman who "sees to oars and oarlocks for the dinghy," while the mistress is "momentary./A luxury. A bright red sloop in the harbor."[36] The wife's solidity is her power and yet her sinecure is won at a terrible price: "She is so naked and singular./She is the sum of yourself and your dream/Climb her like a monument, step after step" (For, 190). In contrast to the impassive wife who is possessed and conquered, the mistress is free and unencumbered, "As for me, I am a watercolor," she confesses with a mixture of irony, hostility and candor, "I wash off" (For, 190).

If aggressive or ambivalent sexuality was one way women dealt with issues of autonomy in contemporary literature, another equally pervasive alternative was a new feminist chastity. Some female poets and fiction writers in the sixties and seventies viewed heterosexuality with suspicion or outright hostility, often cautioning women to avoid its entrapments, as does Fleur Adcock in her vitriolic "Against Coupling" (1971) which describes sexual intercourse as "a trespassing tongue/ forced into one's mouth, one's breath/smothered, nipples crushed against the/ribcage ... unpleasure."[37] Likewise, the mistress who awaits her lover's telephone call in Edna O'Brien's short story "The Call" (1979) decides to end her liaison with her lover who manipulates her both psychologically and sexually: "Always when he lay above her, about to possess her, he seemed to be surveying his pasture, to sniff like a bloodhound, making sure that no other would pass through to his burrow, making sure that she would be secret and sweet, and solely for him."[38]

A similar alienation from feeling and love is expressed by the mistress in Hortense Calisher's story, "Point of Departure" (1975) who describes her "love" affair with a married man as "two people holding on to the opposite ends of a string, each anxious to let go first, or at least soon, without offending the other, yet each reluctant to drop the curling, lapsing bond between them."[39] The dual narrators, male and female, in the story, suggest the unbreachable alienation of modern love. "It's pathetic, isn't it" the woman confesses to her love, "the spectacle of people trying to reach one another? By any means. Everywhere" (PD, 387).

The couple in Calisher's story separates without even communicating their feelings, "modernly reticent," as the woman ironically notes. The end of the affair, however, is not to be seen as an isolated case of misunderstanding between an insecure mistress and a misogynist man, but rather as symbolic of contemporary relations which are quietly desperate, according to the woman. "It happened everywhere" she explains, "behind the tidy doors of marriage, in the dark bed of adventure, or in the social bumpings against one another in the crowded rooms where people massed together protectively in frenetic gaiety, hiding stubbornly—'I am alone'—using liquor, music, sex, to say — 'You too?'" (PD, 347).

Writers like Calisher, Sexton, Adcock and O'Brien often interpret contemporary sexual relations as a loveless wasteland, full of sexual passion, but little feeling. It is not surprising, therefore, that poets like May Swenson in "Women" (1968) and Jean Tepperman in "Witch" (1969) suggest that women resist the minefields of contemporary heterosexuality. The answer, for some female writers, is separation into a maternal world which would embrace motherhood and children as the source of love and fulfillment while it eschews heterosexual marriage. Within this pervasive literary theme, the family unit is preserved, but it is composed of an almost entirely female cast of characters.

One important book that signalled this philosophical shift towards motherhood but rejection of the traditional nuclear family was Adrienne Rich's *Of Woman Born: Motherhood as Experience and Institution* (1976) which explored this dramatic change in attitude towards heterosexuality, maternity and children. In the "Afterward" to the book, Rich noted that "In the four years of writing this book [1972-76], I have seen the issue of motherhood grow from a question almost incidental in feminist analysis to a theme which now seems to possess the collective consciousness of thoughtful women (Rich, 1976, 4).

One might, therefore, incorrectly conclude that the pendulum, which had moved decidedly away from the traditional family—man, woman and child—had swung back. This new emphasis on children and family might even be misinterpreted as a renewed faith in the future of patriarchal society. However, if one looks more closely at some contemporary literature, a new maternity has evolved which suggests that children born outside of marriage, previously considered "illegitimate" are women's best hope for love in a contentious and divided modern society. Rich's scholarly book-length essay clearly articulates the differences between "institutional" motherhood within the traditional nuclear family and a more positive, life-affirming "experiential" motherhood without men.

Rich encourages women to have out of wedlock children as "one way in which women have defied patriarchy" (Rich 1976,

160). This unsanctioned birth would serve as a liberating force for previously powerless women within a society where "male/female relationships have been founded on the status of the female as the property of the male, or of male-dominated institutions" (Rich 1979, 6). It is not surprising that Rich would use as her support for this belief, Marxist historian Linda Gordon's assessment of the state of heterosexual relations in contemporary life as "always intense, frightening, high-risk situations which ought, if a woman has any sense of self-preservation, to be carefully calculated" (qtd. in Rich 1976, 196).

In *Of Woman Born*, Rich not only criticizes present male/female sexual interactions but also rejects the traditional system of motherhood as a soul destroying "institution" organized and run by what she terms the "Kingdom of the Fathers" (Rich 1976, 56). This kingdom, she defines as the "core of all power-relationships, a tangle of lust, violence, possession, fear, conscious longing, unconscious hostility, sentiment, rationalization: the sexual understructure of social and political norms" (Rich 1976, 39). In 1976, Rich vocalizes a major shift which simultaneously celebrates motherhood, and rejects the patriarchal family in favor of a liberating mother/child prototype.

Yet Rich's position should not be seen as entirely cynical or skeptical. From the mid-seventies to the mid-eighties, there has been a rediscovery of romance, but it is a love affair between mothers and children which often excludes men. The use of the word "romance" in describing the newly formulated mother/child bond is not be taken lightly for there is sometimes an unarticulated, but nevertheless strongly felt belief in some contemporary women's literature that heterosexual love can not exist either within marriage or in alternative, sexually "liberated" heterosexual arrangements. If Rich is correct in her assertion that modern "sexual love is imagined as power over someone" (Rich 1976, 51), then who would blame the woman who flees the traditional family in search of emotional security and fulfillment elsewhere? Critics Rebecca West and Adrienne Rich see desertion and disillusionment throughout contemporary literature and life and seek more positive alternatives elsewhere.

Years before Rich's awakened interest in motherhood became widely known, however, a British novelist, Margaret

Drabble, wrote a novel which would provide a prototype for this new literary maternity. In *The Millstone* (1965) Drabble presents a portrait of Rosamund, a liberated female character cast adrift in a loveless adult world, who becomes pregnant after a one-night stand but rejects both abortion and marriage and elects to raise her daughter alone. Although Rosamund momentarily considers confiding in George, the biological father, she dismisses the option and justifies her action by rationalizing that he was "incidental to my life . . . utterly accidental."[40]

Unlike previous women in literature who must suffer because of an out of wedlock child, Rosamund finds, much to her surprise, that her daughter, Octavia, infuses both love and fulfillment into her otherwise sterile life. Octavia's birth "makes sense of disconnections" (M, 75) in the discontinuous postmodern era. She describes the bond with the baby as one that "links man to man" (M, 79) and most importantly provides "love, for the first time in my life" (M, 114-5). The connectedness that she feels with this child, however, does not help her to rejoin the world of adult relations. At the beginning of the novel, she tells the reader, "I am still not married, a fact of some significance" (M, 7).

Although Rosamund acknowledges the folly of devoting herself exclusively to motherhood, especially a motherhood without men, she fatalistically eschews the traditional nuclear family, and, with it, men in general: "A BAD INVESTMENT, I knew, this affection [with Octavia], and one that would leave me in the dark and the cold in years to come; but then what warmer passion ever lasted longer than six months" (M, 191). Thus, the "illegitimate" child, usually portrayed in literature as a punishment for the erring woman, is revealed as the key to love in a joyless world.

Rosamund, however, is cognizant of the revolutionary nature of her choice as well as its personal and political significance. She views herself as a modern Hester Prynne whose sin represents a "brand-new, twentieth century crime, not the good old traditional one of lust and greed. My crime was my suspicion, my fear, my apprehensive terror of the very idea of sex . . . my selfish, self-preserving hatred of being pushed around . . . I knew how wrong and how misguided it was. I walked around with a scarlet letter embroidered upon my bosom, visible enough in the end, but the A stood for Abstinence, not Adultery" (M, 21).

The scarlet A of abstinence from heterosexual relations to which Rosamund ironically refers is also worn by other female characters mentioned in this study who reject men out of fear, disillusionment or general distrust borne of experience. This flight from men and patriarchy and consequent preference for motherhood, however, comes at a high price. In an essay entitled, "Towards a Feminist Poetics," (1979), Elaine Showalter predicted the potential for violence in the growing sexual separatism: "In the 1970's," Showalter argued, "Mr. Right turns out to be Mr. Goodbar,"[41] previously referred to in this chapter. Rossner's character Theresa Dunn, however, is not saved by maternity. Instead, she succumbs to the hostility of the sex wars as they are waged in the singles' bars of the decade. It was thus not surprising that Showalter called for a new direction in women's literature in the eighties which would take it "beyond the scenarios of compromise and madness and death to a new communion between the sexes" (Showalter 1985, 134).

The call for an end to the violence in both language and literature[42] has also been voiced by Sandra Gilbert and Susan Gubar in their 1987 *New York Times* article entitled "Sex Wars: Not the Fun Kind" in which they, too, ask why "male and female antagonists continue substituting stalemated violence for love and friendship? Can the sexes lay down sword and shield sometime soon, or will the year 2001 witness a war of the words between feminists who are 'not the fun kind' and 'wild men' in search of 'the primitive root' of their maleness?" (Gilbert and Gubar 1987, 23). Gilbert and Gubar, whose three critical volumes on twentieth century literature entitled *No Man's Land* chronicle sexual hostilities and solutions[43] asked in their *Times* article whether "peaceful coexistence between the sexes—a coexistence not predicated on a separatist peace—might [still] become possible" (Gilbert and Gubar 1987, 23).

The dangers of this separatist world have been suggested by a number of other female novelists in the seventies and eighties. Both mothers and children chafe under the claustrophobic relationship which excludes the world. Hilma Wolitzer's short story,

"Waiting for Daddy" chronicles the life of Sandy, a young girl brought up by a mother and grandmother, who fantasizes about her "vanished" father.[44] Her desire for a father, however, is only heightened by her mother and grandmother who "seemed to have no need for men," Sandy observes. As an adolescent, Sandy seeks real and surrogate fathers everywhere, in the homes of her friends and in the back seats of her boyfriends' cars. She rationalizes her behavior by placing herself into the role of helpless victim: "If my father were here, *he* would make the decision, he would be my defender and my strength. But there was no one to protect me from my own bad decisions, no one to lead me from the back seat of cars" (Waiting, 399).

In *The Handmaid's Tale* (1985), Margaret Atwood also speculates about the political as well as the personal ramifications of dislocated familial relationships when she envisions their logical nightmare conclusion: the dystopic society of Gilead, a world in which both men and women are alienated and estranged from each other but also pathologically and fatally obsessed with children and childbirth. Some of the preoccupation with children is a result of diminishing fertility rates and high infant mortality brought about by nuclear accidents and war. Although it is possible to interpret the handmaid's obsession with reproduction in terms of practical survival, that alone is not a satisfactory explanation. What, the reader may ask, created the nightmare world of Gilead? Is it patriarchal religion and society taken to a fascistic extreme? Or, is Atwood's answer found in the subtle but growing estrangement between men and women, children and their mothers that has been an intrinsic factor of contemporary literature and life? How is it, Margaret Atwood asks in 1985, that the free modern feminist world of the sixties and seventies has evolved into this repressive future? In what way is Offred's and Gilead's emphasis on children a hyperbolic rendering of contemporary female character's preoccupation with daughters? In what way is women's "abstinence" from the world of men in *The Millstone* a precursor to the separatism of Gileadean life? At one point in the novel, Offred addresses a rhetorical question to her abducted feminist mother, challenging the older woman's decision to reject men: "Mother, I think. Wherever you may be. Can you hear me? You wanted a woman's culture. Well, now there is one. It isn't what you meant, but it exists."[45]

Atwood's description of the family and heterosexual relations in the seventies and eighties provides a partial clue to understanding Gilead. During the pre-Gilead period, women and men were reluctant to commit themselves to each other or marriage and, instead, moved in and out of superficial relationships, often deserting each other even before the six months which Rosamund gives for most contemporary unions. Offred, like many female literary characters describes these casual relations: "if you don't like it, change it, we said, to each other and to ourselves. And so we would change the man for another one" (HT, 293-4).

Ironically, the leaders of the Gilead establishment use the decadence and confusion of modern life to justify their present authoritarian regime: Offred's Commander and primary stud, argues that women have benefitted from the new Gileadean age: "Think of the trouble they [women] had before. Don't you remember the singles' bars . . . [women] got no respect as mothers. No wonder they were giving up on the whole business" (HT, 283-4). Even Offred, who enjoyed the freedom of seventies' promiscuity, admits that "At that time men and women tried each other on, casually, like suits, rejecting whatever did not fit" (HT, 67).

A closer analysis of Offred's feminist mother provides additional insight into the eventual division of Gilead into two separatist societies, female and male. Offred remembers her mother's antipathy about marriage and men: "I don't want a man around," she said to Offred. "What use are they except for ten seconds' worth of half babies. A man is just a woman's strategy for making other women . . . Just do the job, then you can bugger off . . . I make a decent salary, I can afford daycare" (HT, 156).

From her newly acquired vantage-point in Gilead, Offred sees the confusion and loneliness of her mother's world and tries to understand her mother's dismissal of men and emotional dependence on her daughter. However, when Offred describes her troubled relationship with her mother, she seems very much like an eighties version of Octavia in Margaret Drabble's

The Millstone—grown up and fed up and rebellious after a claustrophobic mother/daughter only family. Offred concedes in her narrative that she admired her mother, "although things between us were never easy. She expected too much from me ... She expected me to vindicate her life for her, and the choices she'd made. I didn't want to live my life on her terms. I didn't want to be the model offspring, the incarnation of her ideas. We used to fight about that. I am not your justification for existence, I said to her once" (HT, 157). Offred, likewise, dismisses the separatist philosophy of her lesbian friend Moira: "If Moira thought she could create utopia by shutting herself up in a women-only enclave she was sadly mistaken. Men were not just going to go away. You couldn't just ignore them" (HT, 223).

In *The Handmaid's Tale*, Atwood warns that the chaos and disillusionment of contemporary sexual and family life will prepare people for the repressive, puritanical, separatist patriarchy that is Gilead. Critic Cathy Davidson, therefore, may oversimplify the complexity of the dilemma when she describes Gilead as "an allegory of what results from a politics based on misogyny, racism and anti-semitism."[46]

Although Offred's participation in Gilead is the direct result of coercion and imprisonment, another character in a different novel willingly enters a repressive religious cult rather than suffer the confusion and violence inherent in the "free" world. In Anne Roiphe's *Lovingkindness* (1987), a twenty-four year old American named Andrea joins an Israeli patriarchal Jewish sect whose values and power structures ironically resemble those of Gilead. Andrea rejects the feminist autonomy of her mother, Annie, and enters the Yeshiva Rachel, a fundamentalist Hasidic sect. In the novel, Annie must confront and eventually accept her daughter's decision to reject the modern world of choice in favor of a "handmaid's" existence at the Yeshiva.

The Yeshiva Rachel, which bears an uncanny resemblance to the Rachel and Leah reeducation center in *The Handmaid's Tale*, provides a stability and serenity for the confused and self-destructive Andrea who has now (like Offred) adopted a new name—Sarai, the wife of Abraham in the Old Testament and the first mother of Judaism. Like Offred, Andrea will serve both the patriarchy and nation by acquiescing to an arranged marriage with another group member. Unlike Offred, however, Andrea does it willingly. It is Roiphe's purpose in the novel to explain why.

When Annie analyzes her daughter's pre-Yeshiva existence, she believes that "choice, too much choice, a world without boundaries, has pushed Andrea overboard."[47] And most importantly, Annie, a self-appointed representative of a modern philosophy which deified freedom and equality, carefully avoiding the traditional patriarchal God, confesses, "I am not sure I can save her" (L, 87). Annie helped to create what she believed would be a new world of equality, a world decidedly superior to her own mother's existence in the forties and fifties. However, she seems convinced now that her daughter and her generation will reject the feminist ideal in favor of a life of servitude: "This admission of failure," Annie confesses, "is a negation of all I imagined, invented, aspired; it is as if I were an architect who had built a city that no one could inhabit. I hear the loosening of bolts, the falling of beams, the breaking of glass as the city rots" (L, 80).

Andrea, like Offred, will also devote herself to a motherhood which is an instrument of a patriarchal regime—not Atwood's Gilead (although Gilead is a biblical city found in the Old Testament), but to the Jewish nation as interpreted and run by Rabbi Cohen. Ironically, as different as she is from her feminist mother, Andrea's life will be relatively free of men as well; she will be preoccupied with children as a means of salvation, "I will take good care of my children because that is all that matters to me" she writes to her mother. Frustrated and angry, Annie accuses Andrea of being nothing more than "a baby machine" and asks "do you know what you are giving up?" Andrea, who has lived in the violent and often meaningless contemporary world, cynically retorts, "A wonderful life like yours?" (L, 207-8).

Pitifully few men or women who inhabit Annie's free world live anything that approaches a "wonderful life." Although Annie tries to convince her daughter to abandon the Yeshiva Rachel and return to New York, Annie doesn't really have faith in her own suggestion: "I know how insane you have to be to stay in my world, how much loneliness you have to bear as you walk among the ruins of other households, knowing that the future may be just as bad as the past. I know how difficult it is to balance when the ground is always spinning and you have to be able to accept losing" (L, 271).

In an interview in 1985, Margaret Atwood describes the evolutionary process which will transform embattled or loveless families into repressive, religious clans:

> Every dictator with any pretensions has a set of slogans that he thinks are going to be appealing to a certain number of people in order to get enough support to run his dictatorship.... That's what happens in religious takeovers. You may enlist the support of certain affiliated groups in order to do the takeover, but then you get rid of them because they are your challengers.[48]

Rabbi Cohen, too, is "selling" the security of the illusory nuclear family to his new converts, the disillusioned, the abandoned and the battered children who inhabit the bus stations and vagrant hotels of the world. He provides them with God's "lovingkindness" because it is, the stuff which sells in the confused and fragmented eighties.

Although both Roiphe and Atwood are clear about the evolutionary process which will create Gilead, neither author blames feminism as a primary agent. "People have asked if I'm saying feminism will cause this upheaval," Atwood noted in an interview. "Feminists are not a cause, they are a symptom. If there were no social disease there would be no feminism" (qtd. in Battiata, G6). Blaming either men or women for the current discord in sexual and familial relations is unproductive because it obscures the real problem—a social system which envisions power relations as a struggle for hegemony rather than a sharing of responsibility.

The world of contemporary black sexual and familial relations is no less demoralizing than the white, but solutions are usually not found in feminine estrangement or separatism, but rather in attacking an economic, racial and social framework which encourages inequality. In her autobiographical *I Know Why the Caged Bird Sings* (1969) Maya Angelou chronicles the destructive consequences of her relations with economically disenfranchised men in her life. After several traumatic experiences, the young Maya learns to be wary of romantic love: "There was that hateful word [love] again," she exclaimed after receiving a valentine card. "That treacherous word that yawned up at you like a volcano"(Caged, 121). She tells her friend that she will never love a man again, although she does want a baby, something to love in a harsh world.

Although the birth of her son is a happy and fulfilling event, it does not provide a safe harbor for the embattled Maya who has, at sixteen, experienced more than her share of male violence and rape. Although Angelou never excuses or condones male misogyny and certainly characterizes the black woman as caught "in the crossfire of masculine prejudice," she also notes that this crossfire is "tripartite" because it also includes "white illogical hate and Black lack of power" (Caged, 231). Her analysis of the destruction of the African-American woman and the black family, does not end with naming the obvious and most immediate victimizer—the black male—but goes beyond to a condemnation of the political order that breeds such behavior. In order to transform the future of black heterosexual relations, the social hierarchy which ranks people according to skin color and money must be scrapped for it is this system which encourages powerless black men to transfer their frustrations onto the safest and nearest objects—their wives and daughters. The critic Jane Miller, characterizes this destructive scenario as "a world where men are threatened and weakened and become threatening and weakening to women."[49]

Toni Morrison's handling of sexual and familial violence in her novel *The Bluest Eye* (1970) provides a similar analysis of the problems confronting black women and men in contemporary society. Morrison delineates the character of Cholly Breedlove, an abusive black man who hurts and abandons his wife and daughter because he cannot defeat the real source of his impotence—white society. Cholly's traumatic first sexual experience when he is humiliated by white men who find him making love to his girlfriend in the woods demonstrates how hatred can be transferred from one object to another: "Sullen, irritable, he cultivated his hatred of Darlene. Never did he once consider directing his hatred toward the hunters. . . . For now, he hated the one who had created the situation, the one who bore witness to his failure, his impotence."[50]

Angelou and Morrison neither condone nor condemn their male characters' actions; instead, they regard the white society which engenders this destructive misogyny as the primary enemy and agent of sexual violence. Escaping into a female culture will not eradicate the political situation which generates the threatening male behavior in the first place. Although black female writers, like Alice Walker are incorrectly accused of "male-bashing," they do not regard separatism as a solution. In fact, Walker defines her "womanist" philosophy as "a woman who loves other women, sexually and/or nonsexually. Appreciates and prefers women's culture . . . Sometimes loves individual men, sexually and/or nonsexually. Committed to survival and wholeness of entire people, male *and* female. Not separatist, except periodically, for health. Traditionally universalist" (In Search, xi).

In 1977, the National Black Feminist Organizations noted that sexual separatism was "not a viable political analysis or strategy for us. It leaves out far too much and far too many people, particularly black men, women, and children" (qtd. in Miller, 236). Since African-American contemporary writers identify the personal problems between men and women in terms of political and social inequities, they are more likely to seek change outside of marriage—in the political rather than the personal area. Individual transformation, therefore, begins in the greater world, the macrocosm.

If contemporary women's literature has witnessed the development of a "woman's culture" whose inhabitants are often mothers and daughters, it is a justifiable reaction against a 150 year old tradition of fatherhood without women described by critic Leslie Fiedler in *Love and Death in the American Novel* (1966) as the "homoerotic fable" which rejects heterosexual marriage and establishes adult male/boy bonds which are "innocent" and "untainted" by the corrupt forces of feminine civilization.[51] After analyzing male writers from Washington Irving to William Faulkner, Fiedler conceded that "there is finally no heterosexual solution which the American [male] psyche finds completely satisfactory, no imagined or real consummation between man and woman found worthy of standing in our fiction for the healing of the breach between consciousness and unconsciousness, reason and impulse, society and nature" (Fiedler, 338).

Neither American male writers in their "homoerotic fables," nor many contemporary female writers can envision satisfying and untainted heterosexual relations in a modern world. As has been stated previously, heterosexuality is often pictured as a battleground associated with war and brutal competition. Ironically, however, despite its seemingly iconoclastic stance, the contemporary theme of a feminist motherhood outside of the patriarchy, seems like the continuation of the homoerotic fable's "fatherhood without women."

Adrienne Rich has given this new motherhood a name when she designated it the "lesbian continuum" in her important essay, "Compulsory Heterosexuality and Lesbian Existence" (1978). The same-sex and thus "safe" love of Fiedler's "buddies" is replaced by Rich's "lesbian continuum," which is also a desexualized single-sex relationship thought to be purer and, therefore, untainted by civilized corruption (Rich 1978, 156-7).

Although the lesbian continuum and the homoerotic fable may signal the cease fire to the sex wars, many modern women writers see it as a troubling and ultimately unworkable peace. When asked about her purpose in creating the nightmare vision of Gilead, Margaret Atwood explained that her novel was a "work of speculative fiction, a logical extension of where we are now . . . this particular genre is a walking along of a potential road, the reader as well as the writer can then decide if that is the road they wish to go on. Whether we go that way or not is going to be up to us" (qtd. in Battiata, G6).

The Mid-Eighties and Nineties: Motherhood as Creativity

Although the theme of motherhood in contemporary literature is problematic and often ambivalently treated by writers, it is also a symbol of artistic inspiration and creativity—the "kunstlerroman"—the novel of the artist's development. Women's literature provides many portraits of motherhood, both negative and positive. In the maternal role, one woman may become frustrated and self-deceived, while another may find the feminine equivalent of heroism, as Kathryn Allen Rabuzzi suggests in her important critical work, *Motherself: A Mythic Analysis of Motherhood* (1988). Rabuzzi argues that classical heroism as described by Joseph Campbell and others is an "androcentric"[52] construction not readily accessible to women. Motherhood is linked in Rabuzzi's thesis with a newly defined feminine, spiritual quest, a new mythos which provides women with a heightened awareness about themselves and others.

Positive images of mothers and children abound in contemporary women's writing as women learn from their children and children, often daughters, gain important perspective and inspiration from their mothers. Sometimes, the literature portrays actual mothers and daughters, but just as often, the mother is a "spiritual" source of feminine creativity, as found in E. M. Broner's novel *Her Mothers* (1975) or Alice Walker's essay "Looking for Zora" (1975) in *In Search of Our Mother's Gardens* (1983).

The experience of mothering and being mothered provides many female writers with insight into themselves and their tradition—as Virginia Woolf notes in her essay *A Room of One's Own* (1929): "A woman writing thinks back through her mothers" (Woolf, xx). Fifty years later, the poet Maxine Kumin analyzes the spiritual and biological dimensions of motherhood in her poem "The Envelope" (1978). Although the voice in the poem admits that she is frightened by her own mortality, she believes that her daughters will carry her identity within them forever.[53] This awareness not only provides her with a sense of optimism but also a faith in continuity, even in a fragmented contemporary world. Through her experiences with her daughters, she sees the link with her own mother. Yet, the physical bond is also an aesthetic one too, for the poet describes the relationship between mother and daughter as the creation of a continuing letter which sends a message into the infinite future.

Audre Lorde also connects pregnancy with creativity in her poem "Now That I Am Forever with Child (1976). The birth of her child is symbolized by the movement of the seasons from the old, death of winter to the renewal of spring. The poet's whole body, including her mind, is involved in the birthing process. A continuous bond is created that day between mother and daughter, which convinces the poet that she is eternally with child.[54]

Even in death, the mother is a source of poetic and spiritual inspiration to the daughter who is left without guidance. In her poem "The Thirty Eighth Year of My Life," (1974) Lucille Clifton looks back at her "ordinary" life and wonders why she has not become the extraordinary woman of her dreams. Her words are directed to her mother who dies young and leaves an unhappy daughter behind.[55] The narrator is not bitter at this abandonment, however, for she praises her mother's memory which inspires the daughter to search for a complementary uniqueness in her own identity. Like Maxine Kumin, Clifton sees the continuity in the mother/daughter relationship, linking the living with the dead. It is, in fact, through the process of searching within herself that Clifton realizes the extraordinary in the ordinary, the miracle of rebirth or resurrection in the everyday occurrence of maternity.

As a mature writer looking backward on her youth, Eudora Welty in *One Writer's Beginnings* (1983) also reveres the memory of her mother as the source and inspiration for her own creativity. Welty remembers that her mother taught her "from the age of two or three that any room in our house, at any time of day, was there to read in, or to be read to."[56] Welty's mother provides her with both the concept of a "room of one's own" as well as an appreciation for the grotesque and "appalling" (One, 19) which inspires the precocious Eudora.

"Appalling" secrets also lead to the writer's individual growth in Maxine Hong Kingston's "No Name Woman," (1976). When her Chinese-American mother cautions the young Maxine "You must not tell anyone . . . what I am about to tell you,"[57] it is the beginning of a tale which, ironically, will be repeated to thousands of readers. The aunt's story of independence and family shame influences the young writer who becomes determined to revere her courageous ancestor by writing her story of "illegitimate" pregnancy, social and familial punishment and eventual death by drowning. It is not an optimistic or pleasant tale, but as Kingston recounts, "Whenever she had to warn us about life, my mother told stories that ran like this one, a story to grow up on" (WW, 5).

Grandmothers as well as mothers are spoken of as a source of spiritual and aesthetic connection in Paula Gunn Allen's poem "Grandmother" (1975) which tells of her grandmother, a member of the Oak Indian clan, who was able to weave "the strands/or her body, her pain, her vision/into creation."[58] Although her grandmother has "disappeared," future generations take the strands and fashion them into stories of independence and courage, pleasure and pain which nurture and develop the children.

Coming to terms with one's mother or daughter is an important step in self-development and, sometimes, survival for many literary characters in contemporary women's writing. The Pulitzer Prize winning play, *Crimes of the Heart* (1979) by Beth Henley describes the difficult road taken by three sisters who finally come to understand their mother's and their own isolation and pain. It is a play which begins in literal and metaphoric "disconnection" among the sisters and concludes with a healing communion and "rebirth" at the belated birthday celebration of the sister Lenny. In what Henley describes in the stage directions to the concluding scene as a "magical,"[59] moment, all three sisters see the transforming and transcendent power of familial connection. McGrath women will no longer suffer in silence, but instead reach out to each other. Babe knows she is now "not like Mama. I'm not so all alone" (CH, 289). At the same time, Lenny, whose literal and metaphorical birthday is celebrated has a "vision" of the three sisters joined after years of isolation, "smiling and laughing together . . . it wasn't forever; it wasn't for every minute. Just this one moment and we were all laughing" (CH, 290). Although the sisters find their own way, it is their mother's painful memory which serves as the catalyst for the quest.

The problematic, but nonetheless significant, relationships between mothers and daughters are also the subject of an important novel by Gail Godwin entitled *A Mother and Two Daughters* (1982) which recounts the troubled relations between Nell Strickland and her two daughters, Cate and Lydia. As in *Crimes of the Heart*, a family tragedy, this time the death of the father Leonard Strickland, brings together women who have previously been unable or unwilling to understand the complexity and value of their connection. And yet, this mother's quest for her children and the children's search for their mother are as important as Telemachus' search for Odysseus.

An intuitive understanding of the importance of family unity, however, comes only after considerable pain and experience, including the harsh reality of one's link to and separateness from another—as in the death of a loved one. Nell's ability to rebuild her own life and the lives of her daughters is the outgrowth of her powers of "maternal thinking," a term popularized in the eighties by feminist theorists Sara Ruddick, Carol Gilligan and Kathryn Allen Rabuzzi to suggest "a reverential respect for an immediate, daily, other reality to which one accedes an independent validity, on which one does not attempt to impose total control."[60]

It is this "mysterious"[61] respect and reverence for forces beyond one's control—death as well as communion—which Nell and her daughters experience on the top of Osgood's mountain at the end of the novel: "what a mysterious thing *we* are, all of us gathered here on old Osgood's mountaintop aerie.... if it weren't for me ... and Leonard ... most of these people wouldn't be here. There wouldn't be Lydia, or Leo and his bride, or Dickie playing, or Cate to have this party" (MTD, 562). Yet, despite this focus on unity, there is also respect for separateness. Individuality within continuity is therefore, a major "mystery" which allows people to join together and, yet, maintain their autonomy. The relationship between mother and child, therefore, provides a prototype for all important unions and becomes an important metaphor for women writers who wish to pursue positive definitions of love and family in contemporary society.

When mothers and children appreciate both their bonds with each other and honor their distinctions, they can finally become whole, functioning people—a definition of adulthood and power sharing in women's writing. This theme can be found in novels as different as Mary Gordon's *The Company of Women* (1980), Carolyn Chute's *The Beans of Egypt, Maine* (1985), Jamaica Kincaid's *Annie John* (1985), Terry McMillan's

Mama (1987), Toni Morrison's *Beloved* (1987), Tina McElroy Ansa's *Baby of the Family* (1989), and Amy Tan's *The Joy Luck Club* (1989). Two outstanding anthologies which analyze the almost mystical union between mothers and daughters are Susan Koppelman's *Between Mothers & Daughters: Stories Across a Generation* (1985) and Irene Zahava's *My Mother's Daughter: Stories by Women* (1991). An excellent collection of literary criticism edited by Cathy Davidson and E. M. Broner entitled *The Lost Tradition: Mothers and Daughters in Literature* (1980) also analyzes this complex theme.

The acceptance of flux, disorder and disconnection as well as the belief in the healing power of familial (maternal) love is also a central theme in the many novels of Anne Tyler. In *Searching for Caleb* (1976), *Morgan's Passing* (1980), *Dinner at the Homesick Restaurant* (1982) and *The Accidental Tourist* (1985) mothers and fathers, husbands and wives, parents and children have to learn to accept the ever shifting nature of the universe which is symbolized by the constantly changing reality of family life. The characters who refuse to accept this natural evolution, the ones who seek to hold on, at all costs, to sameness, are those who remain children, within a self-restricting "womb." They find themselves unable to live in the chaotic world.

Many of Tyler's novels analyze an individual's ability to let go in order to create and nurture those around them, a paradox which many of the characters in *The Accidental Tourist* and *St. Maybe* (1991) must accept if they are finally to live autonomous lives. Macon Leary, the main character in the novel, must develop this "maternal thinking" which both his ex-wife Sarah and his new girlfriend Muriel already possess. Macon and his brothers and sisters, however have become "ossified"[62] as they attempt to prevent change and growth. Macon, whose symbol is the armchair with wings—travelling through life but never leaving the security of one's life at home—loses his wife and almost his life because he cannot acknowledge the untimely death of his son, Ethan.

Macon's wife, however, who loved the son and still misses him desperately, has accepted the action as part of the disruption and chaos which both unites and separates family members. In trying to explain why she is divorcing Macon, Sarah exhibits the "maternal thinking" which Macon lacks: "Everything that might touch you or upset you or disrupt you, you've given up without a murmur and done without, said you never wanted it anyhow ... there's something so what-do-you-call, so muffled about the way you experience things, I mean love or grief or anything; it's like you're trying to slip through life unchanged" (AT, 135-6).

When Macon objects to his wife's interpretation of the Leary philosophy which equates order with common sense and stasis with virtue, Sarah comments that he is "ossified. You're encased. You're like something in a capsule. You're a dried-up kernel of a man that nothing real penetrates. Oh, Macon, it's not by chance you write those silly books telling people how to take trips without a jolt. That traveling armchair isn't just your job; it's you" (AT, 136).

It is only by letting go of the Leary obsession with control that Macon can experience life. With the help of Muriel, herself a whirlwind of change, disruption and lack of "good common sense," Macon relents—he loosens his death grip on life and consents to his lack of absolute control over his environment and family; he becomes a "maternal thinker" metaphorically, if not literally. Likewise, Ian Bedloe in *St. Maybe* also exhibits the maternal thinking so crucial to happy family relations. If patriarchal thinking involves a false duality between control and domination on one side and chaos and sharing on the other, then maternal thinking suggests a positive alternative for men like Macon and Ian; it offers the possibility of continuity within diversity—an important life-saving concept in the works of Anne Tyler.

"Maternal thinking," however, is not exclusively the purview of the immediate nuclear family, but rather is a philosophy of care-taking which can be expanded to include one's friends and society as well as one's family. In fact, in the eighties, the definition of "family" is generalized to include all those with whom one shares common values and love. Women, who have long been portrayed as adversaries or competitors for the attention of men, celebrate their love, both platonic and sexual.[63]

For instance, in her poem "Best Friends" (1983), Sharon Olds writes of her love for a girlhood friend, Elizabeth Ewer, who died in 1951 at the age of nine. Olds has named her own daughter after Elizabeth, thus symbolically bringing her friend back into life once more.[64] Although the naming is an attempt by the poet to perpetuate the old friendship, to resurrect the dead and thus defeat the finality of death itself, the poet knows that her daughter is a separate individual, different from her friend. The nine year old Elizabeth had golden hair while Olds' ten year old daughter has brown. And yet, despite the disparities in time and person, Olds' maternity has made it possible to transcend limitations while simultaneously acknowledging their importance.

Although many writers have discussed actual sexual love between women before the seventies and eighties, it is within the past twenty years that the subject has, with the sexual revolution itself, come "out of the closet" and into the consciousness of mainstream literature and life. May Sarton has provided several sensitive and positive portraits of lesbian relationships in the novel, *The Magnificent Spinster* (1985) and the poems in *Halfway to Silence*. (1980). Lillian Faderman's literary and social history *Surpassing the Love of Men: Romantic Friendship and Love Between Women From the Renaissance to the Present* (1981) suggests that women throughout history have found loving relationships outside of socially prescribed heterosexuality: "a refusal to fulfill the male image of womanhood or to bow to male supremacy."[65]

Likewise, an atmosphere of acceptance of alternative familial relationships has made it commercially possible to publish literary anthologies like Kate McDermott's *Places, Please! The First Anthology of Lesbian Plays* (1985), Elly Bulkin's *Lesbian Fiction: An Anthology* (1981) and *Lesbian Poetry: An Anthology* (1981). New critical attention is being paid to writers like H.D. whose poems about life as well as lesbian love are now being reprinted and reassessed. Of particular interest is *HERmione* (1981) which portrays a woman similar to H.D. herself who must choose between heterosexual and lesbian relationships.

Poets Adrienne Rich, Audre Lorde and Olga Broumas as well as novelist Rita Mae Brown are probably the best known writers who portray the ways in which lesbian culture revises and redefines the traditional heterosexual love and family life. Adrienne

Rich's previously mentioned landmark essay "Compulsory Heterosexuality and Lesbian Existence" (1980) as well as her lesbian love poems in *Twenty-one Love Poems* (1976) provide the aesthetic dimension for female sexuality outside of patriarchal strictures.

Significantly, it is in lesbian love poetry, by Rich and others, that sexuality is not viewed skeptically or in politicized ways. The mutual sharing of physical pleasure in Rich's "The Floating Poem, Unnumbered" discusses sexuality not as a battle between adversaries, but as a dance between equal partners.[66] In poem number XI, all opposites and dualities are counterbalanced in perfect lovemaking. Rich's feminine conception of love transcends masculine dualities, creating a lesbian energy which unites women both physically and imaginatively.[67]

Audre Lorde is equally idealistic in her love poem "On a Night of the Full Moon (1976)." The sexual encounter, so often vilified or reduced to struggle in heterosexual embraces, is presented as a coming together of equals in this context. Interestingly, the concept of "waiting" elucidated upon by Ruddick and Rabuzzi as an expression of "maternal love" is here sexualized into a love embrace with maternal overtones.[68]

While Lorde and Rich focus on the platonic ideal of lesbian relationships, Rita Mae Brown and Judy Grahn discuss the political as well as the personal aspects of homosexuality. In "Carol, in the Park, Chewing on Straws," (1978), Grahn describes the hypocritical, intolerant reactions of heterosexuals who gasp when they discover that Carol "has taken a woman lover/whatever shall we do/she has taken a woman love/how lucky it wasn't you." Grahn expresses the rage of the sexually ostracized lesbian couple which is the butt of a homophobic society that does not value the balancing of contraries: "She walks around all day/quietly, but underneath it/she's electric; angry energy inside a passive form./The common woman is as common/as a thunderstorm."[69] Likewise, in *Ruby Fruit Jungle* (1973), Rita Mae Brown's comic heroine, Molly Bolt, expresses the same aggressive defiance at a society which will not allow her to choose her own partners and family arrangements. Her rage in focused against the heterosexual world, "whether they like me or not." No longer seeking society's approval, Molly asserts, "Everybody's stupid, that's what I think. I care if I like me, that's what I truly care about."[70]

Just as motherhood has become an important theme in female heterosexual literature, it has, likewise, been a focus of attention in literature written about lesbian culture as well. A warm, nurturing lesbian couple attempts to raise the neglected and abused child of a heterosexual marriage in Judith Rossner's *August* (1983). The suicidal Dawn Henley is saved, not only by her devoted lesbian surrogate parents, but also by her psychiatrist, Dr. Lulu Shinefeld who provides Dawn with the maternal love and independence she needs in order to survive. These three powerful women all work together to rescue Dawn and thus represent the good which can come from communal action, when lesbian and heterosexual women work together.[71]

"Prisoners of Gender": Sex, Marriage and Family—1985–Present

In her perceptive article, "Postmodernism and Gender Relations in Feminist Theory," (1987) critic Jane Flax criticizes gender restrictions, not the patriarchal culture and men, for the current tension in heterosexual relations and family life. She argues convincingly that "from the perspective of social relations, men and women are both prisoners of gender ... That men appear to be the wardens, or at least the trustees within a social whole, should not blind us to the extent to which they, too, are governed by the rules of gender."[72]

This increased awareness that all people are "prisoners" of gender is found in a variety of female-authored texts in the late eighties and nineties. Psychologist Carol Gillian analyzes the different male and female moral "voices" and suggests that both perspectives are required in a balanced ethical universe.[73] Barbara Ehrenreich in her critical work *The Hearts of Men* (1983) and Francesca Cancian in her article "The Feminization of Love" (1986) both argue that women *and* men desire an end to mutually destructive, unbalanced gender relations.

Cancian also analyzes the differences between male "instrumental" or action-oriented love and female "expressive" or verbalizing love and calls for a theory of love based on both male and female models.[74] Flax, Gilligan, Ehrenreich and Cancian all call for a reevaluation of femininity and masculinity which may lead to a new understanding and rapprochement between the sexes.

This desire for reconciliation and forgiveness is also reflected in late eighties and nineties literature. In her novel, *The Hearts and Lives of Men* (1988), Fay Weldon paints a now familiar picture of masculine malfeasance and female masochism in the marriage of Clifford Wexford and Helen Lally. However, the narrator laments their inevitable estrangement and divorce: "If she and Clifford had stayed together, and faced their own natures, and so been in a position to reform them, she would have been less of a liar now ... And Clifford would have been less cruel, less calculating, less vengeful on the female sex: less concerned with his own image. He would have changed partners less frequently, and changed himself instead."[75]

Weldon's world view emphasizes reconciliation not revenge, understanding not recrimination. At one point in the novel, Clifford and Helen apologize to each other. The narrator, who approves of this action, reveals the political and personal significance of apologies which she describes as "important things. World Wars start because they are not made, because no one is prepared to say you were right, I was wrong" (HLM, 206). In fact, the need for forgiveness—the title of one of the last chapters in the novel—is essential in an ambiguous, imperfect world. Within Weldon's complex handling of good and evil, therefore, is the implicit potential for reform and reunion between the troubled women and men in contemporary literary families.

Weldon's refusal to ascribe sole blame to men is shared by several other female novelists. Although Margaret Atwood, Anne Bernays and Anita Brookner never forget the abuse that women suffer at the hands of patriarchal culture, they share an awareness that men, too, are caught in the web as well. The much-abused Offred in *The Handmaid's Tale* remarks that her book is not really about "control ... who can do what to whom and get away with it," but rather, her story analyzes "who can do what to whom and be forgiven for it." She cautions the reader, "Never tell me it amounts to the same thing" (HT, 174).

Similarly, the narrator in Anne Bernays' satiric novel *Professor Romeo* (1989) feels some compassion for Jacob Barker, the middle-age seducer of young female students. The blind author of his own torment, Barker ends his days in the Arizona desert, in a kind of self-imposed exile from a society he cannot begin to understand or explain.[76] He has lost contact with his gay son while his former neglected wife has run off with Barker's young, male research assistant. All of the characters seem ensnared by gender restrictions over which they have little control; and this, finally, is the source of both the comedy and the tragedy of their lives.

Equally deserving of both blame and understanding is Bertie Vernon, the erstwhile, philandering husband of the passive, but eccentric Blanche Vernon in Anita Brookner's novel *The Misalliance* (1986). In many respects, *The Misalliance* contains all the aspects of the contemporary novel of manners: a non-communicative husband escapes his ordinary life by running off with a younger woman, Mousie. Bertie does not seem worthy of his wife who then makes a series of her own "misalliances" before deciding to transform her own life into a postmodern saga. However, the novel's conclusion—the reunion of Bertie and Blanche—signals a departure from the usual plot scenario in contemporary literature. Despite their past mistakes, Blanche and Bertie are, after all, a proper "alliance" in the shifting, contemporary world of ephemeral relationships. It is, therefore, not surprising that the novel should have a "happy" ending as the repentant and somewhat chastened Bertie enters his old home, puts his suitcase down in the bedroom and announces to his startled, but relieved former wife, "I'm home."[77]

One might ask at this point, how far have women writers come from Kay Boyle's "Winter Night" when mothers and daughters waited for the men to return home. Have contemporary women writers found alternative plot narratives for women on quests? The answer is, ambiguously, yes and no. For instance, in Jill McCorkle's 1992 collection of short stories entitled *Crash Diet*, some of the characters have removed themselves to "lover's purgatory," where they are content to sit in "glorious neutrality" after having survived the "hell" of contemporary sexual combat.[78] In McCorkle's short story

"Crash Diet," Sandra is annoyed that her husband has left her on Monday morning "before I'd even had the chance to mousse my hair."[79] Like Blanche in *The Misalliance*, the main character in McCorkle's story finds herself replaced by a younger woman. But unlike the long suffering and dignified Blanche, Sandra finds herself a shrink/lover and continues on her cynical journey. At the end of the story, Sandra is in bed, alone, thinking about her lover/analyst, Alan, and his desire to grab her hipbones: "it's a real pleasure to have someone find them and hang on," she muses. "You can do okay in this world if you can just find something worth holding on to" (CD, 19).

And, yet, McCorkle can also reject Sandra's protective cynicism in favor of a more idealistic attitude towards love and marriage. Anna Craven, the main character in McCorkle's short story "Departures," is unable to find any one to "hang on to" when her husband dies. Despite her children's injunction that mourning is maudlin and unhealthy, Anna cherishes his memory and refuses to accept a substitute. She rejects her children's new-age alliances, and bed partners of all sexes in favor of traditional monogamy. In this story, McCorkle creates a contemporary Penelope who is determined to maintain her loyalty in a society devoted to immediate gratification and the continuous present.

Anna's quest, therefore, is not to reinvent herself but rather to retain a memory of an idyllic past—real or imagined—which she inhabited with her husband and children. Memory, commitment, monogamy and loyalty are, therefore, her ideals in a world which has made them liabilities. It is, in fact, for this reason that Anna must travel to airports in order to remind herself that people do have relationships which transcend immediate place and time. If her loss has taught her anything, it is that "life is fragile, so very very fragile"[80] and that one needs to treasure and savor it before it is irretrievably lost. While other characters like Sandra find contemporary marriage a bad joke or a living hell, Anna finds it an almost anachronistic refuge. Although it seems puzzling to find two characters as different as Sandra and Anna inhabiting the same collection of short stories, McCorkle's women are indicative of the diversity of viewpoints in contemporary female characterization.

Conclusion

Certainly, many contemporary writers have taken Rachel Du Plessis' challenge to "write beyond" the traditional endings of marriage and death while others have not. If all contemporary characters do not conclude "happily ever after" in marriage, they do not end, as Rebecca West suggests, "unhappily ever after" in death either. Possibly, the best way to define the situation is to analyze Laurie Colwin's guarded optimism towards sex, marriage and the family in *Happy All the Time* (1978), *Family Happiness* (1982) and *Goodbye Without Leaving* (1990). Colwin objects to critics' designation of her novels' endings as "happy," and, instead, interprets her characters as in a "cheerfully anxious state. These people are anxious!!! . . . There is not *one* single happy ending in any book written by me. They are all unresolved endings . . . [which] describe a certain kind of struggle."[81]

In the last two decades of the twentieth century, women writers have turned their attention to the "cheerfully" and not so cheerfully anxious relations between women and men, both inside and outside of marriage. Some social critics, like Elizabeth Fox-Genovese, have recently called for a renewed sense of cooperation between the sexes which would empower all individuals, and resolve gender antagonisms. "Without such a vision," she warns, "we risk a radical fragmentation that realizes the most Kafkaesque nightmares of solitary individuals at the mercy of sinister, faceless power" (Fox-Genovese, 32). Contemporary literature in the nineties and beyond will, no doubt, reflect this struggle with additional imaginative portrayals of modern sexuality and family life. Whether it will come to any resolution or detente, however, is yet to be seen.

Notes

1. Kay Boyle, "Winter Nights" in *Thirty Stories* (New York: New Directions, 1957), 352; hereafter cited in text as "WN."

2. Adlai Stevenson, "A Purpose for Modern Woman," in *Images of Women in American Popular Culture*, ed. Angela G. Dorenkamp et al (New York: Harcourt Brace Jovanovich, 1985), 114; hereafter cited in text.

3. Ferdinand Lundberg and Marynia Farnham, *Modern Woman: The Lost Sex* (New York: Harper & Brothers, 1946), 217; hereafter cited in text.

4. Nancy Woloch, *Women and the American Experience* (New York: Alfred A. Knopf, 1984), 496; hereafter cited in text.

5. Morris Dickstein, *Gates of Eden: American Culture in the Sixties* (New York: Penguin Books, 1977), 50; hereafter cited in text.

6. Several good studies of the impact of Freudian thought on women are discussed in "Feminism and Freudianism" in *Feminist Theory: The Intellectual Traditions of American Feminism* (New York: Ungar, 1985) 91-116).

7. Dorothy Canfield, "Sex Education," in *Contemporary American Short Stories*, ed. Douglas and Sylvia Angus (Greenwich, Conn: Fawcett Publications, 1967), 231; hereafter cited in text as *Sex*.

8. Alfred C. Kinsey, *Sexual Behavior in the Human Female*, by the staff of the Institute for Sex Research, Indiana University (Philadelphia, 1953).

9. May Swenson, "The Centaur," in *New and Selected Things Taking Place* (Boston: Little, Brown and Company, 1978), 239; hereafter cited in text as *Centaur*.

10. Grace Paley, "An Interest in Life," in *The Little Disturbances of Man* (New York: Penguin, 1985), 88; hereafter cited in text as *Interest*.

11. Sylvia Plath, "Daddy," in *The Collected Poems* (New York: Harper & Row, 1981), 224; hereafter cited in text as "D."

12. Erica Jong, *Fear of Flying* (New York: Holt Rinehart and Winston, 1973), 17; hereafter cited in text as "FF."

13. Doris Lessing, *A Proper Marriage* (New York: Plume Books, 1952), 24; hereafter cited in text as *"PM."*

14. Eudora Welty, "Circe," in *The Bride of the Innisfallen and Other Stories* (New York: Harcourt Brace Jovanovich, 1949), 102; hereafter cited in text as *Circe*.

15. Jean Stafford, "Cops and Robbers" in *The Collected Stories of Jean Stafford* (New York: Farrar, Straus & Giroux, 1969), 426; hereafter cited in text as "Cops." 82-97

16. Adrienne Rich, "Living in Sin," in *The Fact of a Doorframe, Poems Selected and New, 1950-1984* (New York: W.W. Norton, 1984), 15-6.

17. Iris Murdoch, *A Severed Head* (New York: Viking Press, 1961), 14; hereafter cited in the text as "SH."

18. Eva Figes, *Patriarchal Attitudes: Women in Society* (New York: Persea Books, 1970), 50; hereafter cited in text.

19. Ti-Grace Atkinson, *Amazon* (New York: Links, 1974), 93.

20. Shulamith Firestone, *The Dialectic of Sex: The Case for Feminist Revolution* (New York: Bantam, 1971), 11; hereafter cited in text.

21. For general background in the increasing hostility and violence against women, see the discussion of men's misogynist literature in Elaine Showalter's essay, "Rethinking the Seventies: Women Writers and Violence."

22. Mary Allen, *The Necessary Blankness: Women in Major American Fiction of the 60's* (Urbana: University of Illinois Press, 1976), 7; hereafter cited in text.

23. Sylvia Plath, "Nick and the Candelstick," in The Collected Poems (New York: Harper & Row, 1981), 240-42.

24. Joyce Carol Oates, "Accomplished Desires" in *The Wheel of Love and Other Stories* (New York: Vanguard Press, 1970), 134; hereafter cited in text as "AD."

25. Joyce Carol Oates, "The Children," *Marriage and Infidelities* (New York: The Vanguard Press, 1972), 216; hereafter cited in text as "Children."

26. Anne Stevenson, "The Suburb," in *Reversals* (Middletown, Conn.: Wesleyan University Press, 1973), 19. hereafter cited in text as "Suburb."

27. Ellen Peck and Judith Senderowitz, eds. *Pronatalism: The Myth of Mom and Apple Pie* (New York: Thomas Y. Crowell Co., 1974), 7; hereafter cited in text.

28. Alix Kates Shulman, *Memoirs of An Ex-Prom Queen* (New York: Alfred A. Knopf, 1969), 8; hereafter cited as *Memoirs*. Also see Shulman's prose essay, "Sex and Power: Sexual Bases of Radical Feminism," in *Women—Sex and Sexuality*, edited by Catharine R. Stimpson and Ethel Spector Person (Chicago: University of Chicago Press, 1980).

29. Judith Rossner, *Looking for Mr. Goodbar* (Pocket Books, 1975), 136; hereafter cited in text as *LMG*.

30. Elizabeth Benedict, *Slow Dancing* (New York: McGraw Hill, 1985), 3; hereafter cited in text as *SD*.

31. Ann Beattie, "Tuesday Night," in *Secrets and Surprises: Short Stories* (New York: Random House, 1978), 285.

32. Ellen Gilchrist, *Drunk With Love* (Boston: Little, Brown, 1986), xiii; hereafter cited in text as *DL*.

33. Denise Levertov, "About Marriage," *O Taste and See* (New York: New Directions Publishing Co, 1962), 68-9.

34. Denise Levertov, "The Ache of Marriage," *O Taste and See* (New York: New Directions Publishing Co., 1962), 5.

35. Rebecca West, "And they all lived unhappily ever after," *Times Literary Supplement* 73 (1974): 779; hereafter cited in text.

36. Anne Sexton, "For My Lover Returning to His Wife," in The Complete Poems: Anne Sexton (Boston: Houghton Mifflin Co., 2982), 189; hereafter cited in text.

37. Fleur Adcock, "Against Coupling," in *Selected Poems* (Oxford: Oxford University Press, 1983), 33-4.

38. Edna O'Brien, "The Call," in *A Fanatic Heart: Selected Stories of Edna O'Brien* (New York: Farrar, Straus, Giroux, 1984), 443; hereafter cited in text as *Call*. 345-48

39. Hortense Calisher, "Point of Departure," in Images of Women in Literature, ed. Mary Anne Ferguson (Boston: Houghton Mifflin, 1977), 344; hereafter cited in text as PD. 344-7

40. Margaret Drabble, *The Millstone* (New York: New American Library, 1965) 20; hereafter cited in text as *M*.

41. Elaine Showalter, "Towards a Feminist Poetics," *The New Feminist Criticism* Ed. Elaine Showalter (New York: Pantheon Books, 1985), 134; hereafter cited in text.

42. See Gilbert and Gubar's discussion of sexual animosity in twentieth century literature in their book *No Man's Land: The Place of the Woman Writer in the Twentieth Century*, Volume One, "The War of the Words," (New Haven: Yale University Press, 1988).

43. For a discussion of sexual androgyny, see Gilbert and Gubar's *No Man's Land: The Place of the Woman Writer in the Twentieth Century*, Volume Two "Sexchanges" in 1989 by Yale University Press. A third volume, "Letters from the Front," is forthcoming.

44. Hilma Wolitzer, "Waiting for Daddy," in *About Women: An Anthology of Contemporary Fiction, Poetry, and Essays*, ed. Stephen Berg and S.J. Marks (Greenwich, Connecticut: Fawcett Books, 1973), 395; hereafter cited in text as *Waiting*.

45. Margaret Atwood, *The Handmaid's Tale* (New York: Ballantine, 1985), 164; hereafter cited in text as *HT*.

46. Cathy Davidson, "A Feminist '1984'" Rev. of *The Handmaid's Tale* by Margaret Atwood. *Ms.* (February 1986), 24; hereafter cited in text.

47. Anne Roiphe, *Lovingkindness* (New York: Summit, 1987), 27; hereafter cited in text as *L*.

48. Mary Battiata, "Atwood's Nightmare New World," *The Washington Post*, 6 April 1985, G6; hereafter cited in text.

49. Jane Miller, *Women Writing About Men* (New York: Pantheon Books, 1986), 236; hereafter cited in text.

50. Toni Morrison, *The Bluest Eye* (New York: Washington Square Press, 1970), 119; hereafter cited in text as *BE*.

51. Leslie Fiedler, *Love and Death in the American Novel* (New York: Dell, 1966) 349; hereafter cited in text.

52. Kathryn Allen Rabuzzi, *Motherself: A Mythic Analysis of Motherhood* (Bloomington: Indiana University Press, 1988), p. 10.

53. Maxine W. Kumin, "The Envelope," in *The Retrieval System*. New York: Viking, 1973, p. 40; hereafter cited in text as "E."

54. Audre Lorde, "Now That I Am Forever With Child," in *Chosen Poems, Old and New* (New York: W. W. Norton, 1982), 13-4.

55. Lucille Clifton, "The Thirty Eighth Year of My life," in *An Ordinary Woman* (New York: Random House, 1974), 93; hereafter cited in text as "Thirty."

56. Eudora Welty, *One Writer's Beginnings* (New York: Warner Books, 1983), 5; hereafter cited in text as *One*.

57. Maxine Hong Kingston, *The Woman Warrior: A Girlhood Among Ghosts* (New York: Vintage Books), 3; hereafter cited as *WW*.

58. Paula Gunn Allen, "Grandmother," in *The Third Woman: Minority Women Writers of the United States*, Dexter Fisher, ed. (Boston: Houghton Mifflin, 1980), 126; hereafter cited as *G*.

59. Beth Henley, *Crimes of the Heart* in *Plays for the Contemporary American Theatre*, ed. Brooks McNamara (New York: Mentor Books, 1988), 291; hereafter cited as CH. 229-91.

60. Josephine Donovan, *Feminist Theory: The Intellectual Traditions of American Feminism* (New York: Ungar, 1985), 175; hereafter cited in text.

61. Gail Godwin, *A Mother and Two Daughters* (New York: Viking Press, 1982), 19; hereafter cited in text as *MTD*.

62. Anne Tyler, *The Accidental Tourist* (New York: Berkley Books, 1985), 136; hereafter cited in text as *AT*.

63. For an anthology of fiction which discusses the differences between women and the necessity of bridging the gap which separates them, *The Things That Divide Us* edited by Faith Conlon, et al. (Seattle: Seal Press, 1985).

64. Sharon Olds, "Best Friends," in *The Dead and the Living* (New York: Alfred A. Knopf, 1983), 27.

65. Lillian Faderman, *Surpassing the Love of Men: Romantic Friendship and Love Between Women From the Renaissance to the Present* (New York: Morrow, 1981), 413; hereafter cited in text.

66. Adrienne Rich, "Twenty-One Love Poems," in *The Fact of a Doorframe: Poems Selected & New, 1950-84* (New York: W. W. Norton, 1984), 243.

67. Adrienne Rich, "It is the Lesbian in Us . . ." in *On Lies, Secrets, and Silence: Selected Prose, 1966-78* (New York: W.W. Norton, 1979), 201.

68. Audre Lorde, "On a Night of the Full Moon," in *Chosen Poems, Old & New* (New York: W.W. Norton, 1982), 20-1.

69. Judy Grahn, "Carol, in the park, chewing on straws," in *The Work of a Common Woman* (New York: St. Martin's Press, 1978), 67.

70. Rita Mae Brown, *Rubyfruit Jungle* (New York: Bantam Books, 1973), 7.

71. Judith Rossner, *August* (Boston: Houghton Mifflin, 1983.

72. Jane Flax, "Postmodernism and Gender Relations in Feminist Theory," *Signs: Journal of Women in Culture and Society* (Summer 1987), 629; hereafter cited in text. 621-43.

73. Carol Gilligan, *In a Different Voice: Psychological Theory and Women's Development* (Cambridge: Harvard University Press, 1982), 22; hereafter cited in text.

74. Francesca Cancian, "The Feminization of Love," *Signs: Journal of Women in Culture and Society* (Summer 1986), 692-709; hereafter cited in text.

75. Fay Weldon, *The Hearts and Lives of Men* (New York: Penguin, 1988), 151; hereafter cited in text as *HLM*.

76. Anne Bernays, *Professor Romeo* (New York: Penguin Books, 1989), 275.

77. Anita Brookner, *The Misalliance* (New York: Pantheon Books, 1986), 191.

78. Jill McCorkle, "Man Watcher," in *Crash Diet: Stories* (Chapel Hill: Algonquin Books, 1992), 29.

79. Jill McCorkle, "Crash Diet," in *Crash Diet: Stories* (Chapel Hill: Algonquin Books, 1992), 1; hereafter cited in text as "CD."

80. Jill McCorkle, "Departures," in *Crash Diet: Stories* (Chapel Hill: Algonquin Books, 1992), 112; hereafter cited in text as "D."

81. Mickey Pearlman and Katherine Henderson, *A Voice of One's Own: Conversations with America's Writing Women* (Boston: Houghton Mifflin, 1990), 146; hereafter cited in text.

Chapter Three

Women and Spirituality: A Journey from Nothingness to New Naming

> We need to know the writing of the past, and know it differently than we have ever known it; not to pass on a tradition but to break its hold over us.
>
> (Rich 1979, 35, 49).

In seeking new solutions to their post-war malaise, some women writers do not limit their critique to secular issues alone. Whether their vision is "orthodox" in its orientation—holding to a prescribed set of traditional religious rules and rituals—or "heterodox"—departing from a specific church doctrine in order to create a personal theological alternative—women authors often revise, reinterpret and transform contemporary religious thought in their literature. In focusing attention on what theologian Mary Daly terms "the transcendent dimension of feminism,"[1] many women writers seek to restructure both their personal spirituality and religious institutions, thereby initiating what might be termed a "theopolitical" journey in contemporary literature.

What must be abundantly clear, however, is that there is no one feminist analysis[2] and perspective on spirituality, nor is there one solution for reviving faith in a time of widespread disbelief. Authors as diverse as Cynthia Ozick, Flannery O'Connor, Simone de Beauvoir, Adrienne Rich, Anne Sexton and H.D.—Catholic, Jewish, Protestant and agnostic—seek a renewal of the spiritual in the contemporary world.

The result of this search for an alternative spirituality is found in the post-war feminine quest, discussed in Carol Christ's important book, *Diving Deep and Surfacing: Women Writers on Spiritual Quest* (1980). In her critique of contemporary literature, Christ provides a means of analyzing widely divergent views on the women's religious journey in the latter half of the twentieth century. In Christ's archetypal pattern, each woman undergoes an "experience of nothingness," an "awakening," "insight," and then a "naming" of self.[3] This personal journey from nothingness to a knowledge of self and God is not simplistically linear, however, but often cyclical and recursive, since both an individual woman or women as a social group can experience levels of the journey over again. Most importantly, however, Carol Christ's mystical framework suggests a means of understanding the unique journey of women as they seek to enrich their spiritual as well as secular lives.

Despite their differences, both orthodox and heterodox women writers encounter Christ's "experience of nothingness" in the late forties and fifties. Orthodox Christians and Jews—writers as dissimilar in background as Flannery O'Connor and Cynthia Ozick—were already dissatisfied with the modern interpretation of their respective faiths in the years immediately after World War II. Orthodox women were frustrated with the ways in which their faith was practiced in modern bourgeois society. Likewise, heterodox writers like Simone de Beauvoir in *The Second Sex* (1949) rejected traditional religious practice altogether and sought alternative paths to spiritual affirmation. If women were considered "other" in secular life, as de Beauvoir suggested in *The Second Sex*, it would follow that patriarchal religion would exclude them too. Barbara Hill Rigney characterizes this experience of nothingness and will to change in her book *Lilith's Daughters: Women & Religion in Contemporary Fiction* (1982) as "perceiving, revising and exorcising archetypal images and ideas of traditional religion."[4] Although the "experience of nothingness" would mean different things to orthodox and heterodox writers in the forties and fifties, the goal would be the same—the "transformation of nothingness into insight" (Christ 1980, xix).

The awakening process is crucial for believers and agnostics alike because it prepares women to encounter their true natures. Carol Christ suggests that female spiritual awakening is different from a male version because women describe a "coming to self" instead of a "surrender of self" (Christ 1980, 19). Through this awakening process, "women overcome self-negation and self-hatred and refuse to be victims."[5] No longer controlled by oppressive patriarchal religious roles, women gain insight into their proper place in the spiritual world.

Although the pattern of the spiritual quest is similar for orthodox and heterodox women to this point, it is in the nature and type of religious insight acquired that the two groups, orthodox or heterodox, part company in both literature and theology. During this period of "mystical identification" (Christ & Spretnak, 330) or "insight," heterodox authors like Adrienne Rich and Doris Lessing seek alternative theologies such as pantheism, the goddess or Eastern Sufi for inspiration into the feminine quest while orthodox Jews and Christians like Ozick and O'Connor find knowledge in revised or "re-seen" patriarchal religious traditions. Their divergent revelations, however, are not as simple as such a dichotomy would suggest since even within both orthodox and heterodox visions there are significant variations.

Thus, in the 1960s many women authors "awaken" to different visions which provide the foundation for divergent religious journeys in the late 1960s and 1970s. These mystical revelations, an outgrowth of unparalleled ferment and experimentation during this period, provide the stimulus in the 1980s and 1990s for the last and most important phase of the spiritual journey, what Carol Christ calls the "new naming" (Christ 1980, 4) of self and society. This "new naming" has both a personal and a social/political dimension since it acts as the creative stimulus for a contemporary literature which reflects women's newly found spiritual consciousness. Christ links this final stage of the spiritual journey to art because women "have not told their own stories, they have not shaped their experiences of self and world nor named the great powers from their perspectives" (Christ 1980, 4). By naming oneself, women as individuals and artists are able to revise moribund patriarchal religious traditions or revolt against them completely and create new stories. In either case, however, the silent woman who experienced a sense of otherness or nothingness is finally given a voice within the culture.

Moving Beyond Nothingness and War: Breaking the Silence in the Forties and Fifties

Although the late forties and fifties saw an expansion of traditional religion, this post-war phenomenon, according to historian Will Herberg, was a "religiousness without religion ... a way of sociability or belonging" (qtd. in Kaledin, 13). During this period, civic leaders viewed organized religion as one means by which democratic western nations could defeat "godless" Communism. In America, the forces of conformity and religion were particularly strong. In the late fifties, 63% of the population considered itself church affiliated and, in a 1954 survey, four out of five people stated that they would not elect an atheist as President or allow an atheist's book to appear in a public library (Kaledin 12-3). In 1953 and 1954, the Bible appeared on the best-seller list while the second most popular book in 1952 was Catherine Marshall's praise of her chaplain husband in *A Man Called Peter* which sold over 1.5 million copies by 1955 (Kaledin 29).

Many established churches reinforced this new wave of democratized religious fervor. The Catholic Church, in a series of Papal encyclicals beginning in the thirties with Pius XI's *Casti Connabii* on the subject of marriage through Pius XII "The Apostolate of the Midwife" in 1951 and Pope Paul VI's Second Vatican Council and publication of *Humanae Vitae* (1968) tended to enforce the ideas of woman as subservient to man in both the home and the church. In 1948, a Committee on the Life and Work of Women in the Church of the World Council of Churches surveyed women's roles in Christian churches and proclaimed that women should, indeed, be excluded from positions of power. Although some churches such as Methodist, Congregationalist and others allowed women into the clergy, most demanded that they, according to St. Paul, remain silent, at least in church.

Although the forties and fifties saw no organized feminine challenge to established religion, there were many important women who demanded control over their spiritual lives. Mary Daly praises Simone de Beauvoir's landmark philosophical treatise, *The Second Sex* (1949) for "breaking the silence ... even during the dreary fifties."[6] In de Beauvoir's chapter in *The Second Sex* entitled "Myths: Dreams, Fears, Idols," she argues that the conception of woman as "other" is "dear to the male, and every creation myth has expressed it, among others the legend of Genesis, which, through Christianity, has been kept alive in Western civilization" (de Beauvoir, 159). De Beauvoir cites the Old Testament's Eve as symbolic of women's passivity, alienation and nothingness. In 1949, de Beauvoir argues that women must create their own feminine myths or continue to "have no religion or poetry of their own: they still dream through the dreams of men. Gods made by males are the gods they worship" (161).

Most importantly, however, is de Beauvoir's questioning of the neutrality and universality of a patriarch religious tradition which she believed men "confuse with absolute truth" (161). Although Elaine Pagel's essay "What Became of God the Mother?" (1976) and her book *Adam, Eve and the Serpent* (1988) about the importance of the goddess in the pre-Judeo Christian world were not to be published for another twenty-five or thirty years, de Beauvoir, like Jane Harrison and Helen Diner before her, was already expressing a need for a pre-patriarchal goddess who functions as an antidote to patriarchal religion.

Two other women who sense a pervasive emptiness in religious life during the forties and fifties were theologian Valerie Saiving in "The Human Situation: A Feminine View" (1960) and fiction writer Flannery O'Connor in *Mystery and Manners* (1957-63). Although both authors were disillusioned with the current state of religion and spirituality in the forties and fifties, each reflects a divergent tradition; Saiving, following de Beauvoir in *The Second Sex* and Margaret Mead's theories of gender difference in *Male & Female* (1949), rejects patriarchal religious language as sexist and exclusionary. Like many writers in the heterodox tradition of feminist theological thought, Saiving calls for new myths to counteract women's sense of nothingness because, she believes, "a feminine society will have its own special potentialities for good and evil, to which a theology based solely on masculine experience may well be irrelevant."[7] Although historians may overestimate Saiving's importance as "the first open challenge to traditional religion" (Wandersee,

57) Saiving does lead the way for direct and open confrontation between heterodox feminists and established religion.

Another critique of organized religion—and one as equally impassioned in its attack on the status quo—is the orthodox view as expressed by Flannery O'Connor in the late fifties and early sixties. O'Connor, a practicing Catholic, adheres to the church's ideals, but not, she believes, its present bourgeois practices. O'Connor confesses that she is "no vague believer," but rather a person whose orthodoxy is "centered in our Redemption by Christ."[8] In the late fifties, she characterizes the religious world as an "unbelieving age ... Man wanders about, caught in a maze of guilt he can't identify, trying to reach a God he can't approach, a God powerless to approach him" (Mystery, 159). However, O'Connor's sense of nothingness does not emanate from her position as "other" or "woman." In fact, even when O'Connor writes about her own beliefs, she uses the generic "he" to represent both Christian women and men. Instead, O'Connor blames spiritual disillusionment on the "intellectual" and materialist approach to religion which seeks an "Instant Uplift" but lacks true "religious sense." She castigates the modern desire to make religion into an educational experience and worries that, in contemporary society, God "will suffer the ultimate degradation and become, for a little time, fashionable" (Mystery, 165-66).

Although O'Connor's orthodox vision of spirituality is not to become the mainstream heterodox view which is decidedly feminist and iconoclast, it remains a prevalent voice in women and spirituality and continues to be heard in the writings of Cynthia Ozick, Anne Sexton, Mary Gordon and a variety of minority and ethnic writers who maintain their ties with an established patriarchal church. And yet as disparate as the orthodox and heterodox perspectives remain, both agree that women authors should critique contemporary spirituality, using literature as their vehicle. In her essay, "The Church and the Fiction Writer," O'Connor maintains that "the Catholic sacramental view of life is one that sustains and supports at every turn the vision that the storyteller must have if he is going to write fiction of any depth" (Mystery, 152). The importance of literature as a means of alleviating modern despair is paramount in both heterodox and orthodox views; despite their disparate interpretations of "nothingness," women writers in the forties and fifties are "believers" in the importance of the spiritual.

Despite their divergent theological perspectives, many women writers in the late forties and early fifties react with horror and angst to the tragic events of World War II and its aftermath. Doris Lessing's novel *Martha Quest* (1952) provides one of the best contemporary analyses of heterodox spirituality in the decade immediately after World War II. Martha, the protagonist for Lessing's series of novels entitled "Children of Violence," is very much a child of her generation, contemptuous of organized religion and yet desirous for transcendence which will free her from the strictures of her mundane, materialistic society.

The youthful, nonconformist Martha sees the ways in which organized religion has reinforced and supported segregation and the colour bar in her native Rhodesia. In an argument with her parents about a male neighbor's sexual exploitation of his black female servants, Martha decries her parents' hypocrisy: "Anything for peace, you and your Christianity, and then what you do in practice" (MQ, 55). Although Martha is unfair to implicate her parents in her neighbor's miscegenation, she is correct to see the ways in which the Rhodesian church reinforced the status quo and its oppressive racial and class theories. And yet, despite her cynicism about organized Christianity, Martha seeks in the veld or jungle a "moment," a sense of wholeness and unity which Christianity should provide but does not. In her moment of "illumination," Martha understands "her smallness, the unimportance of humanity" (MQ, 52-3). This initial transcendent experience, however, does not last. It is not until *The Four-Gated City* (1969), Lessing's last novel in the series, before Martha is able to create a satisfactory spiritual life for herself.

H.D. (Hilda Doolittle) is also horrified as she surveys the effects of World War II in her poetic epic entitled *Trilogy* (1944-46). Like Lessing, H.D. expresses both the post-war sense of nothingness and a vision of hope in her second book of poetry in this series, *Tribute to the Angels* (1945). In this work, H.D. reimagines the New Testament's Book of Revelations and sees its symbolic angels. She reinvents the Virgin Mary, "Our Lady of the Pomegranate," whom she associates with the goddesses Persephone and Demeter.[9] H.D.'s Mary is no staid vision, but rather "a wisp of a girl/trapped in a golden halo" (T, 30). Associated with fertility, this virgin goddess is dressed in "apple-green" and "apple-russet" (T, 214-5), but is not a fallen Eve. An antidote to the meek and humble New Testament matriarch, H.D.'s Mary is both aggressive and delicate, awesome and peaceful: "not shut up in a cave/like a Sibyl . . . not imprisoned in leaden bars/in a coloured window," but instead a "Psyche, the butterfly" (T, 37). H.D. does not want an awe-inspiring Mary, "not even over-whelming/like an Angel," but instead "one of us, with us . . . with our purpose, a tribute to the Angels" (T, 39-40). Mary will not be "vas spirituale" a spiritual vessel nor "rosa mystica" Dante's spiritual rose, but instead the "flowering of the rood" or cross which would make it possible for humans to "rise again from death and live" after the despair and suffering of the war. (T, 41-2).

Although Elizabeth Bishop's complex, ambiguous and artful treatment of the spiritual predicament immediately after the war in *North & South* (1946) is not decidedly feminist in perspective, it makes an important analogy between patriarchal religion and political violence. For example, Bishop's poem "Roosters" (1946) equates the rooster's crowing with political aggression and religious conformity. The speaker of the poem asks the braying cock, a symbol of an authentic Christ, "what right have you to give/commands and tell us how to live . . . wake us here where are/unwanted love, conceit and war?" The "virile presence" of the cock is felt everywhere, "over our churches/where the tin rooster perches,/over our little wooden northern houses." The frustrated speaker, however, finally confronts the "tin rooster"—the spiritually unauthentic: "Roosters, what are you projecting?"[10] she asks. Bishop's ironical, critical vision is especially appreciated during the fifties when she is awarded the Pulitzer Prize for her poetry in 1955.

Like Bishop, poet Muriel Rukeyser surveys the moral destruction of World War II in *Beast In View* (1944) and *The Green Wave* (1948) and feels both helpless and hopeful. In her poem, "Who in One Lifetime" (1941), the speaker describes "Herself dismayed and helpless, cities down." Despite the surrounding "madnesses," however, there is some degree of distant hope found in the symbol of the goddess. At the end of the poem, the goddess still "holds belief in the world . . . though her whole world burn." And yet, the fertility goddess described by the speaker is "childless" and, therefore, incapable of restoring or regenerating the world.[11] She is a part of the fertility cycle which seems broken and unable to return the world to fecundity as in old myth. Rukeyser, who was Jewish, particularly felt a sense of apprehension after the holocaust.

Following World War II, many female authors write about their sense of religious and spiritual desolation during the holocaust of six million Jews and several million other victims by the Nazis, so many authors, in fact, that it is possible to mention only one or two here. Born in Germany to Jewish parents who escaped to Sweden during the war, Nobel Prize-winning poet Nelly Sachs speaks most powerfully and forcefully for a generation of holocaust writers who see the personal implications of political annihilation. *In the Habitations of Death* (1947) and *Eclipse of the Stars* (1949) contain poems like "O The Chimneys" (1949) where Sachs recounts the crematoria in which millions of victims were gassed and burned to death. The speaker confronts the chimneys themselves and asks, "who devised you and laid stone upon stone/The road for refugees of smoke."[12] Despite the unmitigated suffering of her people, Sach's epigraph to the poem—from the Old Testament's Book of Job— provides a sense of hope amid despair. A desire for redemption or renewal, implicit in Bishop and Rukeyser, seems explicit here. It is a message which is communicated quite dramatically through the popular culture as well in *The Diary of Anne Frank* (1947).

In the forties and fifties, many writers, however, feel unsure about how to confront the spiritual world or initiate their quest for redemption. The early poetry of Denise Levertov in *With Eyes at the Back of Our Heads* (1958) also uses biblical allusion to symbolize a sense of ominous despair in poems like "To the Snake." Having "hung" the snake around her neck, the speaker of the poem acknowledges "the weight of you [snake] on my shoulders."[13] Although seemingly oblivious of the consequences of her actions, the speaker, like Eve, swears to her companions that the snake is "harmless" despite any assurances to the contrary.

Some women writers on a spiritual quest in the forties and the fifties are unable to find even Levertov's glimmer of hope. In her novel, *Ship of Fools* (1962), Katherine Anne Porter dramatizes the plight of Western society on its self-destructive voyage by fictionalizing the actual trip of the North German Lloyd S. A. Vera which sailed from Mexico to Bremerhaven, Germany in 1931. Although the ship could have been the means of salvation for the Jewish passengers and others who wished to escape the Nazi holocaust, it was instead their tomb. An ancient image of free passage from the time of Homer, this modern vessel is only a "ship of fools." In discussing the novel, critic Lewis Simpson concludes that "the modern ship of fools sails not into eternity but into the Nazi dream of the thousand-year Reich."[14]

Several female writers, including Tillie Olsen and Margaret Walker, view religion as not only helpless to correct injustice, but as an obstacle to righteousness. Tillie Olsen's main character "Eva," like many of the other Eves in fifties literature desires a transcendence, but is unable to achieve it in the life she leads in "Tell Me A Riddle," written in the fifties and awarded the O. Henry Prize for the best short story of 1961. When she is dying in the hospital, Eva refuses to see a Rabbi and asks her child to write on the hospital form, "Race, human; Religion, none" (Tell, 80) Eva blames Judaism for her inability to control her personal and political life and thus feels contempt for a "religion that stifled and said: in Paradise, woman, you will be the footstool of your husband, and in life—poor chosen Jew—ground under, despised, trembling in cellars. And cremated. And cremated" (Tell, 81). Biblical sexism and racial intolerance are intertwined as Eva merges political, religious and sexual oppression. Although Eva returns imaginatively to the innocence and beauty of her youth at the end of the story, her spiritual reawakening is not possible on earth. In this work as well as in her extended prose essay *Silences* (1962-71), Olsen feels the need to break the silence which keeps women from attaining their creative visions.

In *For My People* (1942), Margaret Walker analyzes the plight of her own African-American people and, like Olsen, looks beyond organized religion for salvation. Like Doris Lessing's Martha Quest, the speaker in these poems seeks a means of transcendence apart from the established church which has been used to restrain or pacify women. In the title poem, "For my People," the speaker rejects the traditional church spirituals for their passivity and wishes to replace them with "martial songs."[15] In the poem "Since 1619," the speaker asks the reader "How many years since 1619 have I been singing Spirituals?/How long have I been praising God and shouting hallelujahs."[16] The speaker, not unlike the early Martha Quest, is influenced by thirties' Marxist antipathy towards the established church, a view which rejected religion as the "opiate of the masses."

In her collection of essays entitled *In Search of Our Mothers' Gardens* (1974), Alice Walker also looks back on the struggle of African-American women who suffered under religious and racial bigotry. Abused by both men and society, these women are described as "crazy saints [who] stared out at the world, wildly, like lunatics—or quietly, like suicides," women who look to a God that is unable to help them. According to Walker, this God is "as mute as a great stone." Like Eva and her sisters in the post-war era, these beleaguered women "dreamed dreams that no one knew . . . saw visions no one could understand. . . . They were Creators, who lived lives of spiritual waste" (In Search, 232-3). However, it is not for another decade or generation—until the publication of Olsen and Walker in the 1970s—that many of these abused saints are given a voice and a place in literature.

Although the heterodox writers mentioned above utilize biblical or classical images to discuss their spiritual quest, they do not adopt Judeo-Christian doctrine. In most cases, therefore, heterodox women authors while searching for spiritual salvation use traditional myth for new purposes. However, there are also other female authors—Flannery O'Connor, Mary McCarthy and Caroline Gordon—whose traditional religious visions guide them through a sense of nothingness immediately after World War II. Despite the fact that O'Connor and Gordon were practicing Catholics and McCarthy considered herself "lapsed,"[17] all of these women possess a faith in a specific church's ability to combat the forces of chaos in the post-war world.

Southern novelist and short story writer Caroline Gordon's conversion to Catholicism after World War II has a major impact on her fiction including *The Strange Children* (1951), and her *Collected Stories*. Gordon, like O'Connor, believes in the universal fall of mankind and the need for traditional redemption through Christ. And yet, despite the possibility of divine grace through the church, many of her characters do not achieve salvation because they neglect their communities and commit the sin of pride.

Much of Flannery O'Connor's best fiction, novels like *Wise Blood* (1952) and *The Violent Bear It Away* (1960), as well as powerful short story collections like *A Good Man Is Hard to Find, and Other Stories* (1955) reflect the orthodox writer's dilemma in the 1940s and 1950s of portraying the power of faith in a disbelieving age. The struggle, which is graphically, if not grotesquely presented in such short stories as "A Good Man is Hard to Find," "Greenleaf," "Revelation," and "Good Country People" is not a fight in which good triumphs over evil. Instead, these stories, according to O'Connor, only dramatize "our broken condition, and through it, the face of the devil we are possessed by" (Mystery, 168). Although O'Connor would like to provide her readers with more successful modern spiritual quests, she is content to shock and awaken the atheistic world.

A "modest" spiritual recognition is the best which the grandmother in O'Connor's well known story "A Good Man is Hard to Find" can achieve in the post-war world. The grandmother, who has led a foolish and non-reflective life is both the agent of her own destruction and salvation when she gives her son incorrect driving instructions on a rural road in Georgia. Through the grandmother's indiscretion, the family encounters a modern day version of the devil—the misfit—who kills them all and steals their car. However, before the old woman succumbs to the misfit's violence, she begins to see her kinship with him; she calls him "one of my babies"[18] and has a moment of illumination, closely followed by oblivion and death. Although the grandmother has no opportunity to apply her newly found insights, she has been able to acknowledge, as O'Connor would state, her own spiritually "broken" condition. And for this reason, the misfit says of his elderly victim, "She would of been a good woman if it had been somebody there to shoot her every minute of her life" (Good, 143). O'Connor's confrontation, however, between good and evil seems, in the fifties, to conclude without resolution; there is no triumph for Christ or the devil, and the believer glimpses only momentary illumination.

O'Connor's many other imaginative works of fiction follow a scenario similar to the one described above. The moments of spiritual insight are often given to characters who cannot understand or appreciate their impact. According to O'Connor, modern peoples' desire for empirical confirmation of God leads to disillusionment, moral relativism and, finally, nihilism, as evidenced by the Misfit's statement that "it's nothing for you to do but enjoy the few minutes you got left the best way you can—by killing somebody or burning down his house or doing some other meanness to him. No pleasure but meanness" (Good, 142).

Why would O'Connor—the devout Catholic—present such a grotesque, violent image to modern readers? As she explains in her essay "The Fiction Writer and His Country," the presentation of modern evil must be both shocking and exaggerated to the dulled, bourgeois mind because "to the hard of hearing you shout, and for the almost blind you draw large and startling figures" (Mystery, 34).

Another writer whose spiritual questing meets with many obstacles in the forties and fifties is Mary McCarthy. Her satiric stories in *The Company She Keeps* (1942) as well as her novels including *A Charmed Life* (1952) and the highly celebrated *The Group* (1963) present the dilemmas of women and men who have great difficulty finding their way in modern life. Although McCarthy acknowledges in her autobiography, *Memories of A Catholic Girlhood* (1957) that she is "lapsed" from the faith, her Catholicism provides her with insights into the nature of life, even if it does not guarantee the expected salvation. Her vision, therefore, is similar to the more orthodox O'Connor since both authors view religion as an ideal which few in contemporary life are capable of attaining—a sense of both the nothingness of the present and the missed potentiality of the religious ideal, fused into a single ironic vision.

This complex attitude towards religion and the spiritual can be seen in McCarthy's personal aside "To the Reader" which introduces her autobiographical *Memories of a Catholic Girlhood*. Although her mother's Catholicism made her feel that "religion was a present to us from God" (M, 16), years later, a psychoanalyst would blame McCarthy's adult "complacency" on her early religious training. The "lapsed" author, however, rejects this interpretation and instead praises religion for providing her with "a sense of wondering," (M, 16) a statement echoed by other orthodox writers like Cynthia Ozick and Mary Gordon in the sixties and seventies. McCarthy believes that, as an orphan, her despair and sense of "nothingness" were mitigated by the church's early influence: "It was religion that saved me," she concedes in the autobiography. "Our ugly church and parochial school provided me with my only aesthetic outlet," she explains. Despite the fact that this brand of Catholicism was, according to McCarthy, "cheapened and debased by mass production" she nonetheless embraced "with ardor, this sensuous life, and when I was not dreaming that I was going to grow up to marry the pretender to the throne of France and win back his crown with him, I was dreaming of being a Carmelite nun, cloistered and penitential" (M,20). Like orthodox Jewish author Cynthia Ozick who also uses the identical word "ardor" to describe her feelings about religion, McCarthy's imagination is inspired by the sensuosity and mystery of her faith.

Therefore, one would wonder why McCarthy would allow such a positive force in her life to "lapse." And yet, in her description of her first communion—the actual practice of religious doctrine in ordinary life—the reader sees the problem. The young McCarthy sips some water before the communion service, an action proscribed by the nuns who interpret Catholicism for the children. Overcome with guilt for drinking on a fast day (a mortal sin), the guilt-ridden young girl allows herself to receive the communion so as not to disappoint her family and teachers. McCarthy views this hypocrisy as paradigmatic of her entire life. The church taught her how to become a moral hypocrite, to care more for appearances than inner virtue. When she lies to her husband about a pregnancy, she describes her actions as "the same fix, morally, as I was [in] at eight years old" (M, 22).

Like O'Connor, Mary McCarthy does not object to the ideal Catholic faith, but rather to its contemporary bourgeois interpretation and practice in the forties and fifties. She makes some specific distinctions between two "strains" (M, 22) of Catholicism. The first strain is utopian and theoretical—aesthetically elegant and moral; the other, implemented by the earthly church, is tawdry and disillusioning, a religion which "bring[s] out some of the worst traits in human nature and ... lend[s] them a sort of sanctification"(M, 23). Modern Catholicism as well as Christianity as a whole should be capable of salvation, but in contemporary life, McCarthy argues, it is disappointing and impotent. In her autobiography and fiction, religion and virtuous action are often unconnected: the "average Catholic perceives no connection between religion and morality," McCarthy suggests, "unless it is a question of someone *else's* morality" (M, 24).

Cynical and alienated from her early spiritual path, and yet loyal to the remnants of a lost moral order, McCarthy feels herself a spiritual as well as a literal orphan. What she retains in adulthood is an ephemeral but powerless "sense of mystery and wonder ... all this ritual, seeming slightly strange and having no purpose" (M, 26). Many writers in the forties and fifties who do have personal faith are not sure that they live in a world which will support their vision. And for a great number of heterodox authors, the modern world, with its political and cultural chaos immediately after World War II, is a place in which spirituality is, at best, problematic, and at worst a manifestation of political oppression. Writing about fifties society, Betty Friedan in *The Feminine Mystique* (1963) contends that women must eschew philosophies which limit their freedom, even if these ideologies are "enshrined in the canons of their religion, in the assumptions of their own and their husbands' childhoods, and in their church's dogmatic definitions of marriage and motherhood" (FM, 339). As orthodox and heterodox women enter the sixties and seventies, it is obvious that they have their spiritual work cut out for them.

Sixties and Seventies: The Dead Awaken to Insight

When Carol Christ in her book *Diving Deep and Surfacing* (1980) describes the second stage of women's spiritual journey as "awakening" and "insight" (19), she could easily have the decades of the 1960s and 1970s in mind. Politically, culturally and theologically, women—both orthodox and heterodox—awakened to a new consciousness during this period. Christ, herself, defines "awakening" as "a time when the light begins to dawn, when we begin to see the world in a new way" (Christ 1980, xx). Although many women authors write about feminine spiritual awakenings in the sixties and seventies, there are distinct differences between the orthodox and heterodox visions which signal a parting of the road in women's spiritual quest.

The orthodox writers of the sixties and seventies "awaken" to a new light, but they maintain their ties to male Gods and established church principles. Heterodox women seek alternative conceptions of the divine and new rituals. It is this "parting of the ways" which accounts for women's divergent paths in the eighties and nineties. After acquiring both consciousness and insight, many women writers will undergo Christ's final stage of "new naming"; however, orthodox writers will come to a new self through a reunion with the Judeo-Christian tradition. Heterodox women writers's search leads them to seek a new entity such as a Goddess. Their definitions of divine transcendence and self-discovery, therefore, differ greatly.

In some respects, women's spiritual "awakening" is a theological extension of the civil rights and women's rights movement in the early and late sixties. The "consciousness-raising" groups which begin in the sixties help crystalize feminine discontent in a variety of spheres, including the spiritual. In an essay entitled "When We Dead Awaken: Writing As Re-Vision" (1971), Adrienne Rich characterizes the philosophical changes as a time when "the sleepwalkers are coming awake" (Rich 1979, 35). This process of "coming awake," will finally provide women writers with the potential to revise or "re-see" the myths (both theological and cultural) which have shaped them.

This revising process will also offer a radical critique of pre-existing literature and the impetus to imaginatively move forward into what theological Mary Daly will term the "exodus community."[19] Rich and Daly—spokespersons for the heterodox view towards religion in the sixties and seventies—both believe that the old patriarchal order is beginning its final chapter in the seventies.

Published in the same year as "When We Dead Awaken," and cited by Rich in her Preface to that essay, Mary Daly's revolutionary theological treatise, *Beyond God the Father* (1971) launches her own assault on the patriarchal Judeo-Christian tradition. Daly, who began in the late sixties as a religious reformist intending to revise Christianity's patriarchal emphasis on God as a male parent, becomes increasingly political and iconoclastic in the late seventies and eighties. Historians describe Daly and other revolutionary feminist theologians' transformation as a "crucial breakthrough ... the community out of which Daly spoke [in the seventies] was no longer the church but the women's movement" (Wandersee, 60).

Religious institutions both within and outside of established churches, therefore, were beginning to feel the influence of this new "theopolitical" thought in the late sixties and early seventies. In the same year that Rich and Daly published their aesthetic and theological critiques of patriarchy, the Women's Caucus of the American Academy of Religion formed its first feminist group. Only a year before, in August 1970, a Joint Committee of Organizations Concerned with the Status of Women in the Roman Catholic Church had accused the Church of discriminating against women (Wandersee 59). The connection between the theological and the political was nowhere more evident than in Daly's book *Beyond God The Father* which calls for a revolutionary separatist movement, an "exodus" community which would provide a "cosmic sisterhood" (Daly 1971, 155). This emphasis on sisterhood was discussed by numerous literary and theological writers including Adrienne Rich in *Of Woman Born: Motherhood as Experience and Institution* (1976), Naomi Goldenberg's *Changing of the Gods: Feminism and the End of Traditional Religions* (1979), Alice Walker *In Search of Our Mothers' Gardens* (1974), Merlin Stone's *When God Was a Woman* (1976). Many of these texts—both fiction and non-fiction—sought to repair the damage done to women in order to create a new spiritual bond between women of all generations.

Many contemporary heterodox writers seek to re-see classical myths of female bonding, such as the Greek myth of mother Demeter and her grief at the rape of her daughter Persephone. Critic Myra Jehlen characterizes this movement well when she defines "feminist thinking" as "really *re*thinking ... [about] the fundamental assumptions that organize all our thinking."[20] French novelist Monique Wittig captures the spirit of this period when she encourages women to use their imaginations to restructure the symbolic world: "There was a time," Wittig writes in the novel *Les Guerilleres*, "when you were not a slave, remember.... Or, failing that, invent."[21] And "invent," they did, as can be seen in any analysis of women's writing in the sixties and seventies. Re-formulated old myths, new matriarchal traditions of the goddess, an increased awareness of "mother" earth inform the heterodox writings of women in the sixties and seventies. In their award-winning critical work, *The Madwoman in the Attic*, Sandra Gilbert and Susan Gubar characterize some of the "best-known recent poetry" as a "parody in the cause of feminism: traditional figures of patriarchal mythology like Circe, Leda, Cassandra, Medusa, Helen and Persephone have all lately been reinvented in the images of their female creators, and each poem devoted to one of these figures is a reading that reinvents her original story."[22]

In 1976, theologian Elaine Pagels wrote a ground-breaking essay entitled "What Became of God the Mother? Conflicting Images of God in Early Christianity." The essay—the origin for her book length treatment of the Gnostic gospels in *Adam, Eve and the Serpent* (1988)—discusses the feminist aspects of the banned Gnostic gospels which would have feminized patriarchal Christianity. Pagels notes the loss of a maternal concept of God in the New Testament and suggests that early Christians excised this feminine imagery by 200 a.d. when they buried *The Gnostic Gospels*, both metaphorically and literally. For Pagels, one of the greatest differences between the orthodox and heterodox view, therefore, is found in the intentional male gendering of God.

Orthodox and heterodox imaginative literature in the sixties and seventies reflects this difference between masculine and feminine images of the divine. Orthodox writers like Flannery O'Connor and Cynthia Ozick retain the patriarchal imagery of the Judeo-Christian tradition with its emphasis on God's androgynous or paternal omnipotence. In her collection of essays entitled, *Art and Ardor* (1965-77) Cynthia Ozick maintains her unquestioning faith in a Jewish, ungendered, universal conception of both religion and art. In "Previsions of the Demise of the Dancing Dog" (1965) Ozick attacks the "Ovarian Theory of Literature" which makes distinctions between male and female art.[23] Ozick even goes so far as to state that making gender distinctions in literature and religion is heresy: "Biology is *there*: it does not need our praise, and if we choose to praise it, it is blasphemous to think we are praising not God but ourselves." Although Ozick does acknowledge that women experience discrimination in the academic world and elsewhere, she views art and God as above the material world, "an unknowable abstraction" (Ozick 1984, 271).

Ozick, therefore, agrees that one must praise God's creation as a means of worshipping the divine itself; to do any less is, in her estimation, "idolatry" (Ozick 1983, 206). Ozick would probably agree with Flannery O'Connor's characterization of modern people as "lopsidedly spiritual" (*Mystery*, 159) because they worship the object which God produced (art, nature, themselves) instead of the power which created the sacred things of the world. For Ozick, there is no theopolitical conflict in Judaism, no male God to overthrow. She views the divine, not as a tyrannical father who excludes women from his kingdom and church, but rather as the creator of everything positive, worthy of infinite praise and regard.

In addition to the orthodox and heterodox traditions, however, there are a host of other writers in the 1960s and 1970s who are neither overtly orthodox nor heterodox—Mary Gordon and Margaret Atwood[24] to name a few—who seem caught between the two conflicting perspectives, accepting neither the universalist/masculine nor the feminine rendering of the Divine. Margaret Atwood's response to an interviewer in 1979 typifies this independent vision. Skeptical of any spiritual dogma, Atwood asks, "Would a matriarchal theology exalt women and give men a secondary place? If so, I'm not interested because it would be the same problem in reverse" (qtd. in Rigney 1982, 57). In 1984, critic Nina Auerbach also expresses reservations about what she fears is fast-becoming women's moral self-righteousness, a "self-glorifying separatism so extreme that it meets the extremes of patriarchy, purging women of all violence and ego until we become a gush of sheer nurturance in an angry world."[25]

So pervasive is the heterodox tradition of female literary spirituality in the sixties and seventies, however, that in her book, *Lilith's Daughters: Women and Religion in Contemporary Fiction* (1982), critic Barbara Hill Rigney presents only heterodox views as the predominant religious literature of feminism, clearly overlooking the orthodox vision. Rigney views the 1960s and 70s as a "revolution" in the "sexual politics of theology . . . [a] new literature of protest which is often vehemently iconoclast" (Rigney 1982, 4).

In many respects, Rigney is correct about the predominance of women's heterodox spirituality. Some of the most revolutionary literature surfaces in the late 1960s. In 1968, with the creation of radical feminist organizations like WITCH, covens of women appear around the United States, taking their name from the Old Testament's Samuel, I. 15:23 which states that "Rebellion is as the sin of witchcraft." These covens were formed to "spook" the patriarchy, according to Mary Daly, by devising a mixture of political and cultural "weapons" which included: "theater, satire, explosions, magic, herbs, music, costumes, cameras, masks, chants . . . your own boundless, beautiful imagination."[26] And, many women inspired by the rebellion and political upheavals of the late sixties, responded by creating a literature of radical theology, unprecedented in modern times and, possibly, as iconoclast in its own way as the Gnostic gospels were in the first century a.d. Poet June Jordan voices this new theopolitical spirit in *Things That I Do in the Dark* (1980). Jordan's poetry, intended to "spook" the patriarchy, is both threatening and intimidating. Poems in this volume speak of bloody revenge and signal the end of feminine politeness.[27]

A similar hostility towards all "fathers"—divine or biological—can be felt in Sylvia Plath's poem "Daddy." (1963). The speaker in the poem is in open rebellion against the Daddy who is described alternately as a "bag full of God," a Nazi "man in black with a Meinkampf look" and a "devil." And yet the speaker believes she can "kill" the Daddy once and for all because he is "Not God but a swastika/So black no sky could squeak through." Plath, like Betty Friedan in *The Feminine Mystique*, makes the analogy between women and the Jews under the Nazi regime. Her "Daddy" is "An engine, an engine/ Chuffing me off like a Jew. A Jew to Dachau, Auschwitz, Belsen," concentration camps which exterminated six million Jews and millions of others during World War II (D, 222-23). The speaker's struggle is not only personal, but political and theological as well. It is not simply a matter of teenage rebellion, but a matter of survival for a race and gender.

Jean Tepperman's poem "Witch" also typifies the angry sixties rebellion against traditional religion and society. "They told me/I smile prettier with my mouth closed," the speaker of the poem confesses. "They said—/better cut your hair—/long, it's all frizzy,/ look Jewish." Society's injunctions against both her spirit and her body, however, only enrage the sixteen-year-old girl who was "buttoned . . . into dresses/covered with pink flowers." Despite the oppression, however, the girl carries a "hand grenade/in my pants pocket," while waiting to become visible as a human being. "I have been invisible,/weird and supernatural" the speaker notes, but a change is coming. "I want my black dress . . . I want my broomstick/from the closet where I hid it." In her witch-like state, she is empowered where previously she was impotent: "We are screaming,/we are flying,/laughing, and won't stop."[28]

The "laugh" of the witch or of the medusa, as in French feminist Helene Cixous important article "The Laugh of the Medusa," (1976) is a statement of open rebellion against *status quo* religion. "Let the priests tremble," Cixous says in her essay, "we're going to show them our sexts,"[29] a conflation of the words "texts" and "sex." Cixous encourages women writers to create texts which are "subversive" and "volcanic" in order to "smash everything, to shatter the framework of institutions, to blow up the law, to break up the 'truth' with laughter" (Cixous, 292). This revolutionary laughter can come from the reinterpretation of myths previously held taboo. Cixous wishes to incite women to write their own stories and not be influenced by male interpretations of women and feminine virtue. In a complete re-vision of Odyssean myth, Cixous asks women "to stop listening to the Sirens (for the Sirens were men) ... You only have to look at the Medusa straight on to see her. And she's not deadly. She's beautiful and she's laughing" (Cixous, 289). Cixous wishes women to awaken to a reality untainted by male opinion and reject both patriarchal myths or the values which support them; only then will they finally become creators of their own lives and literature.

In the 1960s and 1970s, Cixous as well as other artists and critics believed that the Medusa, witch and crone were manifestations of the pre-patriarchal goddess supplanted by the Hebrew God Yahweh and the Christian Jesus. When theologian Mary Daly looked "beyond God, the father," she needed to find something to take its place or risk a feminist spiritual nihilism. As heterodox feminist writers rejected traditional religious imagery, they were often left with a void, or as Barbara Hill Rigney terms it, the "anxiety" and "loneliness" of the iconoclast who must "fill spiritual and psychological gaps" (Rigney 1983, 5-6). As Charlene Spretnak explains in her speech "Why Women Need the Goddess" (1978): "symbol systems cannot simply be rejected, they must be replaced."[30]

Therefore, many of the poems, short stories, novels and plays written in the sixties and seventies reflect this awakened desire for new myths and values to replace moribund ones. The goddess who emerges as a woman with an innate ability to both create and destroy is a powerful entity, not the weaker half of a male dualism. She embraces contraries and rejects hierarchies which insist that certain people have dominance over others. Heterodox writers contend that the goddess represents a harmonious, balanced view of life and death, good and evil, female and male which allows women to reacquire some of the energy lost in patriarchal religions.

One particularly influential collection of poetry entitled *No More Masks! An Anthology of Poems by Women* (1973) was published at the height of interest in the goddess and the re-mythicizing movement of the seventies. The book took its title from a poem by Muriel Rukeyser which ended with the injunction to women: "No more masks! No more mythologies!/ Now, for the first time, the god lifts his hand,/the fragments join in me with their own music."[31] The editors of the anthology, Florence Howe and Ellen Bass, reject patriarchal mythologies and publish a number of poems which focus on the goddess and new revisions of old myths.

One particular myth—the focus of much feminist literary revision in the seventies—is the story of Demeter and Persephone. The Greek myth recounts the story of Persephone (Kore), the goddess of fertility, who is stolen by the God of the underworld, Hades, who makes her his bride. Demeter, Persephone's mother, searches endlessly for her lost daughter and bargains with Hades for her daughter's life. Demeter is able to persuade Hades to allow her daughter to live for eight months of the year on the earth's surface, thereby making the harvest possible. The rest of the year she must "die" and live in the underworld. For many heterodox women artists, the myth is a testimonial to the love of a mother for her daughter, a symbol of women's power and tenacity and a mythicizing of positive, feminine creative power. For this reason, the goddess and the myth of Demeter and Persephone are retold in countless poems, novels and essays.

The myth is incorporated into a praise of the mother-daughter relationship in Kathleen Raine's poem "Kore in Hades" (1965) in which the Persephone/Kore figure pledges an allegiance to the beloved mother. It is this alliance between mother and daughter that produces the "roadside green" and "golden gentle and bright light of the living" in spring's renewal. Kore's love for her mother embodies none of the traditional antagonism directed towards a mother in complicity with the patriarchy; instead Kore's love is all peace and fecundity. The dualistic thinking of patriarchy is exorcised as mother and daughter recapture "the garden/lost from time."[32]

Although Raine's use of the Demeter/Persephone myth is quite obvious, many other authors incorporate it into their novels, including an inversion of the tale in Margaret Atwood's *Surfacing* (1972) where the daughter goes in search of the lost mother. In Judith Rossner's *August* (1982), a female psychiatrist rescues her youthful female patient from an underworld of suicide, and in Atwood's novel *Cat's Eye* (1989) Elaine Risley's mother, a cross between Demeter and the "virgin of lost things," saves the young Elaine from drowning in a ravine (CE 361).

The retrieval of the valuable daughter by the powerful mother is also the subject of a poem by Adrienne Rich entitled "Diving Into the Wreck" (1973). Like a courageous Demeter, the speaker in this poem must submerge herself in the ocean or underworld in order to survey the wreckage of the society, the fragments from which she will recreate her life. Although she takes with her a book of myths, the speaker realizes that this journey will be made unaided and alone; the old values and patriarchal stories cannot serve as models. At the conclusion of the poem, the speaker has found someone—a symbolic daughter like Persephone, or possibly just her actual self. In any case, she knows that the book of old myths provides no help because it does not contain women's names or their identities.[33] If women are to find what lies under the wreck of patriarchal society and thus renew the earth, they will have to use new stories for guides; the old ones are of little use in this contemporary quest.

However, five years later, in *The Dream of a Common Language* (1978), Rich begins to provide further insights to guide women on their spiritual journey. Although the speaker in "Transcendental Etude" is still searching for the truth which will make sense out of her life, she describes her dilemma in music terms as the problem inherent in trying to memorize a piece of music which the musician cannot read or play quickly enough.[34] Despite the speaker's isolation, however, she wishes to reach the goal of a common language which will enable women to name the world and create themselves anew, overturning the patriarchal Adam who named Eve and thus possessed her.

In their quest for spiritual salvation, many heterodox female authors in the sixties and seventies do not give up the old biblical myths, but instead revise and reinterpret them. In Australian poet Judith Wright's amusingly cynical poem "Eve To Her Daughters" (1966) Eve, is finally given a voice and a point of view. She speaks to her "daughters," providing them with her version of the fall, a punishment which she takes philosophically and fatalistically. Wright's Eve is not a passively constructed "rib" of Adam, but rather his chief critic. She names him as the archetypal "egotist" who refuses to comprehend his own failings and flaws. She would like to correct her husband's arrogance but realizes the futility of such an action. "It's useless to make/such a suggestion to Adam," she contends. "He has turned himself into God,/who is faultless, and doesn't exist."[35] Wright's Eve, however, is too enlightened to mistake Adam for God and does not worship at her husband's altar.

Another reinvented portrait of Eve is presented by Canadian poet Dorothy Livesay in her poem "Eve" (1967). Livesay's revised Eve finds an apple tree, "the last survivor of a pioneer orchard" which grows brazenly "beside the highway/at the motel door." Unlike the apple in the biblical fall from paradise, this apple furnishes Eve with a resurrection and rejuvenation. She picks it up and bites into it "spurting juice/earth-sweet!"[36] And, instead of bringing death and destruction into the world, Eve feels herself youthful again. As Livesay and other female authors "rewrite" or reimagine biblical myths, they reject religious myths which denigrate or repress women.

British poet Stevie Smith also revises the story of Adam and Eve with her characteristic irony in "How Cruel Is the Story of Eve" (1966). The speaker castigates the male author of Genesis for his role in the historical victimization of women. Smith contends that the story of Eve's temptation of Adam and their subsequent fall creates a lasting resentment between women and men. Anticipating the reader's possible objections, the speaker asks, "It is only a legend/You say? But What/Is the meaning of the legend/If not/To give blame to women most/ And most punishment?"[37]

Although many feminist heterodox writers devote their attention to revising the Genesis myth in order to make it less misogynist, other writers focus on female biblical characters like Mary and Ruth or the heroic martyrdom of Christ. One example is African-American poet Pauli Murray's "Ruth" (1970) which presents a new interpretation of the Old Testament's Book of Ruth. The biblical Ruth is a loyal wife and daughter-in-law of the Hebrew tribe, although she is not Jewish. In the original version, when Ruth's husband dies, she pledges faithfulness to her mother-in-law Naomi and is ultimately rewarded with a new husband and family. When Pauli Murray reimagines the story, she makes Ruth into the "Queen of ghetto, sturdy hill-climber" who chants "Te Deums [prayers to God] on Sunday." This brown-skinned Ruth waits for no masculine protection; she is her own hoped for "Gallant challenger, millioned-hope bearer."[38] The speaker of the poem praises her courage, her strength and determination but this contemporary woman is the personification of a feminine autonomy which waits for no man.

Denise Levertov's increasingly political anti-Vietnam war poetry during the sixties also makes use of such biblical inversions. In the poem, "Advent 1966" (1966) Levertov compares the burning infant victims of the Vietnam war to Christ's metaphorically burning flesh in a painting by Southwell. The poet's eye, however, sees the ironic difference between the painter's theoretical Holy Infant and the Vietnamese babies who are "living on/moaning and stinking in hospitals three abed."[39] Levertov's contemporary portrait of the Trinity and Christian martyrdom is graphically reimagined in her presentation of the "Advent" or birth of Christ in the modern world.

Equally nightmarish is the sacrifice of Jesus which Sylvia Plath re-sees in her poem "Mary's Song" (1962). The speaker in the poem compares the sacrifice of her own heart to Mary's sacrifice of her son Jesus. In the speaker's world, all female lovers are martyrs, innocents with little hope for redemption. Once again Plath conflates sexual, religious and political martyrdom. As the speaker cooks a Sunday lamb in the oven, the images of death flood over her—Sunday dinner, the lamb of God and exterminated Jews all coalesce into one image of spiritual suffering—a contemporary song for Mary. The speaker refers to the world as "this holocaust I walk in," a holocaust which will "kill and eat" the "golden child" which is her "heart."[40] Although many readers may consider Plath's comparison between her own personal suffering and that of concentration camp victims to be exaggerated, the poem derives its power from its transformation and translation of biblical myth into a contemporary idiom.

Although women writers in the heterodox tradition are drawn to traditional religious iconography, they often do not utilize the images in a literal or orthodox manner. To explain, Plath compares her suffering to Mary's, but emphasizes the Virgin's pain and not her sense of redemption through the birth of her son. There is not a sense of hopefulness in Plath, that one would find in the writings of a more orthodox handling of traditional Christian imagery. Irish fiction writer Edna O'Brien provides additional examples of this heterodox tradition in her trilogy of novels, *The Country Girls, The Lonely Girl* and *Girls in Their Married Bliss* (1960-64).

O'Brien's novels and short stories dramatize the influence of Catholicism on family life in her native land. But, her use of religious imagery often emphasizes the failure of spiritual ideals, the corruption of theological principles as they are practiced in Irish society. In O'Brien's short story "A Rose in the Heart of New York" (1979) an unnamed protagonist and her mother, Delia, suffer Christ's martyrdom at the hands of a violent, abusive father/husband. For a short time, the young girl looks upon her mother as the redemptive Virgin Mary who is capable of saving her soul: "Her mother was the cup, the cupboard, the press with all the things in it, the tabernacle with God in it."[41] However, her mother dies silently, leaving her daughter neither a note of explanation or a token of love. At her mother's death, the young woman does not see any transcendent Christian redemption which would traditionally be derived from suffering; instead, both the story and the main character's relationship with her mother end inconclusively—an aborted journey. Mother and daughter are never reconciled. Even as the young woman kisses her mother in the coffin she wonders, "So soul . . . where are you, on your voyaging and oh soul, are you immortal?" (Rose, 175). Delia wants a transcendent communique from the dead to the living, but knows, "there was no such thing" (Rose, 177).

Other heterodox writers like Alice Walker agree with O'Brien that if women desire salvation, they will have to find it on earth and not in a speculative after-life. In a 1973 interview, Walker analyzes her preoccupation with the theological: "Certainly I don't believe there is a God beyond nature. The world is God. Man is God" (In Search 265). Walker, who will expound upon this theme in detail in her Pulitzer Prize winning novel, *The Color Purple* (1985) developed her heterodox theories during the sixties and seventies when she wrote many short stories included in *In Love and Trouble* (1973). One story in particular, "Everyday Use," shows Walker's distrust of established theology and insistence on a self-determined spirituality. The narrator of the story is an older woman with two daughters, Maggie and Dee, who refuses to accept any systematic belief system, even Dee's new Afro-centricism. Instead, God comes to her through love and personal creativity, in this instance through her disfigured daughter Maggie's quilting. The mother praises her daughter's quilting in language usually reserved for the theological: "It was Grandma Dee and Big Dee who taught her [Maggie] how to quilt ... This was Maggie's portion. This was the way she knew God to work."[42]

In her essay, "Saving the Life that is Your Own," (1976) Walker argues that personal salvation is achieved through personal not divine interaction. It is the imperative of the black female writer, Walker contends, to write her own stories, tales which praise and redeem her culture. Interestingly, Walker compares her own religious aesthetic to that of orthodox writer Flannery O'Connor because both women explore salvation through literature. According to Walker, story-telling "is our only hope—in a culture so in love with flash, with trendiness, with superficiality, as ours—of acquiring a sense of essence, of timelessness, and of vision" (In Search 8). Although Walker's vision does not insist on the adherence to a specific doctrine of an established church, and would probably be repudiated by the Catholic O'Connor, Walker's sense of mission is no less spiritual. It is Walker's means of achieving this redemption that separates her from O'Connor and the orthodox tradition.

Personal and group salvation are also important to black playwright Ntozake Shange in her award winning play/choreopoem entitled *for colored girls who have considered suicide/when the rainbow is enuf* (1974). Initially many of the seven women of color dramatized in the play seek redemption through masculine rescue—both divine and mortal; however, they become increasingly despondent and disillusioned when salvation or enlightenment elude them. Some even consider suicide in a world which cannot or will not meet their needs. The "lady in brown's" self-awareness, however, requires no less than a resurrection since "she's been dead so long/closed in silence so long/she doesn't know the sound/of her own voice."[43]. The woman further expands the metaphor theologically when she asks that a speaker appear who can "sing the song of her possibilities/sing a righteous gospel . . . let her be born/let her be born" (for, 5).

Many of the women in the play speak of their betrayals by lovers who use and abandon them. The "lady in yellow" describes her condition as a "metaphysical dilemma" (for, 45) while all the women feel that they are "missing something" (for, 61). Finally, the "lady in purple"—in almost a foreshadowing of Alice Walker's message in the 1983 *The Color Purple*—provides the ladies with the means to achieve their personal resurrection, not through an established church or the myth of romantic love, but through the self: "i found god in myself/& i loved her/i loved her fiercely" (for, 63) she tells the other women at the play's conclusion. Symbolically, this naming of the god or goddess within becomes one of the guiding forces of the heterodox tradition in the eighties and nineties although it is fictionally introduced earlier.

In the seventies, many authors see the need for independent spiritual action, the theological corollary to the civil rights and women rights movements. In Mary Gordon's novel *Final Payments* (1978), the main character and narrator Isabel Moore, cannot wait for a male rescue but must "resurrect" herself after an eleven-year living death as the caretaker of her dying father. Like Mary Daly's newly liberated woman who must survive the death of God the Father, Isabel must recreate her existence: "After they lowered his body, I would have to invent an existence for myself. Care of an invalid has this great virtue: one never has to wonder what there is to do."[44] And yet in "inventing" a life for herself, Isabel rejects the predetermined spiritual roads set forth by her Catholic church. She refuses to continue her martyrdom as the parish's nurse, nor will she immediately marry in order to produce Christian children.

Isabel's new freedom, however, is as frightening as it is liberating. She must confront a "sickening expanse of potential" (FP, 65) in the modern world, and decide her place in it. Caught between the end of traditional roles and the creation of new ones, in the seventies, Isabel and her friend Eleanor bemoan their situation. Eleanor confesses to Isabel that she would like some assurance, "to do something I was entirely sure of." Isabel, too, feels nostalgic for the absolute faith of the church. "It's so unfair. There's nothing like it, nothing takes its place . . . I miss that sureness," she tells her friend. "But I don't miss the people and what it does to them" (FP, 58). Although both women "miss the sureness" of church sanctioned feminine roles like devoted martyr and servant, they also know that there is no returning to the patriarchal fold. They will have to awaken themselves and invent modern identities for themselves or die.

In order to save herself, therefore, Isabel begins a painful resurrection with her two friends by her side. Isabel, who has previously invoked church doctrine to deny herself pleasure, now uses it to launch herself into a new life. She interprets Christ's words "The poor you have always with you: but me you have not always" (FP, 298) to validate her decision to enjoy both life and sexuality. No longer will she have to make "final payments" for her pleasures. At the conclusion of the novel, she stands in a newly fashioned trinity of community with her friends Eleanor and Liz, the three women forming a new "cosmic community" (Daly 1973, 155) which Mary Daly predicts will take the place of the church in the hearts of women. Isabel praises this friendship which she describes as "a miracle," (FP, 307) the feminine equivalent of the resurrection.

Many of the female writers in the seventies come to realize that while women's spiritual lives are circumscribed by an oppressive patriarchal church, it is within their own power to change. From this insight comes the need for women to work in concert with each other instead of at the behest of men. In the Introduction to E.M. Broner's novel Her *Mothers* (1975), Marilyn French describes the purpose of Broner's book as the recreation of "an entire generation's experience of growing up as a Jewish female in the forties and early fifties, subject to a male-dominated social and religious tradition that is enforced by females—mothers."[45] The recurring plot scenario involves a dialogue between a pregnant woman and her mother about the imminent birth of a daughter. The mother—an enforcer of the Jewish patriarchal tradition—generally tells the pregnant woman not to give birth. In one instance, the mother asks her pregnant daughter if her fetus has a "date for New Year's Eve? . . . a date for the Senior Prom?" When the pregnant woman answers, "No," the patriarchal mother retorts, "Then tell her not to be born" (HM, 34).

Despite this inauspicious beginning, however, the main character Beatrix—named for Dante's spiritual Beatrice in *The Divine Comedy*—is determined to be born and to bear new daughters who refuse to be defined and named by patriarchal traditions. Beatrix is even willing to give birth to herself or allow her new daughters to retroactively "birth" their foremothers, thereby retrieving and resurrecting women from history who will act as role models. One such heroine or foremother worthy of imaginative resurrection is nineteenth century author Margaret Fuller. In the novel, the pregnant woman imagines a conversation with "Mother Margaret" who symbolizes the mother independent of patriarchal influences. When Beatrix informs Mother Margaret that she is "pregnant with a baby girl and she's religious," Margaret queries, "Has she been a minister, a priest, a monk, a rabbi? . . . Is she at the pulpit? Does she open the Holy Ark?" When the pregnant woman answers, "No," mother Margaret skeptically retorts, "Then she's not religious. She's stupid" (HM, 88-89).

As Beatrix becomes increasingly aware of her inferior position in the religious hierarchy, she turns her anger towards the complicitous "mothers" who uphold and enforce what Broner cynically calls the "old testicle." "Mothers! Sara! Rivka! Lea! Rachel! You have taught your daughters that women fight for the penis of a man. . . . Who named *you* my mothers? Who named *this* a matriarchy?" (HM, 168).

In order to complete her spiritual journey, Beatrix must find a new communion between herself and her mother, an awakened sense of feminine religious community like those which conclude both *Final Payments* and Beth Henley's play *Crimes of the Heart*. Broner's *Her Mothers* provides just such a heterodox communion ceremony when an aging Beatrix requests that her spiritual foremothers "birth" her. In this world, all the musicians and creative powers are female as the last woman announces to her mother, "Mother, I'm pregnant with a baby girl ... [and] she is singing.... Because she's unafraid" (HM, 241).

The need to transform female competitiveness into communion is a major mission for the heterodox religious writer in the seventies. This is especially evident in Maxine Hong Kingston's powerful autobiography *The Woman Warrior: Memoirs of a Girlhood Among Ghosts* which won the National Book Critics Circle Award. In the first essay, entitled "No Name Woman," Kingston tells the tale of her aunt who drowns herself when she is humiliated by her community after giving birth outside of marriage. Kingston's mother tells her the story of the aunt as a warning about disobedience. "You must not tell anyone" (WW, 3) about the nameless aunt who has been erased from family history for giving birth out of wedlock. In giving voice and "name" to her aunt, Kingston begins her own spiritual rebirth as she breaks the vow of silence which separates women from each other and their power. In the process of naming her foremother, Kingston also begins to name herself—an action which has political, aesthetic and spiritual importance.

The orthodox religious vision in the 1960s and 1970s differs from the heterodox in many ways, not the least of which in the former's insistence on the universality or androgyny of religious experience. Cynthia Ozick and other orthodox writers do not seek alternatives to the Judeo-Christian traditions, or other established churches; they generally see their faiths and deities as gender neutral. They stress both the universality of the divine and the aesthetic and consider any attempts to discuss the gendered nature of god or art as idolatry—making material objects out of something which should be worshipped as an abstraction.

It is thus not surprising that orthodox writers like Ozick and Flannery O'Connor take little notice of women's struggle in their art. Ozick, in fact, calls the entire notion of the "woman" writer "this myth-fed condition of segregation" (Ozick 1984, 285). She clearly separates the political, the religious, and the aesthetic and argues that "outside its political uses, 'woman writer' has no meaning—not intellectually, not morally, not historically. A writer is a writer" (Ozick 1984, 285). Unlike the heterodox writers, Ozick does not believe in an expressly feminine spiritual journey. Rather her ideal is one which is sexless and universal. Where many heterodox writers see women's creativity stifled by patriarchal traditions—divine or secular—Ozick seems to reject even the notion of a patriarchy. Great women artists will not emerge until women can "forget" their sexuality, "until woman-as-person becomes as flat and unremarked a tradition as man-as person" (Ozick 1984, 279).

In order to dramatize the dangers of idolatry, Ozick presents literary characters who worship other gods—the gods of experience, physical beauty and knowledge—with devastating and tragic results. One in particular, Isaac Kornfeld, in "The Pagan Rabbi" (1966) rejects the entire Judaic tradition in favor of paganism, thereby relinquishing his life and endangering his eternal soul. The epigraph to the story sets forth the theme quite explicitly. It is a quote from the book *The Ethics of the Fathers* which states that "He who is walking along and studying, but then breaks off to remark, 'How lovely is that tree!' or 'How beautiful is that fallow field!'—Scripture regards such a one as having hurt his own being."[46]

In Ozick's short story, the learned Rabbi Kornfeld who rejects his own faith to follow a female dryad into the park, commits suicide, leaving behind a notebook and a letter praising Pan and nature. Rather than revering God, Kornfeld has turned inward, infatuated with understanding and exploring his soul, unaided by divine light. In his notebook, Kornfeld states his newly found purpose: "To *see* the soul, to confront it—that is divine wisdom . . . To see one's soul is to know all, to know all is to own the peace" (PR, 21). Kornfeld speaks of this adventure in sexual terms, as coupling with a dyrad, a goddess like the biblical Lilith. However, unlike the heterodox writers who consider Lilith a positive symbol of female rebellion against patriarchal oppression, Ozick regards Lilith and the dryad as detrimental to the Rabbi's soul. In fact, Ozick uses the traditional male (soul) female (body) dichotomy to represent the struggle within Kornfeld's psyche. The dryad is, therefore, the temptress, the traditional Old Testament "foreign woman" of Proverbs who overcomes men and confuses them, convincing them that nature and sensual experience are more important than God's law.

Thus, the picture of the observant male succumbing to the wayward foreign female—so often portrayed in Jewish scripture—is given a contemporary perspective by Ozick who has few qualms about perpetuating negative female stereotypes. Although one may agree with Edmund White's assessment that "Judaism has given to her what Catholicism gave to Flannery O'Connor—authority, penetration and indignation,"[47] Ozick's faith has also provided her with a rationale for bypassing gender issues in favor of "higher" ultimate concerns. In her novels *Trust* (1966) and *The Cannibal Galaxy* (1983) as well as in her three volumes of short stories, *The Pagan Rabbi* (1971), *Bloodshed* (1972), and *Levitation* (1982), Ozick analyzes the complexities of the orthodox vision, but does not seem to question gender disparities inherent in the tradition.

Although Anne Sexton's attitude towards orthodox Christian principles varied greatly over the course of her tragically short career, many of the later poems, particularly in *The Book of Folly* (1972) and *The Awful Rowing Toward God* (1975), provide a searing portrait of one woman's search for a God who would provide the answer to her suffering. In the Introductory remarks to Sexton's *The Collected Poems*, published posthumously in 1981, friend and fellow poet Maxine Kumin explains Sexton's lifelong fascination with God. After several unsuccessful suicide attempts, Sexton turned to a God who was, according to Kumin, "a sure thing, an Old Testament avenger admonishing his Chosen People, an authoritarian yet forgiving Father decked out in sacrament and ceremony." Kumin believes that Sexton desperately needed authority figures who would provide direction for her life and work: "the psychiatrist and then the priest put an imprimatur on poetry as salvation, as a worthy goal in itself."[48]

Sexton's series of poems entitled "The Jesus Papers" in *The Book of Folly* (1972) present just such a portrait of the artist herself, someone who suffers in order to survive. According to Kumin, however, Sexton would not place ultimate trust in an inner God or a heterodox "goddess"; instead, she was an ambivalent seeker on "a quest for a male authority figure to love and trust . . . identifying herself through her relationship with the male other" (Kumin 1981, xxx).

The results of her quest can be found in *The Awful Rowing Toward God* (1975), the last book of poetry to be published during Sexton's lifetime. Kumin characterizes the poems in the collection as Sexton's "final effort to land on 'the island called God'—in the person of the patriarchal final arbiter" (Kumin 1981, xxx). In the opening poem "Rowing," the speaker describes her increasing awareness of the divine which inhabits a distant island. Although the speaker knows that the "island will not be perfect," she still hopes for a redemption which comes from outside the self. On the divine island "there will be a door/and I will open it/and I will get rid of the rat inside of me." Peace and fulfillment will be the reward for the exhausted rower who will no longer carry her rat self which god will "take . . . with his two hands/and embrace."[49]

In another poem from *Rowing*, entitled "The Play," the speaker compares her life without God to a play with only one actor—herself. Her alienated life is a "solo act . . . All I am doing onstage is running,/running to keep up, but never making it." The audience "boos" her performance because "there are few humans whose lives/will make an interesting play." The speaker summarizes the problem inherent in both her play and existence: "To be without God is to be a snake/who wants to swallow an elephant."[50] The missing second playwright/actor is God, or Jesus, someone to provide additional "lines" in an empty life.

In the last poem "The Rowing Endeth" the speaker has finally reached the island of God, but she finds that he is not an amiable shepherd or even a benevolent father, but rather a duplicitous poker player who holds all the "wild cards." When she realizes that her straight flush is no match for his five aces—God is not above "cheating"—the speaker laughs and addresses her God as "Dearest dealer." She acknowledges her inferiority to the ultimate card sharp in what must be one of the most unorthodox supplications to the deity in contemporary letters: "I with my royal straight flush,/love you so for your wild card,/that untamable, eternal, gut-driven *ha-ha*/and lucky love."[51] God's wild card, his mystery and superiority, have been worth the "awe-full" rowing finally completed by Anne Sexton on her spiritual journey.

During the sixties and seventies, many minority writers who have been brought up within the Judeo-Christian religions also returned to their ancient, pre-European faiths. However, unlike Ozick, Sexton and O'Connor, these female writers sought a pre-conquest, pre-Christian spirituality which was lost when their people were overtaken by the white Europeans. Many women of color, including Chicana writers who are descendants of Native American mothers and European/Spanish fathers, began to trace their religious heritage back to the Aztecs. These writers incorporated symbols like Tonantin, the Aztec goddess of fertility or La Malinche, "the violated mother" or La Llorona, "the legend of the weeping woman" into their religious poetry.[52] In their work, poets like Lorna Dee Cervantes and Ana Castillo imaginatively resurrect the Gods who were a source of strength to the indigenous peoples of North America before European occupation.

Ana Castillo's poem "Our Tongue Was Nahuatl" (1976) recalls a moment before the Spanish invaders, "a time/of turquoise blue-greenness,/sky-topped mountains,/god-suns/windswept rains;/oceanic deities." Castillo recounts a time when her language was Nahuatl when she and her people "were content —/With the generosity/of our gods." The "white foreign strangers" who "made us bow to them," overtook the land and its indigenous peoples and became the new gods who replaced the older fertility deities. Having betrayed both their heritage and their Gods, the proud contemporary Chicana people must now bow down to the white people on buses and in factories where they are derided and humiliated. "WE BOW!" Castillo confesses, but she remembers a time "much different than now" when the Nahuatl language, its gods and people were powerful.[53]

Native American writer Janet Campbell who grew up on the Yakima Reservation recalls her own rebellion against Eurocentric religions, and her longing for Yakima religion and spirituality in her poem "On a Catholic Childhood" (1975). As a young child at catechism, Campbell is made to feel guilty for rejecting the maudlin statues and pictures of Christ. In order to revenge herself against this tradition, Campbell steals her sister's artificial, glow-in-the-dark Virgin Mary and hides it under a lilac bush. She knows better than to confess this sin to the priest because she is sure that the white cleric would find her actions incomprehensible.[54]

Campbell, however, does not abandon the spiritual life altogether, but like other Native American writers, Leslie Marmon Silko and Louise Erdrich, seeks the older pre-European traditions of her ancestors. In the poem, "Desmet, Idaho, March 1969," Campbell recalls hearing her tribe's ancient language being spoken by the old people at her father's wake. Although she does not understand their conversation, she believes that its spiritual force quickens something within her, awakening the soul which has long been suppressed by white people.[55] And it is that language and its magic which awaken her to a transcendence unattainable through white Christianity.

Paula Gunn Allen in her many books of poetry including *The Blind Lion* (1975) and *A Cannon Between My Knees* (1978) also desires to preserve the stories and language of her pre-Christianized ancestors. In her essay, "The Sacred Hoop: A Contemporary Indian Perspective on American Indian Literature," Allen contends that the transmission of spiritual values comes through "song, ceremony, legend, sacred stories (myths), and tales ... [which] verbalize the sense of the majesty and the reverent mystery of all things."[56] In order to retain their sense of the religious in the European world, many of the women from different Native American tribes including Gunn (Laguna Pueblo), Wendy Rose (Hopi), Roberta Hill Whiteman (Oneida) just to name a few, have written contemporary literature based on the ancient religious myths of Spider Woman, as well as the matrilineal Creation myths. The urge to return to pre-Judeo/Christian transcendent values is evident in Allen's poem "Moonshot: 1969" when the speaker compares white and Native American attempts to conquer the moon. While Anglo astronauts conquer the literal moon, she strives for a mystical experience of the universe within. Her emphasis is not on conquering land, an age-old goal of white society, but rather on discovering the soul within.[57]

Some writers during the sixties and seventies experience a renewal of orthodox faith, after a period of doubt or outright rejection. Black poet and essayist Margaret Walker comes to a renewed appreciation of her childhood faith later in life. Walker, who rejects the submissiveness and docility of the African-American Christian Church in *For My People* (1942), makes a decided turn towards orthodoxy in the late sixties when she writes the poetry included in *Prophets for a New Day* (1970), a collection of civil rights poems written from a Christian perspective. Biblical references abound in her later work as civil rights leaders are compared to Old and New Testament prophets for the new world order. She revises her earlier Marxist view of religion as the opiate of the masses in favor of a new spirituality which sees parallels between Martin Luther King and the prophet Amos. The oppression of the Jews by Pharaoh and their liberation by Moses find contemporary parallels in the events and circumstances surrounding the black peoples' struggle for freedom within American society. And most importantly, the hope and optimism inherent in the messianic Bible permeate Walker's vision.[58]

Both the reverence for and ultimate rejection of organized religious principles are also presented in critic Carolyn Heilbrun's autobiographical essay *Reinventing Womanhood* (1979). In it, Heilbrun chronicles her spiritual journey as she becomes increasingly aware of the role that Judaism—for better and worse—has played in her intellectual and emotional life. After graduating from college in the late forties, Heilbrun takes a position at the Jewish Theological Seminary where she overhears a conversation between two rabbis who are discussing the name of the Seminary president's granddaughter. "What did they name her?" one asks the other. The second rabbi off-handedly remarks, "Who thinks of names for girls?" The overheard conversation becomes a personal and professional epiphany for Heilbrun who notes, "I handed in my resignation [from the Seminary] that afternoon."[59]

And ironically, the religion which denigrated her also made her a feminist and an intellectual because it gave her an understanding of the "outsider" (Heilbrun 1979, 20). This alienated perspective made it possible for Heilbrun to find her own personality, separate from fifties and sixties' gender roles. Heilbrun believes that women must bond together to form what theologian Dorothee Soelle calls "the solidarity of the sufferers," (qtd in Heilbrun 1979, 66). From this alliance will come the final stage in women's quest to recreate both themselves and their society. In fact, the goal of Heilbrun's book is to, as the title suggests, "reinvent" (Heilbrun 1979, 29) the very conception of womanhood. Writing at the end of the seventies, Heilbrun looks forward to an active era for all women, a time to recreate and, as Carol Christ describes it "rename" themselves as the final stage of women's spiritual quest.

In her novel, *Ceremony* (1977), Leslie Marmon Silko imaginatively presents this mission to tell one's own spiritual and secular stories, to write one's own genesis or to be the interpreter of one's sacred texts. Silko and many other women writers awaken in the sixties and seventies to the power to name and thus have dominion over their lives. This revelation is immediately apparent in the epigraph to Silko's novel which begins with a story from the Laguna Pueblo tribe: "Thought-Woman, the spider,/named things and/as she named them/they appeared./She is sitting in her room/thinking of a story now./I'm telling you the story/she is thinking."[60]

"The Courage to Name": Literature of the 80s and 90s

Despite their varied perspectives on the nature of the divine, many women authors in the sixties or seventies agreed with Mary Daly's belief that women needed to take back the power to define their existences. In *Beyond God the Father* (1973), Daly contended that "women have had the power of naming stolen . . . To exist humanly is to name the self, the world and God" (Daly 1973, 8). One of the major insights in the post-war period, therefore, concerned the degree to which women were excluded from the process of naming and, thus living as mature, empowered individuals.

Recently, Carol Christ has found the ability to name oneself through the goddess in her book, *Laughter of Aphrodite*: *Reflec-*

tions *On A Journey To The Goddess* (1987). However, in the 1980s and 1990s, female orthodox writers who wished to express themselves found their "names" or role models by reinterpreting classical and biblical female characters. Carol Ochs in *Women and Spirituality* (1983) re-sees Old Testament women like Hagar and Leah as archetypal models for Jewish women while Rosemary Ruether in *Sexism and God-Talk: Towards a Feminist Theology* (1983) synthesizes and reformulates biblical traditions in order to create a theology which is both Christian and feminist.

One of the best collections of essays from all perspectives—Judeo-Christian, Goddess, Eastern, Third-World and cross-cultural—is Judith Plaskow and Carol Christ's edition *Weaving the Visions: New Patterns in Feminist Spirituality* (1989). Although these essays run the gamut from clearly orthodox to heterodox or pagan, in one major respect they are similar; all the authors believe in the essential power of the spiritual and its importance for contemporary women. Their strategies for experiencing the spiritual, however, may be clearly different. Yet, in every essay one sees a common thread—rethinking and revising the established tradition.

This new theological rethinking is clearly evident in eighties literature—poetry, fiction, drama and essays—as women authors confront and revise the basic assumptions about their places in the religious order. During this period there is also a heightened awareness among literary critics who begin to write about the revisionist phenomenon. Some of the important studies of this re-mythicizing are: Alicia Ostriker's excellent book *Stealing the Language: The Emergence of Women's Poetry in America* (1986); Annis Pratt, *Archetypal Patterns in Women's Fiction* (1981); Carol Pearson and Katherine Pope, *The Female Hero in American and British Literature* (1981); Barbara Hill Rigney's *Lilith's Daughters: Women and Religion in Contemporary Fiction* (1982); Rachel Brownstein, *Becoming a Heroine: Reading about Women in Novels* (1982); Elizabeth Abel, Marianne Hirsch and Elizabeth Langland, eds., *The Voyage In: Fictions of Female Development* (1983); Lee Edwards' *Psyche As Hero: Female Heroism and Fictional Form* (1984); Joanne Frye's *Living Stories, Telling Lives: Women and the Novel in Contemporary Experience* (1986).

Both Alicia Ostriker and Barbara Rigney explain the dilemma of women writers who reject traditional myth as patriarchal and demeaning to women. Ostriker argues that although traditional patriarchal mythmaking is "inhospitable terrain"[61] for women, the need for myth is essential. Rigney believes that there is always a need to "fill spiritual and psychological gaps" (Rigney 1982, 6) left after the rejection of a patriarchal God. Ostriker defines this revolutionary reformulation as "stealing the language" in order to "make it say what we [women] mean," thereby equating the poet's personal aesthetic vision with larger political action. "Revisionist mythmaking in women's poetry," she argues, "may offer us one significant means of redefining ourselves and consequently our culture" (Ostriker, 10-11).

Yet both Ostriker and Rigney focus primarily on heterodox writers who eschew the god of patriarchal religions. Ostriker even speaks of a "female anti-authoritarianism" (Ostriker, 27) in contemporary religious literature which looks to the goddess for spiritual strength. Although Rigney discusses the possibility of feminizing the myth of Christ and adapting it to female experience, she, too, defines contemporary fiction as a "new literature of protest which is often vehemently iconoclastic" (Rigney 1982, 4). Rigney is often hostile to traditional feminine archetypes like the Virgin Mary, whom another heterodox critic, Naomi Goldenberg, defines as the "Good Girl of Christianity" (Goldenberg, 75). Instead, Rigney focuses on apocryphal figures like Genesis' Lilith as more representative of the new "free women" who desire both sexual and social freedom (Rigney 1982, 97). Neither critic, however, deals in depth with orthodox women writers and their aesthetic quest.

In fact, a great deal of the literature of the 1980s and 1990s is heterodox, iconoclastic and antiauthoritarian in its attitude towards established religion even as it searches for a spiritual dimension. One good example can be found in Margaret Atwood's *The Handmaid's Tale* (1985) which provides a contemporary indictment of the traditional gender roles dictated by the Judeo/Christian Bibles. Offred, the novel's narrator has no name since "Offred" means "of-Fred," identical to the Old Testament way of naming wives. The novel summarizes her harrowing escape from the futuristic Republic of Gilead—a cross between an Islamic, evangelical Christian and Hebraic theocracy.

Although Gilead is unmitigatingly religious—with its "Ceremonies," "Prayvaganza's" and mottoes proclaiming "God is a National Resource" (HT, 276-77)—it is far from a moral or ethical environment. Religion becomes a political weapon as men and women battle each other for control of the theocratic hierarchy. Although some critics have correctly emphasized the misogynist nature of patriarchal Gilead, Atwood demonstrates through the use of the "aunts" and "Marthas" that women, too, are capable of creating religious tyrannies. The Marthas, who derive their names from the New Testament parable of Mary and Martha in which Martha objects to Mary studying while she cooks, are prime beneficiaries of Gileadean spiritual despotism.

Although Gileadean religiosity is both objectionable and repugnant, the need for spirituality is not dismissed in the novel. A dangerous lack of transcendent values was, Offred believes, what was missing from the contemporary world which precedes Gilead. Offred remembers a world devoid of any absolutes, divine or secular, a world in which women's magazines replaced Bibles as sources of spiritual strength and hope for "immortality" (HT, 201). In the modern world of the absolutely secular, people were incapable of discriminating between authentic and commercial salvation.

In another novel, *Cat's Eye*, (1989) Atwood remains suspicious of an empowered religious establishment and yet desirous of spiritual revelation. Elaine's lack of identity is due to her amnesia—both personal and cultural. Since she cannot recover the buried past when she "lost power," she does not have the ability to reclaim her identity. As an adult, Elaine sees a statue of the Virgin Mary, the "Virgin of lost things, one who restored what was lost" (CE, 210) and would like to pray to her; however, she is at a loss. She walks away from the statue because she confesses "I didn't know what to pray for. What was lost, what I could pin on her dress"(CE, 211). For the narrator, organized religion has lost its mystery and, thus, its ability to offer redemption. Elaine notices a church sermon announced on a billboard identical to the kind for supermarket specials. She cynically notes that "Theology has changed, over the years: just desserts used to be what everyone could expect to get, in the end. Now it's a restaurant specializing in cakes. All they had to do was abolish guilt, and add an s" (CE, 328).

Despite Elaine's disillusionment with religion in the eighties, however, she does not wish a return to the Christian church of her childhood in the forties, and the unforgiving God of Mrs. Smeath, her friend's mother. Instead of providing love, Mrs. Smeath's God inflicts guilt upon everyone, hates Catholics and Jews and provides a haven for hypocrites.

Consequently, Elaine's heterodox conception of redemption at the end of the novel is somewhat problematic, as is the nature of religious identity and spirituality in contemporary fiction. Did Elaine survive her nearly fatal experience at the bottom of an icy ravine because a mystical entity—a mixture of Demeter and the "Virgin of lost things"—interceded on her behalf? Was the voice she clearly remembered her mother's or her own? Although Elaine insists at the end of the novel that "there was no voice. No one came walking on air down from the bridge, there was no lady in a dark cloak bending over me" (CE, 442), the truth is illusive and ambiguous. There seems to be a mystical world outside the self which promises hope but no tangible salvation. An unknowable force beyond the rational has named Elaine and called her back to life—this may be the closest any contemporary person can get to redemption in Elaine's world.

This ambivalence towards religion—a mixture of skepticism and faith, alienation and desire—is also seen in Mary Gordon's novels in the eighties including *The Company of Women* (1980); *Men and Angels* (1985); *Temporary Shelter* (1987); and a collection of essays, *Good Boys and Dead Girls and Other Essays* (1991). In *The Company of Women*, the main character, Felicitas moves into the communal home of her mother and friends when she gives birth to a daughter out of wedlock. Although initially alienated from the community of women directed by the patriarchal Father Cyprian[62], Felicitas comes to appreciate its spirituality, despite her initial reservations about its leader.

An equally conflicted and ambivalent attitude towards orthodox religion is expressed by Anne Foster, a successful art historian in Gordon's novel *Men and Angels* (1985). In her desire to complete an important book on artist Caroline Watson, Foster hires a young governess named Laura to look after her children while she is in Europe. Foster, however, does not realize the extent to which Laura has been damaged by her unloving parents. When she discovers the truth about Laura's fatal lack of love, however, it is too late since Laura has committed suicide. Feeling both guilt and shame for her insensitivity to human need, Foster revises the meaning of the biblical passage in the New Testament from which the novel derives its title: "Though I speak with the tongues of men and angels, and have not charity, I am become as sounding brass, or a tinkling cymbal" (1 Corinthians 13:1).

The need for "charity," "charitas" or Christian love is secularized by Foster who interprets the passage as a divine injunction to love one another or die. God's love alone is insufficient, in Foster's opinion. At Laura's funeral, Foster hears the psalm, "I will lift up mine eyes unto the hills, from whence cometh my help?/ My help cometh from the Lord, which made heaven and earth."[63] Foster cynically reacts to this biblical promise by reflecting that the psalm's message "was so beautiful, and it was such a lie" because people cannot trust God to fulfill a divine commitment (MA, 234). While scattering Laura's ashes after the funeral, Foster takes final responsibility for her own part in the drama; "This was what was left of the girl who died because she [Foster] could not love her" (MA, 235).

In her essay, "Getting Here from There: A Writer's Reflections on a Religious Past" (1988) Gordon's ambivalent attitude towards her Catholic past provides a key to understanding her fiction. Although she believes in no "systematic theology" and confesses that "the religious impulse unmediated by reason terrifies me,"[64] she writes convincingly in this and other essays about "the riches of the Catholic background" (Gordon 1988, 171). Her religious training provides her with a complex source of metaphor which can be understood in secular terms. As a contemporary woman, Gordon is able to transform or reformulate Christianity's message of love while rejecting what she believes is Catholic intolerance, fear of the body and patriarchal misogyny.

The power to re-see Christian imagery for modern readers is also undertaken by Southern fiction writer Ellen Gilchrist in her collections of short stories, *In the Land of Dreamy Dreams* (1981), *Victory Over Japan* (1983), *Drunk With Love* (1986), and her novel, *The Annunciation* (1983). Like Atwood in *Cat's Eye*, Gilchrist transforms the image of the Virgin Mary into a symbol of an empowered secular femininity in *The Annunciation*. In the novel, Amanda McCamey's first daughter is taken away from her when she gives birth at fifteen in a convent for unwed mothers. However, Amanda, who grows up to be a skilled linguist working on literary translations of scandalous religious texts, is not able to erase the birth from her memory. Like a piece of her lost identity, the abandoned baby girl haunts Amanda's adult life. Embittered by her early experience with the nuns who force Amanda to renounce her child, she believes that "only idiots believe in God. If there was a God I'd hate his guts."[65] The scar that remains from the cesarean operation is both physical and symbolic. Amanda's first traumatic birth experience convinces her that she desires no further "annunciation," no more babies, not even with her husband, Malcolm.

Despite her hardened resistance to God, babies and love, however, Amanda does receive an unsolicited "annunciation" in the form of another child. Born on Christmas Day, Amanda's daughter is the antidote for postmodern despair: "all this old depressing stuff . . . Anne Sexton and Sylvia Plath and Berryman . . . and the whole goddamn life-hating death-wish trip" (A, 281). The baby girl connects her with her Southern past, generations living and deceased. At the end of the novel, Amanda names her "Noel" or "good news" and recites her own version of the Lord's prayer—as she gives birth to herself and presumably a new era of spiritual optimism.

A woman's divine right to create and name—actions which many heterodox feminists believe were stolen by patriarchal monotheism—is a prominent theme in the literature of the eighties and nineties. Retrieving lost spiritual power, in fact, is a subject of two Pulitzer Prize winning novels in the eighties, Alice Walker's *The Color Purple* (1982) and Toni Morrison's *Beloved* (1988). Both Walker and Morrison synthesize Christian and African conceptions of divinity or the goddess in order to empower their main characters. Slavery, either literal in Morrison or metaphorical in Walker, becomes a symbol of female bondage in both novels. In each book, women seek freedom from the constraints of their societies in order to speak, name and, eventually, rebirth themselves as autonomous individuals.

The goddess who helps free Celie is Shug Avery in *The Color Purple*. Half African goddess Kali and half Madonna, Shug—who is named Lily, for the Christian Lily of the fields—helps Celie to see the god within herself. In order to retrieve her spiritual way, however, Celie must give up waiting for the white god whom she begs for deliverance in her letters. Early in the story, Celie pictures divinity as "angels all in white, white hair and white eyes, look like albinos. God all white too, looking like some stout white man work at the bank."[66] With Shug's guidance, however, Celie finally realizes that if a white god does exist, he "must be sleep" (CP, 163).

Interestingly, Celie's use of the dialect "sleep" for "asleep" has symbolic importance in this context, for Celie's white god is the god of the underworld—oblivion or "sleep." In order to awaken herself and complete her quest, she must move beyond white unconsciousness to Shug's pantheistic conception of a universal divinity which lives in all things and all people. Shug explains her own spiritual awakening to Celie as: "When I found out God was white, and a man, I lost interest. . . . God is inside you and inside everybody else. You come into the world with God. But only them that search for it inside find it. . . . God ain't a he or a she, but a It." After this revelation, Celie describes Shug as "a big rose," (CP, 177-8), the traditional symbol for the Virgin Mary or Dante's Beatrice, earlier versions of the female spiritual guide. And, despite the fact that Shug—a bisexual and a pantheist—is certainly an unorthodox version of Mary, she is Celie's heterodox mentor. Shug is the first to love and name Celie, the first person to write a song for her, the first person to show her the true residence of the divine in contemporary life.

The goddess as a spiritual guide for a lost female questor is also seen in the fiction of Native American author Louise Erdrich in her novels *Love Medicine* (1984), *The Beet Queen*

(1986) and *Tracks* (1988). In a short story "Fleur" (1986) which is the basis for her later novel, *Tracks*, the reader encounters the mythic, goddess/witch Fleur. The young narrator, Pauline, idolizes the card-playing Fleur who is rumored to metamorphose from a woman to an animal: "the tracks of her bare feet . . . changed, where the claws sprang out, the pad broadened and pressed into the dirt."[67]

Like many goddesses in contemporary literature, Fleur mates with men but is not owned by one. It is rumored by the townspeople that she has become the wife of the mythic water monster Misshepeshu and has metamorphosed into a Medusa-like woman. While the narrator Pauline is at the mercy of the village, Fleur seems invulnerable, able to destroy and create at will. But what is most important about Fleur is her response to and effect on the powerless Pauline. Fleur is the only one to acknowledge the "invisible" young girl, actually calling her by name and providing her with money from gambling. But Fleur's impact on Pauline has a spiritual dimension as well. Fleur, the mythic "spider" woman of Native American legend, represents the hope for Pauline's resurrection. She is the goddess who topples the town's Catholic church steeple and upsets the patriarchal order, a cosmic force which sets things right—a female "Paul" for a new messiah.

Much of the heterodox poetry of the eighties also reflects this faith in the redemptive power of the heterodox goddess. In her anthology entitled, *She Rises Like The Sun: Invocations of the Goddess by Contemporary American Women Poets* (1989), Janine Canan brings together the poetry of twenty-nine women who "constitute a new body of Western religious poetry. . . . a potent religious and moral force."[68] Canan's anthology includes a wide variety of artists from different generations, as well as ethnic, racial and religious groups; however, the vast majority of the poems included in the volume were originally published in the 1980s a high point in the goddess' power as aesthetic and theological symbol. In the Introduction to the collection, Canan argues that "the image of the Goddess is everywhere in our culture today: in our art and literature, our mythology, our psychology, our history, our anthropology, our politics, our philosophy and, most significantly, our theology"

(Canan, xxi). Popular culture has also reflected an interest in the goddess, particularly Estes' best-selling *Women Who Run With The Wolves*.

Canan's anthology of American authors as well as several other international collections of women's poetry including *A Book of Women Poets from Antiquity to Now* (1980), *The Faber Book of 20th Century Women's Poetry* (1987) and *Longman Anthology of World Literature by Women* (1989) contain a wide variety of religious poetry, some of which is devoted to goddess mythology. Although there has been a consistent interest in goddess poetry since the 1960s, it is important to note that many political and realistic poets have become interested in goddess mythology in the eighties. Maya Angelou's book length poem, *Now Sheba Sings the Song* (1987) speaks of the mystical Queen of Sheba as divine spirit while Denise Levertov focuses on a mythic "Dragonfly-Mother" in her poetry collection *Candles in Babylon* (1982).

In Levertov's "The Dragon-Fly Mother," the speaker of the poem is about to leave her home to engage in political action "for a good cause," but is kept inside by the dragon-fly mother, her own conception of the goddess. This deity is not a righter of social wrongs, but rather, the speaker's own best inner spiritual voice who helps her to focus her life and art. Although the rewards for listening to this goddess may not be politically tangible, the goddess is the vortex of artistic fertility. She is the self-namer, the original story-teller: "When she tells/her stories she listens; when she listens/she tells you the story you utter." Like many of the embodiments of the goddess in contemporary literature, Dragon-Mother symbolizes the woman's ability to give birth to herself. The speaker describes her union with this feminine deity as keeping "a tryst with myself,/... if I don't trust her/I can't keep faith."[69]

Although some poets envision the mythic goddess outside of Western tradition, Carolyn Kizer, Judy Grahn and Marge Piercy focus on deities associated with Greek, Judaic or Christian cultures. In her poetry collection *Mermaids in the Basement* (1984), Kizer reformulates the patriarchal myths of the Greek Hera and Persephone in such poems as "Hera, Hung from the Sky" and "Persephone Pauses." Judy Grahn's poem "The Queen of Wands" (1982) fuses all the ancient goddesses into one

"Queen" who is "the tree/with candles/in its fingers/the tree with lights/Menorah/Yule-flame/tree of life." In the poem, the Queen speaks to the audience, explaining her omnipresence: "I am the Queen of Wands/who never went away" she informs the reader, "where would I go?/the flame is central/to any civilization/any household/any bag of bones."[70]

Marge Piercy who was well-known for her satirical and political fiction in the sixties and seventies, provides a serious portrait of the goddess in the eighties. In a poem on the Jewish sabbath, published in *Available Light* (1988) Piercy emphasizes the importance of naming the eternal goddess, Shekinah, who is the queen of the Jewish sabbath. The speaker in "Wellfleet Sabbath," describes the energy and sensuosity of the Shekinah who inhabits her home on the Sabbath, "raising her song and bringing/down the fresh clean night."[71] The Shekinah is not a patriarchal shadow of a woman, but a presence associated with the strength and dynamism of the sea surrounding the Wellfleet, Massachusetts home.

African-American and Native American poets also search for the ancient goddesses as a source of spiritual and political regeneration for all contemporary women, regardless of race, religion or national origin. In their recent poetry collections, Audre Lord, Joy Harjo and Paula Gunn Allen all write of the goddess traditions which transcend narrow cultural divisions created by the Western Judeo/Christian traditions. In her poem, "He Na Tye Woman" from *Shadow Country* (1982), Gunn, a member of the Laguna Pueblo tribe, sees the goddess as an "undulant woman river"[72] who represents all rivers and nations. She is a cleansing storm who washes away the dryness of the modernist "wasteland" and refreshes the world. The speaker refers of her as "Rain. The Rain that makes us new," and wonders aloud, "How did I wait so long to drink" (H, 125).

In the poem "Call" from *Our Dead Behind Us* (1986), Audre Lorde invokes the African goddess Aido Hwedo, the Rainbow Serpent, as the source of religious and political resurrection. Naming the goddess, the speaker provides a password which unlocks the prison of spiritual and political prejudice. The speaker names such political activists as American Civil Rights workers Rosa Parks and Fannie Lou Hamer as "daughters" of the goddess. All of these women are inspired by a feminine divinity who provides a language which is learned by heart and never taught.[73]

The political and spiritual importance of this new naming is especially evident in Joy Harjo's poem "The Book of Myths," (1989). The speaker views her union with the goddess as a rebirth and thus does not want to act precipitously or unwisely. Harjo's goddess reopens the "book of myths" Adrienne Rich found in 1973 when she was "Diving Into the Wreck" of masculine culture. However, while Rich could not find women's names in the patriarchal book, in 1989 Harjo does find women's names inscribed in the stories of the goddess who has "everyone dancing, laughing and telling the stories/that unglue the talking spirit from the pages."[74]

To be sure, the heterodox tradition of the goddess is alive and well during the last twenty years of the twentieth century. Authors as diverse as Toni Cade Bambara in *The Salt Eaters* (1980), Tina McElroy Ansa in *Baby of the Family* (1989); Eleanor Wilner in *Shekhinah* (1980), Sandra Cisnero's in *The House on Mango Street* (1983) and Ethel Johnston Phelps'in her collection of fairy tales, *The Maid of the North: Feminist Folk Tales from Around the World* (1981) all suggest the richness of the goddess' presence in contemporary literature.

The orthodox tradition of feminine spirituality, however, is also represented in the work of many important writers in the eighties and nineties. Writers like Cynthia Ozick, Lore Segal, Anne Roiphe, Lucille Clifton as well as countless other female novelists, poets, playwrights and essayists maintain their spiritual quest within an established religious framework. Rosemary Radford Ruether's philosophy illustrates this orthodox feminist perspective which acknowledges the historical sexism of the Judeo-Christian tradition but seeks a return to a purer theology, untainted by patriarchalism.

In her extremely important book, *Sexism and God-Talk: Toward A Feminist Theology* (1983), Ruether concedes that "all the categories of classical [Christian] theology in its major traditions—Orthodox, Catholic, and Protestant—have been distorted by androcentrism."[75] However, she is unwilling to reject the Judeo-Christian God in favor of an earlier goddess. Ruether believes that the return to the goddess does not achieve what women seek in a spiritual dimension and calls this quest "historically inaccurate and ideologically distorted" (Ruether 1983, 39).

Instead, orthodox female authors in the eighties and nineties are resacralizing religious texts—reinterpreting the work in light of a new understanding of the "sacred." One major project in which many female writers have participated is David Rosenberg's collection of original essays entitled *Congregation: Contemporary Writers Read the Jewish Bible* (1987). Among the female novelists, short story writers, essayists and playwrights interpreting Jewish biblical texts are: Daphne Merkin, Cynthia Ozick, Francine Prose, Anne Roiphe, Norma Rosen, Lynne Sharon Schwartz, and Lore Segal. It is important to note that some writers' analyses of the Jewish Bible are not exclusively laudatory.

In her explanation of the prophet Malachi, novelist Francine Prose expresses many objections to the brutal and violent actions of God, "a Father with so little patience or tolerance for His children's missteps, for the ordinary run of human failings."[76] Prose, however, does not criticize Yahweh's harsh treatment of his people, but rather seeks to understand the tribal culture which necessitates his actions. In fact, she describes her own reaction to the text as "squeamish" and "arrogant." Despite Prose's well-articulated initial misgivings about Malachi's version of God, she confesses that, by the end of the text, she has "come full circle, so that now even this [divine] threat has come to seem like further evidence of love. . . . no matter how strong our doubts and misgivings, it is ultimately almost impossible not to be reassured and comforted by what we come to learn of Malachi's God." In many respects Francine Prose would agree with other orthodox authors like Ozick, O'Connor and Sexton since she also marvels at the infinitude of God who embodies "a higher presence, permanent and unchanging" (M, 281).

Humility in the face of the divine is a trait shared by many female orthodox authors in the eighties and nineties. They see the difficulty and complexity of modern faith, but they finally acquiesce in spite of their initial skepticism. In her Pulitzer Prize winning short story "The Shawl" as well as in her short stories and novels in the eighties, particularly *Levitation: Five Fictions* (1982), *The Cannibal Galaxy* (1983) and *The Messiah of Stockholm* (1987), Cynthia Ozick continually depicts the faithful and faithless contemporary men and women who seek assurance in a postmodern world.

In her many novels including *Up the Sandbox, A Season for Healing, Lovingkindness* and *The Pursuit of Happiness*, Anne Roiphe often creates characters who question the meaning of God and spiritual existence. In *Lovingkindness* (1987), Roiphe's cynical character, Annie, has replaced patriarchal religion with liberal philosophy, only to find her daughter returning to a Jewish cult run by the domineering Rabbi Cohen. Her novel *The Pursuit of Happiness* (1991), chronicles the lives of the Jewish Gruenbaum family from the late nineteenth century to the present. Although they cannot understand why their God would allow senseless persecution, they are ultimately faithful to his incomprehensible divinity. Roiphe explores the frustrations and problems of contemporary life, but her characters often find a harmony in the divine which transcends temporal chaos.

The return to a spirituality rooted in an "old" world from which one has emigrated is analyzed in Edith Blicksilver's excellent anthology, *The Ethnic American Woman: Problems, Protests, Lifestyle* (1989). The tensions of dual loyalties—whether religious, social or political—are also the focus of several Asian-American female authors including Maxine Hong Kingston and Amy Tan. In *The Joy Luck Club* (1989), Amy Tan recounts the torturous path walked by children of two cultures—Chinese mystic and secular American. The journey back to China undertaken by one of the modern American daughters reveals the importance of blending the mysterious with the rational, the old myths with the modern stories. Jing-Mei Woo's mother tells her that "the East is where things begin"[77] and it is to the East and China that she must go in order to realize and recapture her identity. Religion and tradition—however "tainted" by old world patriarchies—cannot be discounted or discarded in the new world. The old stories of the mothers should be reevaluated and treasured for their wisdom.

The tension between the old religious world and modern heterodoxy—whether it manifests itself in Asia, Africa or Europe—is one that many contemporary female authors encounter. Alice Walker's novel, *The Temple of My Familiar* (1990) looks to Africa for spiritual nourishment, while contemporary poets like Lucille Clifton conceptualize a religious ideal in traditional Christian images of Mary. Clifton's collection of verse entitled *Two-Headed Woman* (1980) contains a series of poems dedicated to the Virgin Mary. Poems like "the astrologer predicts at mary's birth," "holy night," "a song of mary" and "island mary" all recount the misgivings and joy experienced by the Virgin Mary. In "anna speaks of the childhood of mary her daughter," Clifton imagines the reactions of the impoverished Anna, mother of the Virgin Mary, who dreams of her daughter's transcendent divinity in an adoring world. [78]

And yet other female writers who are brought up in the Christian tradition are not as sure as Clifton of its meaning to marginalized people of color. In her poem "Latin Women Pray" from a collection of Chicano, Puerto Rican and Cuban American poetry entitled *Triple Crown* (1987), Puerto-Rican/American poet Judith Ortiz Cofer articulates the frustration of Latin American women who "pray in Spanish to an Anglo God/With a Jewish heritage." The ironical speaker in Ortiz' poem does not openly reject the conception of a male white god for Hispanic women; however, she does hope that if God is not "omnipotent" at least he is "bilingual."[79] Caught between what seems to be two conflicting traditions—or possibly three if one adds gender—Latin American women, like all contemporary women, look forward to their religious life with a mixture of devotion and skepticism, hope and awe.

Conclusion

What seems quite apparent to anyone studying the spiritual dimension of literature written by contemporary women is its diversity and energy. Although one may make distinctions between the orthodox and heterodox religious visions, even that dualism is ambiguous and often misleading. Writers like Mary Gordon, whose characters often struggle with theologically-sanctioned gender roles, recently wrote her own version of "The Gospel According to Saint Mark" for her the collection of essays, *Good Boys and Dead Girls* (1991). Likewise, in an interview, Alice Walker acknowledged that she is "constantly involved, internally, with religious questions" and yet "the truth is probably that I don't believe there is a God." However, despite this categorical assertion, Walker immediately revises her stance and her perspective: "I waver in my convictions about God, from time to time," she reveals. "In my poetry I seem to be for; in my fiction, against" (In Search, 265).

Although there are many perspectives and degrees of faith in women's spirituality—from woman to woman and even within one author's own discourse—what is most important is the way in which spirituality has become a focal point of aesthetic, political and social concern. Theologians Judith Plaskow and Carol Christ characterize this "new diversity of voice and method" as "a creative and exciting development," even as they acknowledge the "tensions between different views of women's experience, tensions between those who would reconstruct traditional religion and those who would create new religious forms, tensions between those who would name and celebrate women's body experience and those who would emphasize women's transcendence and freedom."[80] That these tensions exist is undeniable to anyone reading contemporary women's literature; however, the discord or flux can be interpreted as part of any revolutionary change in consciousness. And, at the moment, it is just this kind of spiritual upheaval that modern women are experiencing in the texts that they create.

Notes

1. Mary Daly, "Sister as Cosmic Covenant," in *The Politics of Women's Spirituality: Essays on the Rise of Spiritual Power within the Feminist Movement*, ed. Charlene Spretnak (New York: Anchor Books, 1982), 353; hereafter cited in text.

2. Although I discuss "women" as a single theoretical group in the chapter, it should be evident that there is no one voice which speaks for women on any subject. Race, class, religion and ethnic group all play decisive roles in feminist philosophy. For further discussion of this subject see Judith Plaskow and Carol Christ's introduction in their anthology, *Weaving the Visions: New Patterns of Feminist Spirituality* (1989).

3. Carol Christ, *Diving Deep and Surfacing: Women Writers on Spiritual Quest*. Second Edition. (Boston: Beacon Press, 1980), xviii-xx; hereafter cited in text.

4. Barbara Rigney, *Lilith's Daughters: Women and Religion in Contemporary Fiction* (Madison: University of Wisconsin Press, 1982), 3; hereafter cited in text.

5. Carol Christ and Charlene Spretnak, "Images of Spiritual Power in Women's Fiction," in *The Politics of Women's Spirituality*, 330; hereafter cited in text.

6. Mary Daly, "Be-Friending: Weaving Contexts, Creating Atmospheres," in *Weaving the Visions: New Patterns in Feminist Spirituality*, ed. Judith Plaskow and Carol Christ (New York: Harper Collins, 1989), 200; hereafter cited in text.

7. Valerie Saiving, "The Human Situation: A Feminine View," in *Womanspirit Rising: A Feminist Reader in Religion*, ed. Carol Christ and Judith Plaskow (New York: Harper & Row, 1979), 41.

8. Flannery O'Connor, *Mystery and Manners* (New York: Farrar, Straus & Giroux, 1961), 32; hereafter cited in text.

9. Hilda, Doolittle, *Tribute to the Angels* (New York: Oxford University Press, 1945), 30; hereafter cited in text as "T."

10. Elizabeth Bishop, "Roosters," in *The Complete Poems* (New York: Farrar, Straus, and Giroux, 1969), 39-45.

11. Muriel Rukeyser, "Who in One Lifetime," in *The Collected Poems of Muriel Rukeyser* (New York: McGraw-Hill, 1978), 227.

12. Nellie Sachs, "O the Chimneys," in *O the Chimneys: Selected Poems* (New York: Farrar, Straus and Giroux, 1967), 3.

13. Denise Levertov, "To the Snake," in *Collected Earlier Poems, 1940-60* (New York: New Directions, 1979), 131.

14. Lewis Simpson, "Southern Fiction," in *Harvard Guide to Contemporary American Writing*, ed. Daniel Hoffman (Cambridge: Harvard University Press, 1979), 179.

15. Margaret Walker, "For My People," in *This is My Century: New and Collected Poems* (Athens: University of Georgia Press, 1989), 7; hereafter cited in text as "For."

16. Margaret Walker, "Since 1619," in *This is My Century: New and Collected Poems* (Athens: University of Georgia Press, 1989, 22.

17. Mary McCarthy, *Memories of a Catholic Girlhood* (New York: Penguin, 1957), 16; hereafter cited in text as "Memories."

18. Flannery O'Connor, "A Good Man is Hard to Find," in *3 by Flannery O'Connor* (New York: New American Library, 1960), 143; hereafter cited in text as "Good."

19. Mary Daly, *Beyond God the Father: Towards a Philosophy of Women's Liberation* (Boston: Beacon Press, 1973), 157; hereafter cited in text.

20. Myra Jehlen, "Archimedes and the Paradox of Feminist Criticism," in *The Signs Reader: Women, Gender & Scholarship.* ed. Elizabeth and Emily Abel (Chicago: University of Chicago Press, 1983), 69; hereafter cited in text.

21. qtd. in Naomi Goldenberg, *Changing of the Gods: Feminism & the End of Traditional Religions* (Boston: Beacon Press, 1979), 89; hereafter cited in text.

22. Sandra Gilbert and Susan Gubar, *The Madwoman in the Attic* (New Haven: Yale University Press, 1979), 80; hereafter cited in text.

23. Cynthia Ozick, *Art and Ardor: Essays* (New York: E.P. Dutton, 1984), 266; hereafter cited in text.

24. qtd. in Rigney, 1982, 57. See Margaret Atwood's novel *The Handmaid's Tale* which is about just this subject.

25. Nina Auerbach, "Engorging the Patriarchy," in *Feminist Issues in Literary Scholarship* (Bloomington: Indiana University Press, 1987), 155.

26. "Witch: Spooking the Patriarchy during the Late Sixties," in *The Politics of Women's Spirituality*, ed. Charlene Spretnak (New York: Anchor Books, 1982), 428-29; hereafter cited in text.

27. June Jordan, "I Must Become A Menace To My Enemies," in *Things That I Do In The Dark* (Boston: Beacon Press, 1981), 144-5.

28. Jean Tepperman, "Witch," in *No More Masks! An Anthology of Poems by Women*, ed. Florence Howe and Ellen Bass (New York: Anchor Books, 1973), 333.

29. Helene Cixous, "The Laugh of the Medusa," in *The Signs Reader: Women, Gender & Scholarship*, ed. Elizabeth and Emily Abel (Chicago: University of Chicago Press, 1983), 289.

30. Charlene Spretnak, "Why Women Need the Goddess," in *The Politics of Women's Spirituality*, ed. Charlene Spretnak (New York: Anchor Books, 1982), 73.

31. Muriel Rukeyser, "The Poem As Mask," in *The Collected Poems of Muriel Rukeyser* (New York: McGraw-Hill, 1978), 435.

32. Kathleen Raine, "Kore in Hades," in *Selected Poems* (New York: Lindsfarne Press, 1988), 116.

33. Adrienne Rich, "Diving into the Wreck," in *The Fact of a Doorframe: Poems Selected and New: 1950-84* (New York: W.W. Norton, 1984), 162-64.

34. Adrienne Rich, "Transcendental Etude," in *The Fact of a Doorframe: Poems Selected and New: 1950-84* (New York: W.W. Norton, 1984), 264-69.

35. Judith Wright, "Eve to Her Daughters," in *Collected Poems*, 1942-1970 (London: Angus & Robertson Publishers, 1971), 234-36.

36. Dorothy Livesay, "Eve," in *Collected Poems: The Two Seasons* (Toronto: McGraw-Hill Ryerson Ltd., 1972), 291.

37. Stevie Smith, "How Cruel is the Story of Eve," in *The Collected Poems of Stevie Smith* (London: Allen Lane/Penguin, 1975), 482.

38. Pauli Murray, *Dark Testament and Other Poems* (Norwalk, Conn: Silvermine Publishers, 1970), 40.

39. Denise Levertov, "Advent 1966," in *Relearning the Alphabet* (New York: New Directions, 1970), 84.

40. Sylvia Plath, "Mary's Song," in *The Collected Poems* (New York: Harper & Row, 1981), 257.

41. Edna O'Brien, *A Rose in the Heart of New York* (New York: Doubleday, 1979, 157; hereafter cited in text as "Heart."

42. Alice Walker, "Everyday Use," in *In Love and Trouble: Stories of Black Women* (New York: Harcourt, Brace and Jovanovich, 1973), 58; hereafter cited as *EU*.

43. Ntozake Shange, *for colored girls who have considered suicide/when the rainbow is enuf: a choreopoem* (New York: Macmillan, 1975), 4; hereafter cited in text as *for*.

44. Mary Gordon, *Final Payments* (New York: Random House, 1978), 3; hereafter cited in text as *FP*.

45. E.M. Broner, *Her Mothers* (New York: Holt, Rinehart, and Winston, 1975), xiii; hereafter cited in text as *HM*.

46. Cynthia Ozick, *The Pagan Rabbi and other Stories* (New York: Alfred P. Knopf, 1971), 3; hereafter cited in text as *PR*.

47. Susan Cahill, "Introduction to Cynthia Ozick," in *New Women, New Fiction: Short Stories Since the Sixties*, ed. Susan Cahill (New York: New American Library, 1986), 1.

48. Maxine Kumin, "Introduction," in *Collected Poems: Anne Sexton*, ed. Maxine Kumin (Boston: Houghton Mifflin, 1981), xxiii; hereafter cited in text.

49. Anne Sexton, "Rowing," in *The Complete Poems* (Boston: Houghton Mifflin Company, 1981), 412.

50. Anne Sexton, "The Play," in *The Complete Poems* (Boston: Houghton Mifflin Company, 1981), 440-41.

51. Anne Sexton, "The Rowing Endeth," in *The Complete Poems* (Boston: Houghton Mifflin Company, 1981), 474.

52. See Dexter Fisher's "Introduction to Chicana Writers" in her anthology, *The Third Woman: Minority Women Writers of The United States* (Boston: Houghton Mifflin, 1980), 307-313.

53. Ana Castillo, "Our Tongue Was Nahuatl," in *Revista Chicano Riqueña*, 4 No. 4 (Autumn 1976).

54. For additional information about Native American women and spirituality, see Paula Gunn Allen's essay, "The Power of Woman in Native America," in *Weaving the Visions: New Patterns in Feminist Spirituality*, ed. Judith Plaskow and Carol Christ (New York: HarperCollins, 1989), 22-27.

55. For a good introduction to Chicana writers see Dexter Fisher's chapter on Hispanic women in *The Third Woman: Minority Women Writers of The United States* (Boston: Houghton Mifflin, 1980).

56. Paula Gunn Allen, "The Sacred Hoop: A Contemporary Indian Perspective on American Indian Literature," in *The Third Woman: Minority Women Writers of The United States* (Boston: Houghton Mifflin, 1980), 5.

57. For a discussion of women's attitudes towards science and ecology see Carol Christ's "Rethinking Theology and Nature," in *Weaving the Visions: New Patterns in Feminist Spirituality*, ed. Judith Plaskow and Carol Christ (New York: Harper Collins, 1989), 314-325.

58. Margaret Walker, *Prophets for a New Day* (Detroit, Mr: Broadside Press, 1970. For additional discussion of black women and spirituality, see Katie Geneva Cannon's "Moral Wisdom in the Black Women's Literary Tradition," in *Weaving the Visions: New Patterns in Feminist Spirituality*, ed. Judith Plaskow and Carol Christ (New York: HarperCollins, 1989), 281-92.

59. Carolyn Heilbrun, *Reinventing Womanhood* (New York: W. W. Norton, 1979), 63; hereafter cited in text.

60. Leslie Marmon Silko, *Ceremony* (New York: Penguin Books, 1977), 1.

61. Alicia Ostriker, "The Thieves of Language: Women Poets and Revisionist Mythmaking," in *Coming to Light: American Women Poets in the Twentieth Century*, ed. Diane Middlebrook and Marilyn Yalom (Ann Arbor: University of Michigan Press, 1985), 12.

62. Mary Gordon, *The Company of Women* (New York: Random House, 1980.

63. Mary Gordon, *Men and Angels* (New York: Random House, 1987), 234; hereafter cited in text as "MA."

64. Mary Gordon, *Good Boys and Dead Girls and Other Essays* (New York: Random House, 1991), 161; hereafter cited in text.

65. Ellen Gilchrist, *The Annunciation* (Boston: Little, Brown, 1983), 32; hereafter cited in text as *A*.

66. Alice Walker, *The Color Purple* (New York: Washington Square Press, 1985), 91; hereafter cited in text as *CP*. For additional discussion of Alice Walker and religion, see Rudolph Byrd's essay "Spirituality in the Novels of Alice Walker: Models, Healing, and Transformation, or When the Spirit Moves So Do We," in *Wild Women in the Whirlwind: Afra-American Culture and the Contemporary Literary Renaissance* (New Brunswick: Rutgers University Press, 1990), 363-78.

67. Louise Erdrich, "Fleur," in *We Are the Stories We Tell*, ed. Wendy Martin (New York: Pantheon Books, 1990), 291.

68. Janine Canan, "Introduction," in *She Rises Like the Sun* (Freedom, Ca.: The Crossing Press, 1989), xlvi; hereafter cited in text.

69. Denise Levertov, "The Dragon-Fly Mother" in *Denise Levertov: Selected Poems* (Bloodaxe Books: Newcastle upon Tyne, 1986), 152-54.

70. Judy Grahn, "The Queen of Wands," in *The Queen of Wands* (Trumansburg, NY: Crossing Press, 1982), 42.

71. Marge Piercy, "Wellfleet Sabbath," in *Available Light* (New York: Alfred A. Knopf, 1988), 117.

72. Paula Allen Gunn, "He Na Tye Woman," in *Shadow Country* (Los Angeles: University of California Press, 1982), 123; hereafter cited in text as "H."

73. Audre Lorde, "Call," in *Our Dead Behind Us* (New York: W. W. Norton & Company, 1986), 74-5.

74. A complete copy of Joy Harjo's poem "The Book of Myths," can be found in *She Rises Like the Sun*, ed. Janine Canan (Freedom, Ca.: The Crossing Press, 1989), 51.

75. Rosemary Ruether, *Sexism & God-Talk: Towards a Feminist Theology* (Boston: Beacon Press, 1983), 37; hereafter cited in text.

76. Francine Prose, "Malachi," in *Congregation: Contemporary Writers on the Jewish Bible*. ed. David Rosenberg (New York: Harcourt Brace Jovanovich, 1987), 274; hereafter cited in text as *M*.

77. Amy Tan, *The Joy Luck Club* (New York: Ballantine, 1989), 22; hereafter cited in text as *JLC*.

78. Lucille Clifton, "Anna speaks of the childhood of mary her daughter," in *Two-Headed Woman* (Amherst: University of Massachusetts Press, 1980), 35.

79. Judith Ortiz Cofer, "Latin Women Pray," in *Triple Crown* (Tempe: Bilingual Press, 1987), 89.

80. Judith Plaskow and Carol Christ, "Introduction," in *Weaving the Visions: New Patterns in Feminist Spirituality* (New York: Harper Collins, 1989), 6.

Chapter Four

Multicultural Voices: The Intersection of Race, Class and Ethnicity

> It is, in the end, the saving of lives that we writers are about. Whether we are "minority" writers or "majority." It is simply in our power to do this.
>
> (Walker, *In Search of Our Mothers' Gardens*, 14)

In *The Second Sex* (1949), Simone de Beauvoir clearly sees the similarities between racial and gender oppression. Victims of prejudice—whether they are young girls, people of color or Jews—often experience limitations created by a powerful majority which would like to keep them "in their place." Despite the distinct differences in their situations, however, de Beauvoir contends that African-Americans and women of all colors are trained to be docile and meek, objects rather than subjects in their own lives. She compares the young girl's situation to that of the fictional predicament of Bigger Thomas in Richard Wright's *Native Son* (1940) who is trapped by color instead of gender. De Beauvoir interprets his imprisonment as parallel to that of women since African-Americans are "partially integrated in a civilization that nevertheless regards them as constituting an inferior caste" (De Beauvoir, 335); thus, in the post-war world, de Beauvoir views both race and gender as obstacles to personal autonomy and growth.

More than thirty-five years later, literary critic Barbara Smith also noted the intersection of race and gender in literature. In her essay, "Toward a Black Feminist Criticism" (1985)[1], Smith wishes the reader to understand "how both sexual and racial politics are inextricable elements in Black Women's writings" (174). In asserting the importance of race *and* gender, Smith acknowledges both the similarities in black and white women's lives and the differences which make "universal" statements about "women" problematic. Critic Deborah McDowell who also sees the link between gender and race wishes readers to appreciate and understand the disparate cultural "contexts" in which African-American literature is written: "This footing in Black history and culture . . . is not only useful but necessary to Black feminist critics."[2]

It is the purpose of this chapter, therefore, to not only describe the important "contexts" within which multicultural women's literature is written, but also to see its relation to and departure from white, middle-class women's writing after World War Two. In some respects, gender has created a bond among all women; however, in many important ways, women from diverse racial, ethnic and class groups have had a decidedly different experience as victims of dual or tripartite oppression—race, class and gender.

Like women's literature in general, multicultural literature over the past forty-five years has witnessed a dramatic transformation in female characters, from victims of a patriarchal order to capable individuals who define and name themselves. Critic Claudia Tate sees the African-American's woman's "unique" quest as a departure from both the white male and female adventure. The black heroine does not hope for ultimate victory over others, but rather "insists that life is an experience to be lived, a process; as a result, she learns that conflicts are often resolved but are seldom solved."[3] By living her life in this way, the black heroine does not attain any final victory, but instead, "teaches her readers a great deal about constructing a meaningful life in the midst of chaos and contingencies, armed with nothing more than her intellect and emotions" (Tate, xxiv).

Multicultural literature often dramatically illustrates the poor, disenfranchised woman who must wage an economic and class struggle in addition to her battle against racial, ethnic and gender prejudice. In her book *Black Feminist Criticism: Perspectives on Black Women Writers* (1985), Barbara Christian notes that African-American women writers have had to overcome not only racism but sexism and poverty. Their literature, therefore, "call[s] into question the pervasive mythology of democracy, justice, and freedom that America projects itself to be."[4] Literature written by women of color increases every reader's awareness of the powerful stranglehold that race, class and gender have on seemingly autonomous individuals. And it is this communal consciousness that black poet and novelist June Jordan, author of *Civil Wars*, notes "transforms the rhetoric of politics into a personal voice [which] is a powerful example of the feminist concept that the personal and political cannot be separated (qtd. in Christian, 162).

Maud, Lutie and Their Sisters: Progress and Frustration in the Forties and Fifties

Unlike their white, middle-class counterparts, many women of color were not subject to Friedan's "feminine mystique" during the forties and fifties. Historian Eugenia Kaledin argues that "the 1950s, so stultifying for women on many levels, must ultimately be seen as a decade of progress for blacks" (Kaledin, 149). Unlike whites, black daughters were encouraged to seek careers outside the home, to compete for entry into college and the workplace. Gerda Lerner characterizes the black family as "expecting their daughters to work most of their lives" (qtd. in Kaledin, 150).

Statistics on Afra-American college graduates and professional workers support Lerner's thesis. In 1950, 58 percent of all black professional workers were women, compared to 35 percent of white women.[5] Mid-fifties black women married later, had fewer children and were likely to feel ambivalent about their roles as women, especially since the white indolent model was a post-war ideal, if not a reality. Social historian Paula Giddings notes that during the fifties black women were "worried about how they were perceived as women at a time when their white peers were staying at home, having children, and scanning the shelves for the latest appliances" (150). In fact, the resentment of black working women towards pampered white housewives would become a theme in the literature of the period in the works of Gwendolyn Brooks, Ann Petry, Alice Childress and others.

The achievement of African-American women was met with a mixture of pride and fear even within their own community.

Although in 1939, historian E. Franklin Frazier praised black women for their "significant role in the development of our civilization . . . without their economic aid and counsel we would have made little if any progress," they were also accused of emasculating their men, dominating their families and causing the breakup of the nuclear family (qtd in Giddings, 247, 252). Therefore, it is not surprising that African-American women occupied an uncertain role in white America of the fifties.

In addition to their confrontations with white women and black men, many black women were confused about their own sense of definition, their identity as both African and American. The fifties was a decade of African revolution and independence. Within a four year period—from 1956 to 1960, nineteen different African nations declared independence. Yet entrance into white America for the African-American woman and man necessitated assimilation into white America: acceptance of its values and cultural norms. Many of the African-American writers in the Harlem Renaissance movement in the twenties urged integration into white mainstream America as the ideal, and thus, black women and men were encouraged to stress similarities rather than differences between themselves and their white counterparts.

Although some black women made economic progress, their civil rights and political power in the forties and fifties were non-existent. In 1954, the Supreme Court in the landmark school integration case of *Brown v the Board of Education* asked schools across the nation to integrate with "all deliberate speed." On December 1, 1955 Rosa Parks, a member of the NAACP, refused to give up her bus seat to a white man in Montgomery, Alabama and initiated a boycott which would focus national attention on segregation in the South. In 1957, Ella Baker and Martin Luther King Jr. led the Southern Christian Leadership Conference in a "Prayer Pilgrimage" in Washington, D.C., the largest civil rights demonstration ever staged by African-Americans (Giddings, 269). And yet, despite their sacrifice and courage, black women still experienced racial discrimination in the United States. "All deliberate speed" proved to be slow indeed through the fifties and early sixties.

As black women lived through the first generation of the post-war era (1945-65), they would begin to confront the inequities in American society which frustrated their attempts at self-fulfillment and definition; and it is from this dynamic tension that they would develop new characters in literature who were fully realized people, not stereotypes of white, male society.

In order to accomplish this, writers in the forties and fifties like Gwendolyn Brooks, Margaret Walker, Ann Petry, Paule Marshall, Alice Childress and Lorraine Hansberry, to name a few, had to fight against the stereotypical ways in which African-American women were often portrayed in literature by many whites and some blacks before 1940. Black female characters were often presented as either a mammy—submissive, selfless and nurturing or as a figure to be feared or pitied such as the "concubine", "conjure woman" or the "tragic mulatto" (Christian 2-4). The images of women in the works of William Wells Brown's *Clotell* (1850), Frances Harper's *Iola LeRoy* (1892), Jean Toomer's *Cane* (1923), and Nella Larson's *Passing* (1929) reinforce long-standing portraits of black women for white audiences.

The most interesting stereotype from this period, and one which African-American female writers would revise in the late forties and early fifties was the black female victim, the "tragic mulatto," the daughter of a black mother and white father who, as Barbara Christian notes, "reveals the conflict of values that blacks faced as a conquered people" (3). The tragic mulatto was worthy, but not white—forever an outsider in both black and white society. With the exception of Janie in Zora Neale Hurston's *Their Eyes Were Watching God* (1937), many pre-1940 mulatto literary characters were "tragic" victims of white society. It would take the writers of the post-war era to create fresh, resilient characters who transcended the passive role of black victim in order to develop a consciousness quite apart from white society or its values.

Pulitzer-prize winning poet and novelist, Gwendolyn Brooks, was one of the first African-American woman writers of the post-war era to confront the personal and social issues facing minority women; however, she did not resort to literary stereotypes or formulaic plot scenarios in her work. Her collections of poetry, *A Street in Bronzeville* (1945), *Annie Allen* (1949), *The Bean Eaters* (1960) and one novel, *Maud Martha* (1953) develop black female characters who experience the frustration and uncertainty with both private and public post-war life. Although they confront many of the racial, gender and economic problems described in pre-war literature, Brooks' complex characters become thinking, complicated women and men.

In her poem, "The Mother," Brooks presents the inner turmoil of a woman who has undergone several abortions. Neither a sainted "mammy" nor a fallen woman, the speaker in the poem never forgets the pain of her decision. She concedes that she has stolen their "births" and their "names"; however, the mother is not a monster of unfeeling, but rather, a woman trapped by circumstances beyond her control: "Believe me, I knew you, though faintly, and I loved, I loved you/All."[6] This portrait of the ambivalent mother reflects Brooks' handling of a complex moral decision made by a black woman who is neither a self-abnegating "mammy" or a selfish Jezebel, two of the popular stereotypes of the period.

Through her poetry about the small and significant personal ironies in life, Brooks saw, even in 1945, the impact of social injustice on private aspirations. In "Kitchenette Building," the people who inhabit the tenement building have little space for hope within the bleak confines of a kitchenette building. Even if a dream could survive in this environment, the people who inhabit this tenement must accede to practical concerns; when given a choice between abstract hope and a warm bath, the residents choose the later, a small pleasure in a limited world.

If there is anger and disappointment in Gwendolyn Brooks' early books, it is always tinged with irony. There is inequity in the world, but few answers even in "Bronzeville Woman in a Red Hat" in *The Bean Eaters* (1960) or "The Children of the Poor" in the Pulitzer Prize winning volume of poems *Annie Allen* (1949). "What shall I give my children? who are poor/ Who are adjudged the leastwise of the land,/Who are my sweetest lepers?" the mother/artist asks the reader in the poem "The Children of the Poor." The artist/speaker watches as her unfinished creations, her "little halves" wander without direction "across an autumn freezing everywhere."[7] It would not be until the late sixties and a "new turning" in Brooks' philosophy in the 1968 volume *In the Mecca: Poems* that Brooks would dramatize the real violence and anger of ghetto life. As she admitted in an interview in 1970, "Many things that I'm seeing now I was absolutely blind to before."[8]

Therefore, in 1953 when Brooks published her novel *Maud Martha*, she provided few solutions for overcoming white paternalism and exploitation. When Maud Martha reluctantly takes a job as a maid in the home of the imperious Mrs. Burns-Cooper, the rich white mistress tells Maud Martha to use the back entrance only. Powerless because of her financial situation, Maud Martha resolves to hate Mrs. Burns-Cooper in silence. The experience, however, is not entirely negative because it provides Maud Martha with some insight into her own troubled husband's sufferings under his white "boss." In 1953, however, there seems to be no viable political action to remedy the injustice experienced by the African-American worker in white society. Maud Martha can refuse to participate or endure the indignities—direct, ameliorative, political action is not an option.

In the same year that Gwendolyn Brooks published *Maud Martha*, playwright Alice Childress published a series of dramatic conversations between Mildred, a black maid and a friend Marge, in her play, *Like One of the Family* (1953). One particularly important dialogue involves Mildred's speech to Mrs. C., a patronizing employer who abuses Mildred but insists on introducing her to white visitors as "one of the family." In a monologue which seems part reality, part wish fulfillment in 1953, Mildred tells Mrs. C. that she does not wish to be called "one of the family" because she is treated as a servant. To continue the charade is, according to Mildred, a grand hypocrisy. Mrs. C. is described as speechless after her maid's outburst, but promises to ask her husband for Mildred's raise. It is respect, not false camaraderie that the black maid desires in the home of the white woman; while this was possible in literature, it was not always attainable in real life. And yet Alice Childress' plays *Florence, Just a Little Simple, Gold Through the Trees,* and *Trouble in Mind* were received by appreciative audiences at the Club Baron in Harlem in the late forties and early fifties.

Two other important writers who offer more militant solutions to racial oppression in the forties were Margaret Walker and Ann Petry. In an essay entitled "On Being Female, Black, and Free" (1980), Margaret Walker describes the "three strikes" she had against her because she was born female, black and poor in 1911.[9] In *For My People* (1942), Walker takes a somewhat aggressive and optimistic stance against white prejudice and oppression. Her poetic characters are often resilient, courageous women and men who are both mean and virtuous, good and evil. In "Lineage," the speaker describes "strong," black grandmothers who "followed plows and bent to toil." They are nurturing women who "touched earth and grain grew" yet they are also imbued with spiritual and physical strength: "They were full of sturdiness and singing . . . My grandmothers are full of memories/Smelling of soap and onions and wet clay."[10]

However, the characters who appear in *For My People* are often violent and strong. In "Kissie Lee" the speaker describes a sensitive child who grew up to be the strongest woman ever made by God. The mythic Kissie Lee dies as she has lived, aggressive and active, irreverent to the end.[11] Walker's poems about the "Whores" or "Molly Means" describe women who are both powerfully evil *and* good, prototypes for Toni Morrison's enigmatic characters, Sula and Beloved, who are both creative and destructive.

Hope and despair—creativity as well as violent destruction—are also part of the world described by Ann Petry in her important novel *The Street* (1946). Lutie Johnson, the strong, determined female protagonist in *The Street* is, in some respects, the feminine equivalent of Bigger Thomas, the protagonist in Richard Wright's landmark novel of urban ghetto life, *Native Son*. Lutie, like Bigger, is threatened by a white American value system which presumably encourages all individuals to work, sacrifice and plan for the future, but fails to mention that this work ethic applies only to whites. Ann Petry chronicles the Horatio Alger-like ambition of Lutie as she sacrifices her family life in order to work in the rich, white Chandler home; instead of achieving wealth and success, however, Lutie loses her husband to another woman, her son to the poverty and crime of the urban ghetto and her soul to rape. Finally, like Bigger Thomas, Lutie hits back with violence and rage at a society which has tempted her with success and delivered nothing but hardship and frustration. When Lutie kills Boots Smith, the narrator describes her as "venting her rage against the dirty, crowded street. . . . the smashed homes where the women did drudgery because their men had deserted them. She saw all of these things and struck at them."[12]

Although critic Barbara Christian is correct when she says that *The Street* "functions as a transition from the tragic mulatto pattern . . . to a more contemporary view of the black novel" (Christian, 11), there is a naturalistic fatalism in the novel which never allows Lutie to move beyond protest to some sort of social reform. Possibly, the atmosphere in the late forties made a victory impossible, or at the very least, premature. Ann Petry's other novels, *The Country Place* (1947) and *The Narrows* (1953) and *Legends of the Saints* (1970) were followed by *Miss Muriel and Other Stories* (1971), a collection of short stories about other strong, professional women who wage their own protests against social and racial conditions. The importance of Petry, however, is central to the development of African-American fiction since she chronicles the annihilation of the previously cohesive black family in an urban setting and dramatizes "the causal relationship between social and personal crime" (Christian, 11), a theme which would become extremely important in the sixties and seventies.

The characters in Paule Marshall's *Brown Girl, Brownstone* (1959) as well as in her short stories often understand the sociopolitical implications of racial discrimination in America. In the novel *Brown Girl, Brownstone*, set in Marshall's own Barbadian/American community, the desire to own property, and a part of the American dream is thwarted, but the characters are not crushed by their malevolent environments. Through the communication of important Barbadian values from mother to daughter, the characters survive and hope. One particularly powerful influence on Paule Marshall herself and her literature is discovered in ancestral values and dramatically portrayed in the short story, "To Da-duh, In Memoriam" (1967). The grandmother, nicknamed Da-duh, is found in many of her stories and novels, including Aunt Vi in "Reena" (1962) and Mrs. Thompson in *Brown Girl, Brownstones*. Da-duh represents Barbadian, third-world traditions which often clash with her granddaughter's adopted modern, American values. In "To Da-duh," the young narrator visits her ancestor and learns about the lost culture of her Caribbean home. Although the Barbadian world of Da-duh succumbs to American modernity, it is held within the memory of a granddaughter who lives in New York and paints Barbadian pictures of Tutsi warriors.

The influence of Silla Boyce on her young daughter, Selina in *Brown Girl* is also an important step in the realization of fully developed female characters. Like Lutie Johnson in *The Street*, Silla wants to succeed in America and acquire a home and security while her husband Deighton wishes to buy land in Barbados instead. In her parents' battle over the money, Selina is caught between her mother who symbolizes the new world drive and ambition and her impractical father whose soul is still in Barbadian soil. At the end of the novel, Selina begins to appreciate her mother's indefatigable zeal. Silla Boyce lives on in the person and memory of Selina who represents the synthesis of the old and new worlds.

While Lutie Johnson is a victim of the natural/social forces which conspire against her in a prejudiced environment, Selina and Silla in Marshall's *Brown Girl, Brownstones* (1959) have more control. They are not empowered agents in a free society, yet Marshall's characters have some dominion over their world. This sense of personal autonomy is also apparent in another of Marshall's short stories entitled "Reena" (1962) in which a first person narrator recounts her relationship with her friend Reena during the forties and fifties. At age twelve, Reena renames herself, rejecting her old name, Doreen, and creating a new identity. During the forties, this act of self-definition is an historical one which the narrator appreciates: "she made vivid without knowing it why it is perhaps the most critical fact of my existence—that definition of me, of her and millions like us . . . what it has meant, what is means, to be a black woman in America."[13]

Reena, like her predecessors Lutie, Selina and Maud, attempts to enter and succeed in the white world. The narrator empathizes with the struggle that Reena will have to wage, not only against the injustices of the white world, but also against the complacencies of the black bourgeoisie in the fifties. Reena is discriminated against not only by the newspapers which refuse to hire black journalists in the fifties, but by black families who do not want a dark-skinned woman to marry their light-skinned sons. In the story, the narrator interprets the psychological impact of racial prejudice on black men and women who cannot escape easily from a white America: "We live surrounded by white images, and white in this world is synonymous with the good, light, beauty, success, so that despite ourselves sometimes, we run after that whiteness and deny our darkness, which has been made [by whites] into a symbol of all that is evil and inferior" (Reena, 79).

Reena's odyssey into radical, leftist organizations in the fifties symbolizes the quest of many educated black women seeking a place in a white-dominated world. Her personal as well as professional relationships are affected by the all-pervasive racism she encounters. Her white revolutionary boyfriend and frustrated black husband are precursors of the new male characters in the work of Terry McMillan, Toni Morrison, Alice Walker and other writers in the seventies, eighties and nineties.

In addition, Reena's experience as a black *woman* suggests that gender as well as race have become a centrally important issue in black feminism. The narrator describes the plight of the unmarried black professional woman who spends years educating herself for a fulfilling career, only to find that these "advantages" prove to be a liability with black men. Reena learns that professional women are thought of as "too threatening ... castrating ... sexually inhibited ... not supportive, unwilling to submerge our interests for theirs ... lacking in the subtle art of getting and keeping a man" (Reena, 86). Even at the end of the eighties and the beginning of the nineties, Terry McMillan in *Disappearing Acts* and *Waiting to Exhale* is still attempting to resolve this tension between African-American women and men.

In 1962, however, Paule Marshall conceives of no solution to the gender/race inequities her characters encounter. At the conclusion of her story, Reena has divorced her black husband

and is raising her children alone. She, like many white characters who have become frustrated with American society, compensates by developing a special faith in her children: "I will feel that I have done well by them if I give them, if nothing more, a sense of themselves and their worth and importance as black people. Everything I do with them, for them, is to this end.... No white dolls for them!" (Reena, 89). Unlike Lutie who is left at the end of the novel fleeing to Chicago in utter loneliness, Reena is, in the fifties, still optimistic: "I feel, strangely enough, as though life is just beginning—that it's new and fresh with all kinds of possibilities. Maybe it's because I've been through my purgatory and I can't ever be overwhelmed again" (Reena, 90).

During the forties and the fifties, many racial, ethnic, religious and cultural communities emerging after World War Two are equally anxious to assert their identity in American literature and life. By the beginning of the sixties, therefore, a significant theme emerges in multicultural literature in which marginalized people of color refuse to be defined by white, middle-class society. In order to "take responsibility" for themselves and finally begin to solve their personal/political problems, these characters must take action, no longer permitting white society to define or confine their existences. African-American writer Toni Cade Bambara describes this political and aesthetic "breakthrough" in the sixties as "stunning. Characters that have been waiting in the wings for generations, characters that did not fit into the roster of stereotypes, can now be brought down center stage.... now that American history, American literature, the American experience is being redefined by so many communities."[14]

The Sixties: Revolution in Rhetoric, Literature and Life

Critic Barbara Christian describes African-American female poet Nikki Giovanni as a symbol of "the rhetoric of the sixties, a political nationalistic rhetoric ... preceded by a language of protest, revolt, self and cultural investigation that fostered a linguistic correlative to the changing mood in the inner cities of America" (20). Giovanni's angry, nationalistic sixties poetry, which included such lines as "Nigger/Can you kill" in her 1968 volume *Black Feeling, Black Talk, Black Judgement* is, in many respects, a literary projection of the decade's frustration, awareness and consequent activism.[15] Christian describes the literature of this decade as "socio-political"(15) as black women and men begin to capture in literature the dramatic societal changes brought about by the civil rights movement, the militant student protests by the black Student Non-Violent Coordinating Committee (SNCC), the freedom riders and voting registration drives in the South.

This growing pride and self-awareness are two important developments in sixties literature, according to Alice Walker in her essay "The Civil Rights Movement: What Good Was It?" (1966). In both literature and life, the socio-aesthetic political revolution known as the Civil Rights Movement provides African-Americans with an expanded consciousness and a new voice. Walker describes her childhood in the fifties as a period when she was a silent "shadow" in white society: "I waited to be called to life," she recounts of her early years (In Search, 122). In her essay, Walker argues that the tumultuous events of the sixties "gave some of us bread, some of us shelter, some of us knowledge and pride, all of us comfort.... It broke the pattern of black servitude in this country.... It called us to life" (In Search, 128-9).

Consciousness and empowerment, however, come after many legal battles during the early sixties as people of all colors fight for a voice in the American political arena, the workplace, education, and public life in general. Part of the frustration which erupts in the early sixties grows out of disillusionment with the integration promised by rulings like *Brown v the Board of Education* (1954), six years earlier. The Birmingham bombings which killed four innocent black children while they attended their Sunday school, also provided an unexpected catalyst for violent change in 1963 and 1964. Black activists were losing faith in whites and their ability to eradicate injustice. Despite the landmark Civil Rights Act of 1964, the Voting Rights Act in 1965, and the historic Selma-to Montgomery march led by Dr. Martin Luther King in 1965, many black leaders were calling for racial separatism. The chaos of 1965, when Malcolm X was assassinated and the Los Angeles community of Watts erupted in riots, led to the 1967 call by "black power" activists to purge whites from the civil rights movement.

The desire to remove whites from the movement also had sexual as well as political overtones. Fifties antagonism between black and white women was as evident in radical civil rights organizations like SNCC as it was in the fifties kitchens fictionalized in the literature of Brooks and Childress. When SNCC organized the massive voter registration drives in the South, some of the white women who joined the effort incurred the hostility of black women who resented black men's liaisons with white women. Therefore, when the black power movement called for the purging of whites, it was with a certain relief and satisfaction on the part of black women, according to Paula Giddings.

Both hope and disillusionment, communal action and separatism at the end of the decade are reflected in the poetry, fiction and drama of the sixties. Thus, in her 1968 collection of poetry entitled *Riot*, Gwendolyn Brooks portrays the anger and resentment of the ghetto children who have languished in racist America. In "The Blackstone Rangers," gang members are described in all their violent potential as "Thirty at the corner./Black, raw, ready./Sores in the city/that do not want to heal."[16] These young men are no longer vulnerable child martyrs like Brooks' Emmett Till, but rather the calloused, angry men of urban riots.

The impending tension and divisiveness in sixties society are also dramatically portrayed by Alice Walker in her poem "Once" (1968) where a young, African-American radical is feared by whites and passive blacks alike. The world that Walker describes in "Once" is filled with hypocrisy, injustice and hatred. It is a world where innocent children, like the four girls in their Birmingham Sunday school class, are made easy scapegoats for white hatred. In Part ix of the poem, the exasperated black speaker surveys the racial oppression in the South and promises herself that when the South rises again, she will not be present.[17]

In an essay entitled "What It Is I Think I'm Doing Anyhow," black writer Toni Cade Bambara characterizes the period from 1950 to 1975 as "an era hallmarked by revolution, a period in which we experienced a radical shift in the political-power configurations of the globe.... Writing is one of the ways I participate in the struggle," Bambara notes (qtd. in Sternburg, 153). Bambara sees her role in the civil rights struggle as that of a strong, active, forceful, occasionally angry voice—a perspective quite different from those of white women writers: "Sylvia Plath and the other obligatory writers on women's studies lists—the writers who hawk despair, insanity, alienation, suicide ... are not my mentors. I was raised on stories of Harriet Tubman, Ida B. Wells, Paul Robeson, and my grandmother, Annie, whom folks in Atlanta still remember as an early Rosa Parks" (Sternberg 163). Bambara's writing style and tone are tough, direct and resilient, "focus[ing] on resistance rather than despair" (Sternberg 164).

The literary equivalent of the Black Power Movement is seen in the "Black Arts Movement" of the sixties. Like the politically active Black Power movement itself, the Black Arts Movement stressed pride, strength and self-determination, a celebration of African-American heroes and heroines, traditions, language, music and art. Towards the white world it offered the equivalent of a political boycott—passive resistance, but never despair. Bambara as well as Nikki Giovanni, Sonia Sanchez, Alice Walker and a host of other female and male writers in the sixties and seventies would increase the black community's self-esteem through literature.[18] As Bambara notes, " Now that American history, American literature, the American experience is being redefined by so many [different] communities ... I'm attempting to blueprint for myself the merger of these two camps: the political and the spiritual" (Sternberg 167-8).

Bambara would join LeRoi Jones (Amri Baraka) and Larry Neal who in their work *Black Fire* argue that the "artist and the political activist are one,"[19] an African-American version of the feminist principle that the "personal is political."

Revolution, not despair, black pride not self-pity could be the subtitle of Nikki Giovanni's poem "Nikki Rosa" in her collection of poetry, *Black Feeling, Black Talk/Black Judgement* (1968). The poem's narrator refuses to dwell on her childhood problems—the outside toilets, her father's drinking and bankruptcy. Instead, she chooses to remember familial love as she found it in a Chicago ghetto: the comfort she received when she took a bath in a barbecue tub or the "black love" that she received from her mother. Nor does Giovanni want the white liberal's sympathy for her financially deprived childhood. According to Giovanni, no white person is capable of understanding that "Black love is Black wealth."[20]

Giovanni's affection for community and family is also expressed in a series of rural images of country life in "Knoxville, Tennessee," another poem in *Black Feeling*. In it, she associates the peace and tranquility of her childhood home with images of "fresh corn," gospel music from a church picnic and the country life of her grandmother's house, a place she can go "barefooted/and be warm/all the time/not only when you go to bed."[21] For Giovanni, African-American solidarity and love can overcome the deprivations of poverty. Her injunction that "Black love is Black wealth" equally applies in urban and rural settings.

Yet, during the sixties, Giovanni's hostility towards white America could also be focused and overt. In another poem "For Saundra" in *Black Feeling*, the speaker contemplates giving up writing for political action: "it occurred to me/maybe i shouldn't write/at all/but clean my gun/and check my kerosene supply."[22] In another famous poem from that volume, the speaker asks the black reader: "Nigger/Can you kill/Can you kill/Can a nigger kill/Can a nigger kill a honkie/Can a nigger kill the Man/Can you kill nigger/Huh? Nigger can you/ Kill."[23] The emotional volatility of the sixties is evident as Giovanni's tone vacillates between love and tenderness and hatred and violence. Her poems can celebrate the warmth of the country homeplace and the heat of ghetto fires—all within the same volume of poetry.[24]

Art and politics are equally intertwined in Sonia Sanchez' poem "to blk/record/buyers" (1969) when she alternately celebrates black music and denigrates white artists. There is a good deal of irony in her selection of the Righteous Brothers, a sixties white rock group whose style is patterned after black gospel music: "don't play me no/righteous bros/white people ain't rt bout nothing/no mo," the speaker demands in the opening of the poem. Instead, she wants a black music which encompasses the experiences of black people who are "making out/signifying/drinking/making molotov cocktails/stealing/or rather more taking their goods/from the honky thieves." Music, like poetry and guns becomes a means of destroying white culture and creating black pride: "play blk/songs/to drown out the/ shit/screams of honkies. AAAH./AAAH. AAAH. yeah. brothers./andmanymoretogo."[25]

Mari Evans' two volumes of early poetry, *Where Is All the Music?* (1968) and *I am a Black Woman* (1970) also reflect her commitment to art and politics. In her memorial poem to Martin Luther King entitled, "A Good Assassination Should Be Quiet," the speaker remembers the leader who "had/A Dream/ e x p loded/down/his th r o a t." While Evans acknowledges the destructive impact of a single violent assassination such as King's, she also realizes that the greater annihilation of a people takes place through the steady, "quiet" racism that is a fact of American history: "A good assassination/should be quiet," the speaker notes, "and occupy the heart/four hundred /years."[26]

During the sixties, African-American women writers, for a variety of reasons, concentrated their attention on racial, not gender equality. Racial pride and solidarity with men transcended any allegiance with other women, particularly those middle-class white women who had formerly belonged to black liberation organizations like SNCC and had, later in the sixties, created their own women's liberations organizations. Historian Winifred Wandersee characterizes the black woman's "profound distrust of feminism" during this period and suggests that it was, in part, caused by radical feminism's devaluation of the family and middle-class feminism's tendency "to marginalize the black woman's experience or to generalize and universalize the experience of all women" (Wandersee, 137). Another historian recounts a 1966 confrontation between white feminist Betty Friedan and a black member of SNCC who informs Friedan that she doesn't "want anything to do with that feminist bag," and that her primary purpose is to see that "black men . . . get ahead" (qtd. in Woloch, 520).

The tension between white feminists and black radicals during the sixties was also caused by economic disparities as well as racial differences. Paula Giddings notes that "not only were the problems of the White suburban housewife (who may have had Black domestic help) irrelevant to Black women, they were also alien to them. [Betty] Friedan's observation that 'I never knew a woman, when I was growing up, who used her mind, played her own part in the world, and also loved, and had children' seemed to come from another planet" (Giddings, 301).

The animosity towards middle-class feminists was also shared by working-class women. Historians Carol Hymowitz and Michaele Weissman note that "working-class and minority women were largely absent from the early women's movement [because] most identified more strongly along class and race lines than they did on the basis of sex . . . Black and working-class women spoke of feminists as 'spoiled children,' and 'not my sister,' 'man-hating,' and 'wrong in the way they are protesting.'"[27]

Authors Toni Morrison and Alice Walker concur with Giddings' assessment of African-American attitudes towards white feminists in the sixties. Morrison contends that during the decade, black women had "no abiding admiration of white women as competent, complete people," but instead viewed them as "willful children, pretty children, mean children, ugly children, but never as real adults" (qtd. in Giddings 307). In art as well as life, Alice Walker sees the limitations of white critics and writers. In her discussion of literary critic Patricia Spacks (*The Female Imagination*) and graphic artist Judy Chicago (*The Dinner Party, The Birth Project*), Walker notes that "with a few shining examples . . . white women feminists revealed themselves as incapable as white and black men of comprehending blackness and feminism in the same body, not to mention within the same imagination."[28]

The contentious and tense relationships between white and black women are nowhere more evident than in the relationship between white activist Lynne Rabinowitz and black civil rights worker Meridian Hill in Alice Walker's novel *Meridian*

(1976). Meridian joins the "Movement" at its high point—its "meridian" as the introduction to the book defines it—and stays through its decline in the late sixties and early seventies. The demise of the civil rights movement is dramatized through Meridian's personal experience with Truman, a black man, as well as in the political activities in the South. Despite his promise, Truman dissipates both his energies and love on a Northern white woman instead of Meridian. The black men of the movement seem to prefer the exotic other—white women— to their own strong black women.

Meridian assesses the situation with irony and bitterness, linking the sexual to the political and the racial: "It thrilled her to think she belonged to the people who produced Harriet Tubman, the only American woman who'd led troops in battle. But Truman, alas, did not want a general beside him. He did not want a woman who tried, however encumbered by guilts and fears and remorse, to claim her own life."[29] Thus, when Meridian realizes that she is pregnant with Truman's child, she aborts it, rather than experience his rejection. Symbolically, Truman's white lover and wife, Lynne, represents the source of tension which is partially responsible for the aborted union between African-American women and men. When Truman later jokes that he wants Meridian to have his beautiful black babies, she beats him until he bleeds.

In *Meridian*, white people are often held responsible for more than aborted babies. In the political arena, they are also responsible for fallen leaders: white assassins and corporate America are blamed for the demise of the civil rights movement. In 1968, Truman returns to the South in order to persuade Meridian to forsake her political activism. Cynically, Truman tells Meridian that the sixties revolution is dead: "the leaders were killed, the restless young were bought off with anti-poverty jobs, and the clothing styles of the poor were copied by Seventh Avenue" (M, 188-9). It is this attitude towards white America which produces the black separatist Tommy Olds who hates whiteness in all its manifestations. He tells Truman that "all white people are motherfuckers ... I want to see them destroyed. I could watch their babies being torn limb from limb and I wouldn't lift a finger. The Bible says to dash out the brains of your enemy's children on the rocks. I understand that shit, now" (M, 132).

Meridian's response to this separatism and disillusionment is to become a storyteller, not a destroyer; she is the artist who cannot kill, but will—like the traditional singer of epic tales and ballads—preserve the lost collective memory of her people. In fact, the importance of "singing" the song of freedom for future generations is certainly the impetus behind other literary texts which owe their genesis to the early civil rights era including Anne Moody's *Coming of Age in Mississippi* (1968), Maya Angelou's *I Know Why the Caged Bird Sings* (1970) and Nikki Giovanni's *Gemini: An Extended Autobiographical Statement on My First Twenty-Five Years of Being a Black Poet* (1972).

Anne Moody's *Coming of Age in Mississippi* provides both a graphic portrayal of the injustice of poverty and racism in Mississippi during the fifties and sixties, as well as a statement of faith in change. The autobiography is divided into four parts: childhood, high school, college and the movement—steps in the progression of Moody's spiritual education. The destruction and fragmentation of the black family is evident in the description of Moody's early family life in a shack on the Carter's plantation. However, Part Four on "The Movement" creates a new sense of family in almost theological terms as a band of the faithful struggle during the fifties and sixties in the South's civil rights movement. In this way, the autobiography becomes a weapon against the racist white establishment, a literary corollary to the activist's march, sit-in, or demonstration for freedom. As the autobiography concludes, Anne Moody jumps on a bus headed for Washington, D.C. in order to tell the world about her experiences in Mississippi.

Maya Angelou's four volume spiritual autobiography, *I Know Why the Caged Bird Sings* (1970), *Gather Together in My Name* (1974), *Singin' and Swingin' and Gettin' Merry Like Christmas* (1976) and *The Heart of a Woman* (1981) chronicles her life in Arkansas from the depression of the early thirties through the civil rights movement in the sixties and seventies. Like Moody, Angelou sees the political importance of her personal history as a child, adolescent and adult in white America. She views her maturation as representative of millions of African-American women. Angelou equates her own hardships and suffering with those of all women of color who are "caught in the tripartite crossfire of masculine prejudice, white illogical hate and Black lack of power" (Bird, 231). Yet, despite the "crossfire" Angelou finds herself confronted with in *Caged Bird*, she is as determined as Moody or Meridian to survive. In *Gather Together in My Name*, the sequel to *Caged Bird*, Angelou manages to live through a number of harrowing experiences without abandoning her self-respect or her son Guy. Both *Caged Bird* and *Gather Together* end with a hopeful scene of communion between mother and son, a testament to the future.

As the decade of the sixties concluded, the desire for revolutionary change in both literature and life was unabated. Sonia Sanchez in her poetry collection *We a BaddDDD People* (1970) even rejects the pessimism of the African-American blues culture and calls for positive political action in her "liberation/ poem." The poem's speaker skillfully contrasts the defeatedness of the "blues" with black pride and asks the reader to take to the streets: "But. now. when i hear billie's soft/ soul/ful/sighs of "am i blue"/i say/no. sweet/billie./no mo. no mo/blue/ trains running on this track/they all been de/railed." The train moving down the track into the seventies is inevitably moving into a revolutionary era where depression and "blues" are transformed into action and pride. "am i blue?" the speaker asks of Billie Holliday. "sweet/baby/blue/billie. no. i'm blk/& ready," is the answer.[30]

Beyond Anger and Rage: Seventies' Culture, Soul and Style

The sixties' revolution as envisioned by poets, fiction writers and essayists profoundly transformed America's sensitivity to its racial and ethnic minorities. However, during the seventies, the revolution was expressed more in an awareness of cultural heritage and pride in race and culture than in overt, political action. The anger expressed in sixties literature was, obviously, not eliminated; recalcitrant white prejudice and existing racism ensured that animosities were very much alive in both literature and life. However, the emphasis slowly changed in the seventies. No longer preoccupied with whiteness as the norm, many

African-American female and male writers sought to understand their own culture more clearly; its uniqueness and divergence from the white mainstream became part of its value, not its liability.

During the next decade, black writers like Alice Walker, Toni Morrison, Gloria Naylor, and a host of other playwrights, poets and fiction writers would explore the nature of African-American life: its roots in traditional African life; its myths, morals and culture; its solidarity with other oppressed peoples; and, finally towards the end of the decade, its sexism—a condition shared with all women.

The discovery and preservation of a lost African-American culture are of utmost importance to Alice Walker in a number of essays and short stories she wrote during the seventies. In "Looking for Zora" which was first published in *Ms.* magazine in March 1975 and reprinted in Walker's landmark collection of essays *In Search of Our Mothers' Gardens* (1983), Walker describes her search for the Harlem Renaissance writer Zora Neale Hurston's unmarked grave. This quest, however, is of symbolic value; it is only after Walker has placed the tombstone on Hurston's grave—"Zora Neale Hurston/'A Genius of the South'/Novelist Folklorist/Anthropologist/1901-1960" (In Search, 107) that the contemporary novelist Walker can rest. She has begun to "name" her heritage, and retrieve her literary "mothers" from oblivion in order to preserve their rich tradition of story-telling and myth. Therefore, Walker's journey is not something that the white community can accomplish; neither the white graduate student Charlotte nor Hurston's biographer Robert Hemenway are able to find the neglected grave on their own. Walker and other black writers must initiate and fulfill the literal and artistic quest themselves.

Whether Walker is uncovering the grave of Zora Neale Hurston or setting down her own mother's stories, she is making connections with past "mothers" who nurture her creativity. It is from this interaction with the past that Walker and other black writers will create and sustain their future. From this search for the forgotten past, Walker as well as other black women writers learn that they are not alone. In seeking their "mothers" and their heritage, black women writers express a feminist version of the black arts movement, a version which Barbara Christian calls, "a personal voice [which] is a powerful example of the feminist concept that the personal and political cannot be separated" (Christian, 162). This odyssey to the past focuses on reclaiming a lost African heritage, as well as on a celebration of both simple, black rural culture and sophisticated urban "style." But most importantly, the emphasis in the seventies is on the African-American community in all its diversity, *not* on its victimization by the white majority.

One result of this new emphasis is the rejection of the old white stereotypes of black women and the creation of a host of new images. This literary goal is expressed eloquently in 1973 by the newly emerging National Black Feminist Organization whose treatise demands that black women, "not white men or black men, must define our own self image as black women . . . It has been hard for black women to emerge from the myriad of distorted images that have portrayed us as grinning Beulahs, castrating Sapphires, and pancake-box Jemimahs" (qtd. in Hymowitz, 364).

One source of new imagery is from African legends and myths as translated and interpreted by black women writers. Poet Audre Lorde also utilizes African imagery and myth to revitalize the identity of black women. In several poems in her volume *The Black Unicorn* (1978) Lorde envisions a world quite apart from white Judeo-Christian conceptions of masculinity and femininity. Instead of Adam, Eve and the Garden of Eden, Lorde writes about Yemanja, the mother of the Yoruban (West Nigerian) goddesses and gods. Yemanja is a holistic mother who embodies both good and evil, life and death—the progenitor of the oceans and rivers and a symbol of birth and renewal quite apart from the patriarchal Hebrew god. The speaker in the poem describes a mother with two faces who bears no resemblance to the Jemimah figure of white society. Yemanja, the speaker's mother is both a nurturer and a fearsome figure. A symbol of both stability and chaos, the contradictory goddess is an essential life force for the speaker which sustains the speaker in the same manner that rain replenishes the earth.[31]

African myth and legend also provide the basis for alternative conceptions of the family and mother/child relationships in

Lorde's poem "Coniagui Women" in the same volume. The Coniagui mother, who bears a resemblance to some of the divine mothers in Toni Morrison's *Sula* is the embodiment of the earth goddess who nurtures but then emancipates her children. These women are not dependent upon male assistance, like the Old Testament female warriors, but instead they take direct action and are outspoken and warm. The predatory female of biblical myth or white sexist literature is transformed by Lorde into an entirely new source of poetic inspiration.

The influence of African heritage is most evident in the work of Alice Walker who, from the early seventies through the nineties, has incorporated African myths and imagery into her fiction and poetry. Walker's experiences in Africa are given imaginative representation in her first book of poetry, *Once* (1968), the Pulitzer Prize winning novel *The Color Purple* (1982) and her latest novels *The Temple of My Familiar* (1989) and *Possessing the Secret of Joy* (1992). In an 1973 interview, Walker analyzes the influence of Africa on her writing as "the belief that everything is inhabited by spirit. This belief encourages knowledge perceived intuitively ... an awareness of an openness to mystery, which, to me, is deeper than any politics, race, or geographical location" (In Search, 252).

Yet, despite her belief in the importance of African identity for black Americans, Walker also sees the degree to which this identification may seem forced, artificial or detrimental if it obliterates the American past completely. The first person narrator in the short story "Everyday Use" (1973), is a strong, courageous black woman living in the rural South who nervously awaits the arrival of her sophisticated and successful daughter, Dee. "Dee," however has recently metamorphosed into the African "Wangero Leewanika Kemanjo." When her mother asks her why she would change her name, Dee/Wangero replies, "I couldn't bear it any longer, being named after the people who oppress me" (EU, 53). In her enthusiasm to develop a new African identity which would supplant the old "slave" name, Dee has also given up her real ancestors—those strong, rural Southern women named Dicie and Dee for whom the present Wangero was originally named.

The African identity which Dee wears around her like a fashionable garment is, partially, an illusion. In fact, Dee uses her newly attired African self to belittle and intimidate her "backward" mother and sister, Maggie, who, seem primitive to their upwardly mobile city relative.

In many respects, Dee-Wangero is symbolic of the writer herself, trapped between two worlds—the poverty and ignorance of rural black Southern life, with its roots in slavery and injustice and the world of the Northern college educated black woman who has advanced in the world but lost something of herself in the process. Both the brash, ambitious Dee-Wangero (the future) as well as the victimized Maggie (the past) are deserving of love and respect. And it is the artist's goal, Walker seems to be saying, that all black women find a compromise, a middle-ground, between these two ways of dealing with one's heritage.

The strength and pride as well as the impotence and frustration of Southern life are nowhere more in evidence than in Walker's landmark novel *The Color Purple* (1982). In the novel, Celie, a down-trodden and abused character much like the fire-scarred Maggie, learns how to live instead of just survive. Battered by both the white and black communities, Celie has decided to endure through the written word, in this case letters written to her sister Nettie and, sometimes, to God.

Africa and African history play a central role in this novel because it is to Africa that Nettie and Celie's children escape the injustice and defeat of white American racism. It is through her travels in Africa that Nettie begins to learn about the Eurocentricism of the Hebrew and Christian Bibles. In Africa, Nettie discovers that Jesus was a dark-skinned African with lamb's wool hair, a fact which frees her from the second-class status she has experienced in the white American church. Nettie's reinterpretation of Genesis within an African context, gives Celie a way to initiate her own genesis.

Although Nettie's experience in Africa provides her with both an escape from white oppression and a source of spiritual strength, Africa is no panacea for either black or white. As in "Everyday Use" the characters must weigh their allegiances to Africa and America, arriving at a harmonious, unromanticized balance. Nettie reminds Celie that slavery began with the Africans themselves who now, like Americans, must pay the price for their avarice. Nettie writes to Celie that the Africans "having murdered or sold into slavery their strongest folks are riddled by disease and sunk in spiritual and physical confusion. They believe in the devil and worship the dead. Nor can they read or write" (CP, 129), skills which are synonymous with liberation in the novel.

In addition, the sexism which plagues Celie, Sophia and other women in America is even more blatant in Africa. The patriarchal world of the African village indoctrinates its women to serve men and then "protects" them accordingly. When Tashi, a young Olinka girl wishes to learn from Nettie, she is punished. In addition, traditional tribal sexual practices such as female circumcision, a subject discussed in Walker's *Possessing the Secret of Joy*, endanger both the physical and mental health of women. Nettie writes to Celie that some of the Olinka men remind her of their abusive father.

What Nettie does learn from her African experience and what she communicates to her sister, however, is the power of love for all women, men and children. Affection among the many wives of the Olinka tribesmen helps them transcend the hardships of life; it is the basis of the good life between missionaries Samuel and Corrine; and finally, it is the lifeline between Nettie and Celie and one of the crucial elements of their survival. In a world in which those who write to God often, like Celie, find him unresponsive or "asleep" (CP, 163), it is love between people which ensures salvation on earth.

Like many literary texts in the seventies and eighties, *The Color Purple*'s main focus is on African-American, not white culture. However, the Caucasian world is a continuing source of humiliation and tension, even for strong characters like Sophia. Sophia's imprisonment within the home of the white mayor and his wife continues the theme of tension between black and white women in the work of Alice Childress and Gwendolyn Brooks discussed earlier in this chapter. If there is a difference in Walker's treatment of all forms of social injustice, including black-white relations, however, it is found in her peaceful solution. Although Sophia fantasizes about murdering the racist mayor and his manipulative, neurotic wife, Celie reminds her of the impracticality, if not the morality of such an action: "Too many to kill off, I say. Us outnumbered from the start" (CP, 98). Having experienced the rage and riots of the sixties, Walker, in *Meridian* and *The Color Purple*, rejects violence as a means of combatting either racism or sexism. Murder is no more effective against her husband, Albert, who has been hiding Nettie's letters to Celie for years. When Celie threatens to cut Albert's throat with a razor, Shug warns her that "Nobody feel better for killing nothing. They feel *something* is all" (CP, 134).

The most important weapon in fighting injustice, therefore, is self-awareness and consciousness. Celie, like the other characters in the novel, must first know herself, find some meaningful work and develop a sense of self-esteem and independence. Celie even tells the white mayor's grown daughter to get a job and develop some self-reliance. When Albert begins to sew, cook and manage his own life, he, too, redeems himself. In one of the last scenes of the novel, Celie and Albert sit together sewing and smoking pipes, having finally found some peace and mutual understanding in their world.

Strong, creative and perceptive women who defy both their circumstances and the cultural stereotypes are prevalent in African-American women's literature of the seventies and eighties. Whether the setting is the rural South or the urban North, these symbolic "mothers" as Walker would call them in her essay "In Search of Our Mothers' Gardens" (1983), are celebrated in the writing of the major black women writers including Toni Cade Bambara, Toni Morrison, Gloria Naylor and Paule Marshall among others. In particular, many of the feisty, opinionated female characters in Toni Cade Bambara's short story collections *Tales and Stories for Black Folks* (1971), *Gorilla, My Love* (1972) and *The Sea Birds Are Still Alive* (1977) provide sisters worthy of Celie, Sophia and Nettie.

Like Celie, Miss Hazel in Bambara's "My Man Bovanne" is no radical, freedom fighter in the sixties sense. Although Miss Hazel finds herself at a rally for a relative who is running on a Black Power political ticket, she ignores the speeches and dances instead with an old, blind man named Bovanne. With her countrified language, wig and skimpy dress, Miss Hazel scandalizes her children who have adopted African names and serious demeanors. Miss Hazel, however, ignores their scorn and, concerns herself more with black soul: "touch talkin'" and "vibrations" as she moves around the dance floor with Bovanne. Of her children's sixties radicalism, Miss Hazel suggests that "Black Power got hold their minds and mess em around till they can't be civil to old folks."[32]

The clash of pre and post-civil rights generations is given an urban rather than rural setting by Bambara, but the tensions and outcomes discussed in "Everyday Use" are the same. The humorless young people who try to stifle their mother's funk and soul lack her power. In their quest for their African heritage, the younger generation has forgotten its real roots in its old people. By dismissing Bovanne as a "shufflin'" Uncle Tom, or Miss Hazel as old-fashioned and embarrassing, the young generation severs its ties to the old people who have nourished them through adversity. Miss Hazel laments the transformation of her society in which children are estranged from their mothers and their roots—much to the detriment of both.

In her other short stories, novels and essays, however, Bambara writes from a more political stance. An activist herself, Bambara also presents characters who wish to shake the complacency out of the ghetto and teach the children about power relations in white America. In "The Lesson," another short story in the 1972 collection *Gorilla, My Love*, Miss Moore takes a group of poor black children from Harlem across town to the white world of F.A.O. Schwarz, an elite toy store for the rich. The children who treat Miss Moore with a mixture of contempt and respect cannot initially understand the woman's motivation for such an expedition. However, when they see the price tags on the toys—$35.00 for a toy clown or $195.00 for a sailboat—they become angry over the economic disparities endemic in American society. When Sylvia, the quick-witted and perceptive young narrator of the story, questions an economy which allows white children to spend $1,000 on toys but denies black people rent money, Miss Moore smiles. She realizes that she has inspired the previously complacent Sylvia to ask some important questions about money, power and inequality in American society. However painful and disorienting, Miss Moore's "lesson" is an important part of Sylvia's education as an activist. With the lesson firmly burned into her memory, Sylvia goes to sit in a park, determined to think through her response to inequity, and resolved not to let nobody "beat me at nuthin."[33]

The personalized nature of political struggle is the theme for many African-American women writers in the seventies and eighties. For Sherley Anne Williams in *Dessa Rose* (1986) and "Meditations on History" (1976), as well as in her poetry, the goal of the artist is to personalize the political struggle and make it meaningful in human terms. Williams describes herself as "not a very political person in the sense of joining organizations or espousing political philosophies." However, through her recreation of slavery, told from the point of view of a black slave named Odessa, Williams is able to write a story with social impact. Through literature, Williams attempts "to elucidate those elements in our lives in which constructive political changes, those that do more than blackwash or femalize the same old power structure, can be built."[34]

After the public, political rhetoric in sixties poetry and fiction, many black female writers turned their attentions in the seventies and eighties to the personal lives of African-Americans, preferring to tell individual stories which have larger political implications. One of the most important writers of this era —a winner of both the Nobel Prize and the Pulitzer Prize—is author Toni Morrison whose novels from *The Bluest Eye* (1970) to *Jazz* recount the personal histories of African-American characters in many eras and locales. An analysis of Morrison's subjects and themes from the seventies through the nineties demonstrates the shift in her emphasis on black/white relations in the early work to a concentration on the African-American community itself in several works including *Sula* (1974), *Song of Solomon* (1977), *Tar Baby* (1981), *Beloved* (1987) and *Jazz* (1992).

The childhood and adolescence of Pecola Breedlove in *The Bluest Eye* are both unique and representative of many black women's experiences. The novel opens with a recitation of a "Dick-and-Jane" primer of the forties and fifties, the kind of reader many children—black and white—would have read at home and in school: "Here is the house. It is green and white. It has a red floor. It is very pretty. Here is the family. Mother,

Father, Dick, and Jane live in the green-and-white house. They are very happy."[35] Yet Pecola and the other young black girls who live in her neighborhood do not experience the pleasant banality of Dick and Jane's white world. In contrast, to the happy, simplistic white family of the primer, Pecola is, in the fall of 1941, having her father's baby, a fact—which the narrator Claudia suggests—causes the marigolds not to grow. Unlike the happy green-and-white home described in the white children's book, Claudia's house is "old, cold, and green. At night a kerosene lamp lights one large room. The others are braced in darkness, peopled by roaches and mice. Adults do not talk to us —they give directions. They issue orders without providing information" (BE, 12).

Confused by the disparity between the ostensibly beautiful white world and her own desolate black home, Claudia is frustrated and confused. Her solution is to either worship the white world, as Pecola's mother does, or to hate whiteness, mutilate white baby dolls and despise Shirley Temple. Neither emulating or hating the white world, however, provides redemption. The Breedloves are ultimately destroyed by their own sense of inferiority in relation to the white world. Cholly Breedlove projects his own fear and hatred of white men on his wife and children by abusing his family.

However, four years later, when Morrison published *Sula* (1974) her emphasis shifted from white oppression to an in-depth portrayal of a black community over a forty-five year period from 1920 to 1965. The story of a charismatic black woman and her "experimental life"[36] became the focus of Morrison's story-telling. Sula is different spiritually as well as biologically from the ordinary folks in the bottom because of her rejection of materialism and property ownership. Her reluctance to "own" anything extends to marriage and men—Sula is an "experimental" woman who enjoys men but has little permanent desire to live with one.

When the reader compares the character of Sula to Pauline or Pecola Breedlove in *The Bluest Eye*, the change in emphasis is strikingly apparent. Sula sleeps with white men, lives in the white community, but she has little regard for whiteness or its community. The social constraints which stifle creativity in other black characters do not restrain Sula. Even Nel, who seems like the inverted mirror image of Sula, lacks her vitality. Nel admires, even idolizes Sula, but ultimately fears her freedom in the black or white world.

And yet, the terror that Nel and the townspeople of the bottom feel for Sula is not completely unjustified for Sula is both a destructive and creative force. In the early seventies when Morrison conceived of the character of Sula, the opportunities for a woman with an "experimental life" were still few and riddled with danger. Unlike Celie in *The Color Purple*, Sula is an artist without an art form, no outlet for her creativity like sewing which provides Celie with independence, self-esteem and a place within her community. Instead, Sula remains a "pariah" figure in Morrison's novel, a scapegoat who magically benefits the community, but is ultimately destroyed by it (S, 122). On her deathbed, Sula is reminded by Nel that she "*can't* do it all. You a woman and a colored woman at that. You can't act like a man. You can't be walking around all independent-like, doing whatever you like, taking what you want, leaving what you don't" (S, 142).

Morrison's conception of Sula owes more to the world of the seventies, however, than it does to its setting in the late thirties or early forties. Although Sula ultimately succumbs to her environment, she is not defeated like Ann Petry's Lutie. Instead, Sula leaves a legacy of consciousness behind which enlightens and educates others, including her lifetime friend Nel. After Sula's death, Nel undergoes an epiphany, a sudden awareness of kinship and completion with Sula. It is only at this point that Nel realizes the importance of friendship and female bonding; at the novel's conclusion, Nel understands that it was Sula's love—not male love—she was missing throughout her life.

In the literature and essays of the seventies, eighties and nineties, there is an increased awareness on the part of African-American female writers about the importance of gender as well as racial identity. Many of the characters in novels, poetry, drama in the seventies and beyond, therefore, view gender as a decisive issue; however, they will develop their own black feminism which differs somewhat from white, middle-class feminism. One reason for the shift in emphasis is a realization on the part of black women that their economic and social situation, despite political gains in the sixties, had not improved substantially, and had—in certain circumstances—deteriorated.

In 1970, 30% of black families were headed by women; by 1981 the number had risen to 47%. In 1970, 38% of black births were to unmarried women; in 1980, the number had risen to 55%. Since single-female headed households are at greater economic risk, it is not surprising that in 1981, 52.9% of black female headed households lived at or below the poverty level. This had a disastrous effect on the African-American family and its children; as Kathleen Gerson in *Hard Choices: How Women Decide About Work, Career, & Motherhood* (1985) points out, "nearly one-half of all black children—44.9%—were living in poverty, in comparison to only 14.7% of white children" (qtd. in Wandersee 136). When discussing the genesis of the National Black Feminist Organization in 1973, black activist Eleanor Holmes Norton noted that "it took us some time to realize that we had nothing to fear from feminism" (qtd. in Giddings, 344).

Even before the inception of formal political organizations, however, many black women writers were beginning to define their problems along gender lines. In 1970, Toni Cade [Bambara] published an article in her anthology, *The Black Woman* "On the Issue of [Gender] Roles" in which she argued that "one of the most characteristic features of our [black] community is the antagonism between our men and our women. . . . The few semi-permanent relationships that do develop are invariably built on some shaky finance-romance basis, her trying to get into his pockets, him trying to get into her drawers."[37]

Unlike more radical branches of the white feminist movement which equate sexual separatism with women's liberation, however, black feminists, even lesbian black feminists, did not opt for a similar estrangement. The Combahee River Collective's "A Black Feminist Statement"(1979) provides a clear treatise on black feminism, but is also quite specific about its solidarity with black men: the women reject separatism because it ignores the importance of the black family and unequivocally states that the feminist collective "struggle[s] together with Black men against racism, while we also struggle with Black men about sexism."[38] Although the Combahee Collective viewed its position as racially unique, it nevertheless adopted both the philosophy and language of the sixties feminist movement, particularly the stance that personal problems had their origin and solution in political action. The Collective, however, saw itself as expanding this feminist concept in several ways. This alignment of race, class and gender does, in fact, provide an expansion of the "personal is political" in important ways. Although white women realized that individuals acquired power through work and economic independence, the early women's movement was largely a middle-class phenomenon. Black feminism would expand the appeal of feminist principles to many marginalized women providing a basis for a feminism which transcends race and class barriers.

In 1983, when Alice Walker published *In Search of Our Mothers' Gardens*, she coined the word "womanist" to define an African-American, woman-centered art. Walker described "womanist" as the opposite of "girlish." A "womanist" is a "black feminist or feminist of color.... Committed to survival and wholeness of entire people male *and* female" (In Search, xi).

Walker's "womanist" position for black feminists, however, is not the only perspective. Essayist Michelle Wallace's *Black Macho and the Myth of the Superwoman* (1979) and playwright Ntozake Shange's *For Colored Girls* (1977) are openly critical of black men and often characterize the relationships between black women and men as tense and destructive. Wallace's "Black macho," therefore, is as detrimental to black women's self-esteem and psyche as any form of white racism. And it is this new attitude towards black female/male relations which will initiate a provocative and tension-filled theme during the seventies, eighties and nineties as novelists frankly portray domestic violence, rape, and the black male preference for white women.

Ntozake Shange in her play/poem *For Colored Girls Who Have Considered Suicide/When the Rainbow is Enuf: A Choreopoem* (1977) describes the lives of seven black women who are battered by a violent and hostile environment. *For Colored Girls* explores the previous dependence that black women have on black men, a dependence which makes them vulnerable to abuse and neglect. In "no more love poems" # 1, #2, #3 and #4, the orange woman relates the story of her spiritual death "ever since i realized there was someone callt/a colored girl (for, 42) who clings to a man. Despite her love and allegiance, the man abandons her leaving her "sorry & colored at the same time" which she describes ironically as a "redundant" description (for, 43). There is a remedy for this situation which is presented in the scene entitled "no more love poems." The women must give up "love poems" to men and begin to love themselves and look for salvation within.

When Ntozake Shange and Alice Walker write openly about abusive heterosexual relationships, they often encounter angry criticism from the black, male community, however. In an interview, Shange, justified her controversial portrait of the violent Beau Willie Brown by explaining that she has had "to live around people like him. . . . I refuse to be a part of this conspiracy of silence. I will not do it. So that's why I wrote about Beau Willie Brown. I'm tired of living lies."[39] Alice Walker has received similar criticism for her uncomplimentary portraits of black men in *The Color Purple*.[40] Yet both writers, as well as many others would, in the seventies and eighties, speak with honesty and candor about the brutality experienced by women of color in America and Africa. In fact, in her novel, *Possessing the Secret of Joy*, Walker confronts the taboo subject of female circumcision in Africa in order to expand upon the suffering that women experience at the hands of an oppressive patriarchal order. Thus, this intersection of race, gender and class has become a crucial theme in literature written by black women in the last twenty years.

Lesbian poet Audre Lorde explains her own willingness to speak out about other formerly taboo subjects in her essay "The transformation of Silence into Language and Action" (1977). Although she is fearful of the repercussions, she contends that her voice must be heard: "the transformation of silence into language and action is an act of self-revelation, and that always seems fraught with danger." Yet the alternative—silence and repression—is fatal: "you're never really a whole person if you remain silent, because there's always that one little piece inside you that wants to be spoken out, and if you keep ignoring it, it gets madder and madder and hotter and hotter, and if you don't speak it out one day it will just up and punch you in the mouth from the inside."[41]

Racial conflict, gender antagonisms, heterosexual and lesbian love are all themes discussed in Gloria Naylor's *The Women of Brewster Place* (1982), a microcosm of both the difficulties and joys of female African-American urban life. In the seven different stories which comprise the novel, the relationship between black men and women is dramatized and critiqued from a variety of perspectives. In both "Mattie Michael," "Lucielia Louise Turner" and "Cora Lee," men often brutalize and then abandon their wives and lovers. In order to protect themselves from these men, many of the Brewster Place women cling to or acquire transitory lovers, "shadow men," (WBP, 114) as Cora Lee calls them. Shadow men, however, also give Cora Lee babies who keep her from attending the school she loved or living a decent life away from the roaches and decay of Brewster Place.

Although Naylor does not blame the female victim for masculine abuse, she does, in the narrative of Mattie Michael and her son Basil, provide some explanation for the development of black misogyny. The sole joy of his unmarried mother, Basil grows up to be an egotistical, spoiled and manipulative man. Without conscience or remorse, he flees the area after his mother pays his bail bond when he is arrested for murder and resisting arrest. The hard-working, self-sacrificing Mattie, whose entire life's earnings are tied to the mortgage she puts up as collateral for the bond, loses everything when her son abandons her. The overindulged son is her undoing, as completely as Cora Lee's transient lovers. Although the black male's malevolence can be explained partially in terms of his frustration with a white society, his fatal effect on black women is obvious.

The black female community of Brewster Place, however, is not entirely guiltless in its own suffering. While Naylor is not overtly judgmental, she does portray the hostility and intolerance of women towards each other in the story of Theresa and Lorraine, lesbian lovers in "The Other Two." Although Kiswana Browne supports Cora Lee and Eva helps Mattie, few women offer any assistance to the lesbian couple. Instead, the traditional heterosexual women of Brewster Place ostracize the nonconformist women, in a similar manner to the "Bottom's" punishment of the iconoclastic Sula in Toni Morrison's novel.

Economic and class differences are also treated with realism and candor in *The Women of Brewster Place*. The confrontation between the activist Kiswana Browne and her bourgeois mother, a resident of the black suburb of Linden Hills, reflects the often unspoken animosity between rich and poor within the black community. While many African-American writers discuss class disparities between white mistresses and their poor black maids, Naylor dramatically portrays Mrs. Browne's pride in her middle-class materialism and disdain for the black ghetto. Although the confrontation between generations in *Brewster Place* is reminiscent of the intergenerational conflict in Bambara's "My Man Bovanne," and Walker's "Everyday Use," Naylor's scenario is reversed. In the Kiswana Browne chapter, the mother has succeeded while the child chooses not to follow power or monetary success in the white world. In addition, Naylor's characters achieve their ends by direct engagement with each other. While the Walker and Bambara mothers placate their children by remaining silent and passive, Mrs. Browne confronts her daughter and eventually wins her respect. At the end of the chapter, Kiswana has joined her mother in a temporary female solidarity. Although the struggle between Kiswana and her mother is fierce, there is also hope for consensus and peace.

Another writer who looks unflinchingly at both the hope and despair within the black community is Terry McMillan in *Mama* (1987) and *Disappearing Acts* (1989) and *Waiting to Exhale* (1992). In these three novels, McMillan confronts the problems of intergenerational conflict, white racism, alcoholism, drug addiction, cyclical domestic violence, while she celebrates the importance of female bonding, courage and endurance. Like Naylor, McMillan sees the social disintegration of the black family as a manifestation of white racism; however, the focus of her analysis is on the black family's ability to resist a passive acceptance of "fate." If there is to be social equality and change, McMillan's characters will have to find the strength within themselves; in the world of the eighties and nineties, divine justice—like Celie's white banker God in *The Color Purple*—is "sleeping."

Mama, Disappearing Acts and *Waiting to Exhale* span a crucial era in African-American culture, from the early pre-civil rights sixties to the early nineties. Within this period, opportunities for economic and social advancement expand and yet significant improvement is not evident. Although Freda does succeed in gaining an education and some degree of autonomy in *Mama*, the main character in *Disappearing Acts*, Zora, encounters a new set of obstacles. The world presented by McMillan, therefore, is an increasingly complex one; its problems do not have single causes and its characters must overcome both socially imposed norms and their own personal fears.

In order to understand the initial despair of Freda, her mama Mildred and the Peacock family in the novel, *Mama*, the reader must understand the early sixties milieu in which "drinking was the single most reliable source of entertainment for a lot of people . . . It was 1964, and most folks had never heard of Malcolm X and only a few had some idea who Martin Luther King was. They lived as if they were sleepwalking or waiting for something else to happen."[42] Although Freda succeeds in extricating herself physically from the debilitating effects of Point Haven, it is far more difficult to achieve the psychological autonomy she desires. Anti-discrimination and equal opportunity laws enable Freda to go to college and find a job; however, freeing herself from the cyclical destructive behavior she witnessed as a child proves to be far more difficult.

And it is this topic—the individual's struggle to come to terms with her past—which is the focus of McMillan's novel. Freda must battle herself, not just the white racist establishment, if she is to survive in the world. After making a romantic alliance with a self-destructive, drug-addicted and abusive man—a relationship not unlike those favored by her mother—Freda must break the cycle: "Okay, Freda. This is it, she said to herself. You've been drunk for three or four days now—shit, you've been drunk for a year . . . You call yourself a writer, but what you really are is a fucking ugly drunk. You better start making some decisions, and fast" (M, 253). Freda's resolution to change her life, however, involves her mother as well as herself. At the conclusion of the book, both women have resolved to break with their self-destructive pasts and move on. Mildred will return to college while Freda reclaims her life and career.

In *Disappearing Acts* and *Waiting to Exhale*, Terry McMillan continues to focus on the problematic lives and relationships of black women and men. The two narrators, Zora and Franklin in *Disappearing Acts*, are lovers, although their backgrounds could not be more disparate. Zora, named for the Harlem Renaissance writer Zora Neale Hurston is a college educated music teacher, performer and composer while Franklin is a high-school dropout, former cocaine and alcohol abuser and a sometime employed construction worker. And yet, despite their differing grammar and history, Franklin and Zora tell the same story of loneliness, disillusionment and frustration with transient seventies romantic alliances.

At the beginning of the novel, both Franklin and Zora are taking a "vacation"[43] from sexual relationships. Franklin finds his former lovers ignorant and unimaginative, women who see no reason in voting or keeping up with politics. Zora is equally cynical. Yet, despite the almost insurmountable obstacles of rigid gender expectations and white prejudice, Franklin and Zora fall in love and begin to make a life together. This union, however does not prevent them from "disappearing." Both people have all the problems of contemporary couples whose gender expectations clash; but in addition, they must contend with several other racial and class issues which exacerbate their already fragile alliance.

It is thus not surprising that both Franklin and Zora—kind, intelligent and well-meaning people—begin to "disappear" under the pressure of their lives. In her narrative, Zora admits that Franklin is "dying a little bit every day"; however, she doesn't know how to save him" (DA, 184). Ironically, the more Zora tries to compensate for Franklin's deficiencies and handicaps, the greater his resentment and anger. He witnesses his own dissolution: "I just done disappeared," he confesses. "I don't know who the fuck I am no more. . . . I'm taking it out on her, I can see that . . . All this anger I done accumulated. I gotta find the right outlet for it, though" (DA, 353). Her friend, Portia, warns her that she, "better be careful, or you gon' start disappearing a little bit at a time, and before you know it, you gon' be just like them damn Stepford Wives. Won't even remember who Zora Banks was" (DA, 217).

The "disappearance" of Zora and Franklin could be accomplished quite easily, but for one important factor—their love and courage to survive the internal and external pressures which threaten to annihilate them. It is this boundless determination against great odds that saves the black family—Zora, Franklin and their son Jeremiah—from extinction. And it is McMillan's sophisticated dual narrative technique which allows both male and female voices to define and express themselves that gives her work such power. The willingness to endure and the faith in the future are intrinsic components in the literary voices of Terry McMillan, Toni Morrison, Alice Walker and a host of other African-American contemporary women writers. Perhaps it is best expressed in the poem which serves as the epigraph to McMillan's novel *Mama*:

> It takes years to learn how to look at the destruction
> of beautiful things;
> to learn how to leave the place
> of oppression; and how to make your own regeneration
> out of nothing.
>   (M, n.p.)

Asian-American, Chicana, Native American and Third-World Women's Literature—From Protest to Poetry

Although each of the above literatures is quite distinct, with its own myths, style, and history, Asian-American, Chicana, Native American as well as third world women's writing share many similar characteristics. In American history and literature, many of these racial/ethnic groups experienced a brutal period of discrimination in the nineteenth or early twentieth century, followed by an awakening of consciousness in the sixties brought about by the national focus on civil rights and multiculturalism. Like African-American female authors, women of color in America expressed their anger and hostility at a racist white world which marginalized their lives and creativity. And, in a fashion parallel to black women's writing, many of these same writers shifted their focus in the seventies and eighties in order to celebrate their own culture and people instead of dwelling on the white oppressive majority.

Before the War: Literary Reenactments of Political Struggle

The history of Chinese-Americans in the United States provides a prototype for the suffering that many people of color experienced in the United States in the late nineteenth and early twentieth century. The Chinese Exclusion Act of 1882 limited the number of Chinese female immigrants and prohibited immigration of laborers until it was repealed in 1943 when wives and children were permitted to enter the United States. More Chinese wives emigrated when the 1947 War Brides Act was enacted, but a pattern of discrimination for all Asians was almost an American tradition before and during World War Two. The Alien Land Law Act, which prevented Asians from owning land in California and the Asian Exclusion Act (1924) prohibited intermarriage between Asians and Americans. As Dexter Fisher notes in her excellent introduction to Asian-American literature in her anthology, *The Third Woman: Minority Women Writers of the United States* (1980), "this pattern of legislation is only too familiar to America's minority groups" (Fisher, 435).

Native Americans and Chicanos suffered a similar fate to Asian Americans before 1964. When Native Americans were forced on to reservations in 1851, they had already undergone much suffering both politically and culturally at the hands of the white majority. The Indian Removal Act of 1830 evicted native peoples from lands east of the Mississippi River and caused the death of 4,000 Cherokees during the "Trail of Tears" march. In the face of this genocide, Fisher argues that "writing [for Native Americans] became a means to perpetuate tradition in the face of cultural disintegration" (Fisher, 7). A history of political/social oppression is found in the background of Chicana writing too. These literatures of disenfranchised races reflect the political, cultural and personal exploitation of non-white peoples in the Americas and, therefore, increase the consciousness of readers of every color and nationality. Barbara Christian summarizes the impact of these new literary voices as increasingly important to the future of world literature: "women of color can no longer be perceived as marginal to the empowerment of all American women ... [and, therefore,] an understanding of their reality and imagination is essential to the process of change that the entire society must undergo in order to transform itself" (Christian, 185).

The Civil Rights movement of the sixties had as great an impact on other minority people as it did on African-American writers. Chicano writers during the sixties were influenced by Cesar Chavez and the farm workers' struggle in California and the creation of the National Farm Workers' Association in 1963. Forty-three Native American tribes created the North American Indian Women's Association in 1970, as a consolidation of both racial and gender identity.

In the face of cultural dissolution, many writers—male and female, Asian or Native American, Black or Chicano—resolved to save whatever cultural history they could through literature and the arts. Like Alice Walker in her quest for Zora Neale Hurston and other literary black "mothers," Native American writer Paula Gunn Allen searches for own grandmother's stories, "weaving the strands/of her body, her pain, her vision/into creation" (qtd. in Fisher, 12). Her anthology, *The Voice of the Turtle* (1994) is her latest contribution. Likewise, Elizabeth Sullivan, a Creek Indian recounts and, therefore, preserves the old legends and oral histories in her collection entitled *Indian Legends of the Trail of Tears and Other Creek Stories* (1974). Native American autobiographies have also been preserved by the "as told to" method in which the subject—like Helen Sekaquaptewa, a Hopi Indian—tells her life story to Louise Udall in *Me and Mine: The Life Story of Helen Sekaquaptewa* (1969). Wendy Rose, a Hopi poet whose books of poetry include Hopi *Roadrunner Dancing* (1973), *Long Division: A Tribal History* (1976) sees her culture's decimation in "Vanishing Point: Urban Indian" when she describes her people who are languishing in the cities of America, without anyone to mourn their passing or sing their songs.[44]

Asian American women writers are no less adamant about preserving their traditions within an insensitive white society.

In the recent novel *The Joy Luck Club* (1989), Amy Tan recounts the mystical tales of the older generation of "mothers" who pass their wisdom to their daughters through strange "fairy tales" like the "Kweilin" tale told by Jing-Mei Woo. Without these stories, the past—for good or ill—would be lost, a possibility especially feared by the older generation. Despite the conflicted relations between Americanized young women and their traditional Chinese mothers, the new generation is duty-bound and morally obligated to become the American story-tellers, as is Leslie Marmon Silko for the Laguna Pueblo Reservation and Alice Walker for the rural silent inhabitants of the South.

Lorna Dee Cervantes, a Chicana writer also echoes the importance of the ancestral past in her poem "Refugee Ship." She critiques the state of cultural ignorance that she and her generation possess: "mama raised me with no language/I am an orphan to my spanish name/the words are foreign, stumbling on my tongue." The poem's narrator likens this condition of cultural amnesia to a permanent captivity on a refugee ship, "a ship that will never dock/a ship that will never dock."[45] This rootlessness is the fate of those who are unconscious of their heritage and, therefore, lack a sense of tradition that many minority women writers of all colors and nationalities wish to retrieve from oblivion.

In "Anchorage," in *She Had Some Horses* (1983), Native American poet Joy Harjo sees an old woman on the street, "someone's Athabascan/grandmother, folded up, smelling like 200 years/of blood and piss, her eyes closed against some/unimagined darkness" and claims her as her own.[46] Harjo's poetry provides her people with a means of survival in a world bent on their annihilation, where the chance of maintaining one's identity or life amid desolation is slim at best.

Despite the pride in their heritage, many multicultural women writers also have conflicts arising from this dual allegiance to China or Japan, Mexico, Europe or a Native American nation as well as to America. The difficulty of maintaining one's individualistic traditions within a mainstream Anglo-Saxon, white culture provide a major subject in contemporary women's literature. Dexter Fisher characterizes this theme as a "bifocal vision" which creates a "tension between echoes of one's racial past and the present reality" (Fisher, 433) and a complex identity for those who share the vision.

For an Asian-American writer like Maxine Hong Kingston, this tension is graphically portrayed in her autobiographical work *The Woman Warrior: Memoirs of a Girlhood Among Ghosts* (1976). The narrator is a first generation American who is caught between the ancient responsibilities and complicated loyalties of the Chinese world and her own desire to be an independent American. The first section of the autobiography, entitled "No Name Woman" suggests the dynamic tension between conflicting loyalties—the American's preoccupation with the self and the traditional Chinese allegiance to family. The narrator's aunt who becomes pregnant and subsequently commits suicide after being humiliated and ostracized by her family is a symbol of the narrator's own conflicted self. The narrator does not characterize the aunt's sin as adultery or lust, but rather as the capacity for having "a private life, secret and apart from them [her family]" (WW, 14). The narrator's mother tells her the story of the "no name" aunt in order to instruct her daughter in obedience to family norms and punishments.

The narrator, however, obsesses about the aunt's history, and its implications for a Chinese-American girl's life. Instead of "forgetting" the aunt, wiping out her memory and existence, the narrator/writer memorializes her in a story, thereby defying her mother's instructions and the family code. Kingston's refusal to remain in collusion with a conspiracy of silence about her aunt marks her emancipation from the family. And yet, she does so with ambivalence—a mixture of guilt and pride: "My aunt haunts me," she confesses. "Her ghost drawn to me because now, after fifty years of neglect, I alone devote pages of paper to her" (WW, 19).

Reverence for and rejection of one's heritage are presented in a pair of poems by Chinese-American Cathy Song in "Chinatown" (1983) and "Heaven" (1988). In "Chinatown" the narrative voice acknowledges the uniformity of such communities: "They all look alike./In the heart/of cities. Dead/center: fisheyes blinking between/red-light & ghetto." The descriptive imagery suggests sickness and unhealth: "A network of yellow tumors,/throbbing insect wings." If there is rebirth in such an environment, it comes in the form of "cricket bulbs & roach eggs/hatching in the night."[47]

Other multicultural writers experience the same tension between old country and new, the past and the future. Caught between two worlds, two traditions, their experience is not unlike that of the "tragic mulatto" discussed previously in this chapter. In her "Poem for the Young White Man Who Asked Me How I, An Intelligent, Well-Read Person Could Believe in the War Between Races" (1981), Lorna Dee Cervantes sees her life in America as a perpetual struggle against both racist and sexist forces which would annihilate her and her children. "I'm marked by the color of my skin," she notes in the poem. But the "bullets" which would destroy her are more psychological than metal; they create spiritual "wounds" which encourage the narrator's mind to "stumble" and force her tongue to say "excuse me." Although she states quite specifically that she is "not a revolutionary./I don't even like political poems," she, nonetheless, accepts the politics of her personal oppression. Possibly only race war will eradicate the feeling that both she and other disenfranchised writers have that "this is not/my land/and this is my land."[48]

In her novel, *The Woman Who Owned the Shadows* (1983), Paula Gunn Allen, a Lagunda Pueblo/Sioux/Lebanese-American describes the life of Ephanie, a "mixed blood" woman who is alienated from both white and Native American societies. Rejecting despair, however, Ephanie delves into her native traditions for the answers to her identity. Likewise, Roberta Hill Whiteman, a poet from the Oneida Indian tribe also writes of the struggle to maintain one's autonomy while caught between two conflicting traditions. "We are born with cobwebs in our mouths/bleeding with prophecies," as yet unanswered, the narrator states in her poem "Dream of Rebirth" (1984). She views her peoples' passivity in the face of oppression, people who "hug canned meat" and possess "Worn-out hands [which] carry the pale remains of forgotten murders." Although the narrator feels shame about this "four hundred years" of "slow hunger/this midnight swollen," she dreams of another part of her self from which "a spirit kindles/moonlight glittering deep into the sea." Like Cervantes, Whiteman sees her people as "purified by fury./Once more eagles will restore our prayers./We'll forget the strangeness of your pity ... Some of us may wake unashamed./Some will rise that clear morning like the swallows."[49]

Novelist Louise Erdrich of the Chippewa tribe, also writes of the Native American determination to come to terms with the bifocal worlds in *Love Medicine* (1984) and *Tracks* (1988). In *Love Medicine*, which won the National Book Critics Circle Award, three generations of Chippewa Indians must fight the oppression, poverty and violence found on the reservation and in white dominated city life. Her characters in these novels and her book of poetry *Jacklight* (1984) as well as in *The Beet Queen* (1986) must learn to thrive in an environment which often intentionally excludes and alienates them. Erdrich's characters are often supernaturally strong characters who transcend their conditions in almost mystical ways. In her telling of their stories, Erdrich provides the reader with a sense of the powerful nature of the individual who survives the harsh world of the reservation. One representative woman is Marie Lazarre, a main character in *Love Medicine*. As a young girl Marie falls under the influence of the demonic Sister Leopolda whose physical and emotional abuse of Marie ends the young girl's "sainthood." When Marie enters the hill-top convent, the two engage in a struggle for domination, a battle Marie ultimately wins but does not enjoy.

The importance of family life is a high value in multicultural literature. Love between a mother and child or among family members helps characters transcend their victim status, providing them with both hope and dignity in a world which often denies the non-white person both. Such a sense of kinship and love is evident in Louise Erdrich's work as a whole and in the novels and short stories of another excellent Native American author, Leslie Marmon Silko. In the short story "Lullaby," (1981) Silko recounts the story of Ayah, an elderly Laguna Indian who has lost her children but not her dignity at the hands of the white society. Living on an impoverished reservation and speaking no English, Ayah, her husband Chato, and her two young children are at the mercy of disease and the white government. When a white social worker comes to take the children away because they have been exposed to tuberculosis, Ayah, who has learned to sign her name but not to read English, gives her written consent. After she realizes her tragic error, she blames her husband for her loss because he has taught her just enough English to be dangerous: "it was like the old ones always told her about learning their language or any of their ways," she thinks to herself. "It endangered you."[50]

Ayah and her husband are visited by their children who find Native American culture to be increasingly foreign. Fluent in the ways of the white world, Chato, too, regrets his role in the tragedy and seeks oblivion in alcohol, bought with the monthly government check. Ayah, however, does not despair, but instead, forgives both her husband and herself. At the conclusion of the story, she sings a lullaby to her husband and her missing babies. It is a traditional lullaby sung by generations of native women, a song which speaks of the love of the earth and the solidarity among family members. It is Ayah's and her female ancestor's way of coping with the harsh realities and pervasive racism of white society: "We are together always/We are together always" she sings to her sleeping husband. "There never was a time when this was not so" (55).

The importance of story-telling and song is paramount to Silko and the other writers discussed in this chapter. It is their way of maintaining their self-esteem and autonomy within an often sadistic, unforgiving environment. Self-expression can enable the writer to achieve self-empowerment, a way to transform pain and suffering into hope and joy. In the beginning of Silko's novel *Ceremony* (1977), there is a poem which begins "I will tell you something about stories,/[he said]/They aren't just entertainment./Don't be fooled./They are all we have, you see,/all we have to fight off/illness and death." The narrator of the poem knows that "you don't have anything/if you don't have the stories"[51]. The white majority which persecutes the Laguna Indians "can't stand up to our stories." And, thus, it is incumbent upon each member of the tribe to retell and remember all the tales. Without art, without storytelling, the man in the poem knows "we would be defenseless" (2). Therefore, Tayo's quest in *Ceremony* is to retrieve the Native American past—its traditions, witchcraft and source of power. His ability to succeed in this quest makes it possible for him to cure himself and his people of despair. In an interview about the novel, Leslie Marmon Silko likens herself to the "sick" Tayo at the beginning of the story. When she is asked by the interviewer, "Why did you entitle the novel *Ceremony*?" she answers, "That's what it is. Writing the novel was a ceremony for me to stay sane" (qtd in Fisher, 20).

Conclusion

Writing for Silko as well as for Louise Erdrich, Maxine Hong Kingston, Toni Morrison, Alice Walker or many other marginalized authors is a political act of self-assertion in a world which has excluded or stereotyped them in soul-destroying ways. Although it is impossible to generalize about so many different racial and ethnic groups, there are certain similarities. Over the past forty-five years, the writing of women of color has changed in many ways from a rejection of white stereotypes to an angry denouncement of white prejudice and, finally, to a celebration of community and self—a means of preserving one's sanity in a world which often operates in inhumane and incomprehensible ways. Despite the difficulties in their lives, the women writers discussed above do not flee their heritage in order to assimilate into the white mainstream. Instead, they desire a balance between two worlds, a sense of identity which is the birthright of all free people.

There are countless other women authors, writing in both their native languages and English who have begun to contribute their voices and perspectives to world literature. Chilean born Isabel Allende recreates her world in *The House of the Spirits* (1985) while Anita Desai presents her view of India in *Clear Light of Day* (1980) and *In Custody* (1984). Ruth Prawer Jhabvala's *How I Became A Holy Mother and Other Stories* (1976) offers the West a provocative portrait of India's women while Fumiko Enchi's *Masks* (1983) interprets her native Japan. White and black female authors provide their unique pictures of life in African nations in Buchi Emecheta's *The Joys of Motherhood* (1979) and white, South African Nadine Gordimer's *Burger's Daughter* (1979) and *My Son's Story* (1990). In fact, Gordimer won the Nobel Prize for Literature in 1991, one of only three women—along with Nellie Sachs and Toni Morrison—to receive this honor in the twentieth century.

For women of color and their sisters, writing is an act of self-creation, an act of resistance and self-affirmation in a society which prefers passivity from its women and minorities. During a conference discussion on "The Personal and the Political," poet Audre Lorde explained the importance of the writer's work for society by linking her literary creativity to social equality: "In a world of possibility for us all, our personal visions help lay the groundwork for political action."[52] Lorde, therefore, reiterates de Beauvoir's call for a new active woman who refuses to accept silence, passivity and the status quo. The personal and political value of literature is important to women of color, the poor and otherwise marginalized peoples who have, only recently acquired a public literary voice in the twentieth century.

Notes

1. Barbara Smith, "Toward a Black Feminist Criticism" in *The New Feminist Criticism: Essays on Women, Literature and Theory*, ed. Elaine Showalter (New York: Pantheon Books, 1985), 169.

2. Deborah McDowell, "New Directions for Black Feminist Criticism," in *The New Feminist Criticism: Essays on Women, Literature and Theory*, ed. Elaine Showalter (New York: Pantheon Books, 1985), 192.

3. Claudia Tate, *Black Women Writers At Work* (New York: Continuum, 1983), xxiii.

4. Barbara Christian, *Black Feminist Criticism: Perspectives on Black Women Writers* (New York: Pergamon Press, 1985), 160.

5. Paula Giddings, *When and Where I Enter: The Impact of Black Women on Race and Sex in America* (New York: Bantam Books, 1984), 245; hereafter cited in text. By the mid-fifties—the height of the white feminine mystique—the black, female college graduate was working and often supporting what would become "the black bourgeoisie," a term coined by historian E. Franklin Frazier in his book *The Black Bourgeoisie: The Rise of a New Middle Class in the United States* (1962).

6. Gwendolyn Brooks, "The Mother," in *Blacks* (Chicago: Third World Press, 1991), 21-2.

7. Gwendolyn Brooks, "the children of the poor," in *Blacks* (Chicago: Third World Press, 1991), 116.

8. Gwendolyn Brooks, "An Interview," in *Contemporary Literature* II (Winter 1970), 6.

9. Margaret Walker, "On Being Female, Black, and Free," in *The Writer on Her Work: Contemporary Women Writers Reflect on Their Art and Situation* (New York: W.W. Norton, 1980), 99.

10. Margaret Walker, "Lineage," in *This is My Century: New and Collected Poems* (Athens: University of Georgia Press, 1989), 21.

11. Margaret Walker, "Kissie Lee," in *This is My Century: New and Collected Poems* (Athens: University of Georgia Press, 1989), 31-2.

12. Ann Petry, *The Street* (Boston: Beacon Press, 1946), 430. For a further discussion, see Blyden Jackson's essay, "The Negro's Images of the Universe as Reflected in His Fiction," (1959). Jackson describes Lutie's situation as symbolic of late forties and fifties characters who have the will

to achieve, but are constantly thwarted by their environment. Her expectations, like the dreams of what Jackson calls other black "American democrats" are foiled and frustrated.

13. Paule Marshall, "Reena," in *Reena and Other Stories* (New York: The Feminist Press, 1983), 73; hereafter cited in text as "Reena."

14. Toni Cade Bambara, "What It Is I Think I'm Doing Anyhow," in *The Writer on Her Work*, ed. Janet Sternburg (New York: W. W. Norton & Co.), 8.

15. Nikki Giovanni, "My Poem" in *Black Feeling Black Talk Black Judgement* (New York: Morrow Quill Paperbacks, 1979), 95.

16. Gwendolyn Brooks, "The Blackstone Rangers," in *Blacks* (Chicago: Third World Press, 1991), 446.

17. Alice Walker, *Once: Poems* (New York: Harcourt Brace Jovanovich, 1968), 23.

18. In her essay, "What It is I Think I'm Doing Anyhow," Bambara notes that "since the breakthrough achieved in the sixties by the Neo-Black Arts Movement, the possibilities are stunning. Characters that have been waiting in the wings for generations, characters that did not fit into the roster of stereotypes, can now be brought down center stage" (Sternburg, 167).

19. LeRoi Jones and Larry Neal eds., *Black Fire* (New York: William Morrow, 1968), xvi.

20. Nikki Giovanni, "Nikki Rose," in *Black Feeling, Black Talk/Black Judgement* (New York: Morrow Quill Paperbacks, 1979), 59.

21. Nikki Giovanni, "Knoxville, Tennessee," in *Black Feeling, Black Talk/Black Judgement* (New York: Morrow Quill Paperbacks, 1979), 65.

22. Nikki Giovanni, "For Saundra," in *Black Feeling, Black Talk/Black Judgement* (New York: Morrow Quill Paperbacks, 1979), 89.

23. Nikki Giovanni, "The True Import of Present Dialogue, Black vs. Negro," in *Black Feeling, Black Talk/Black Judgement* (New York: Morrow Quill Paperbacks, 1979), 19-20.

24. Erlene Stetson describes the personal and political nature of Giovanni's work in her critical work, *Black Sister: Poetry by Black American Women, 1746-1980* (1981) as "black unity, love, communal spirit, self-determination, personhood, awareness . . . a poet interested not only in the aesthetic significance of her art, but also its cultural and political impact" (51).

25. Sonia Sanchez, "to blk/record/buyers," in *Home Coming* (Detroit: Broadside Press, 1969), 26.

26. Mari Evans, "A Good Assassination Should be quiet," in *I Am a Black Woman* (New York: William Morrow, 1970), 84.

27. Carol Hymowitz and Michele Weissman, *A History of Women in America* (New York: Bantam Books, 1978), 361.

28. Alice Walker, "One Child of One's Own: A Meaningful Digression Within the Work(s)," in *The Writer on Her Work*, ed. Janet Sternburg (New York: W. W. Norton, 1980), 132.

29. Alice Walker, *Meridian* (New York: Pocket Books, 1976), 110; hereafter cited in text as "M."

30. Sonia Sanchez, "liberation/poem," in *We a BaddDDD People* Detroit: Broadside Press, 1970), 54. For a recent interview about the impact of the music and the blues on Sanchez see Zala Chandler's interview with the poet in *Wild Women in the Whirlwind: Afra-American Culture and the Contemporary Literary Renaissance*, pages 353-62. Also of interest in the same anthology is Angela Davis' "Black Women and Music: A Historical Legacy of Struggle," (3-21).

31. Audre Lorde, "From the House of Yemanja," in *The Black Unicorn* (New York: W. W. Norton, 1978), 6-7.

32. Toni Cade Bambara, "My Man Bovanne," in *Gorilla, My Love* (New York: Vintage Books, 1972), 3.

33. Toni Cade Bambara, "The Lesson," in *Gorilla, My Love* (New York: Vintage Books, 1972), 96.

34. Sherley Anne Williams, "Introduction," in *Black-Eyed Susans/Midnight Birds: Stories by and about Black Women* (New York: Anchor Books, 1989), 225.

35. Toni Morrison, *The Bluest Eye* (New York: Washington Square Press, 1970), 7; hereafter cited in text as "BE."

36. Toni Morrison, *Sula* (New York: New American Library, 1973, 118; hereafter cited in text as "S."

37. Toni Cade (Bambara), "On the Issue of Roles, in *The Black Woman* (New York: Mentor, 1970), 106.

38. "A Black Feminist Statement: Combahee River Collective," in *This Bridge Called My Back: Writings by Radical Women of Color*, ed. Cherrie Moraga, Gloria Anzaldua (New York: Kitchen Table/Women of Color Press, 1981), 213-4.

39. Ntozake Shange, "Conversation with Ntozake Shange," in *Black Women Writers at Work*, ed. Claudia Tate (New York: Continuum Publishing Co., 188), 158-9.

40. Robert Staples, "The Myth of Black Macho: A response to Angry Black Feminists," *The Black Scholar* 10 (March-April 1979).

41. Audre Lorde, "The Transformation of Silence into Language and Action," in *Women's Voices: Visions and Perspectives*, ed. Pat Hoy et al (New York: McGraw-Hill, 1990), 177. For a recent article on black lesbian culture, see Barbara Smith's "The Truth That Never Hurts: Black Lesbians in Fiction in the 1980's," in *Wild Women in the Whirlwind*, pages 213-263.

42. Terry McMillan, *Mama* (New York: Washington Square Press, 1987), 19; hereafter cited in text as "M."

43. Terry McMillan, *Disappearing Acts* (New York: Viking, 1989), 184; hereafter cited in text as "DA."

44. The full text for Wendy Rose's poem, "Vanishing Point: Urban Indian," can be found in Dexter Fisher's *The Third Woman: Minority Women Writers of the United States* (Boston: Houghton Mifflin, 1980), 87.

45. Lorna Dee Cervantes, "Refugee Ship," in *Emplumada* (Pittsburg: University of Pittsburg Press, 1981), 41.

46. Joy Harjo, "Anchorage," in *She Had Some Horses* (New York: Thunder's Mouth Press, 1983), 14-5.

47. Cathy Song, "Chinatown," in *Chinatown* (New Haven: Yale University Press, 1983), 61-4.

48. Lorna Dee Cervantes, "Poem for the Young White Man Who Asked Me How I, An Intelligent, Well-Read Person Could Believe in the War Between Races," in *Emplumada* (Pittsburg: University of Pittsburg Press, 1981), 35-7.

49. Roberta Hill Whiteman, "Dream of Rebirth," in *Star Quilt* (Minneapolis: Holy Cow! Press, 1984), 66.

50. Leslie Marmon Silko, "Lullaby," in *Storyteller* (New York: Seaver Books, 1981), 47.

51. Leslie Marmon Silko, *Ceremony* (New York: Penguin Books, 1977), 2.

52. Audre Lord, "The Master's tools Will Never Dismantle the Master's House," in *This Bridge Called My Back: Writings By Radical Women of Color*, ed. Cherrie Moraga and Gloria Anzaldua (New York: Kitchen Table/Women of Color Press, 1983), 100.

Chapter Five

Power and the Female Contemporary Literary Tradition

> The true representation of power is not of a big man beating a smaller man or a woman. Power is the ability to take one's place in whatever discourse is essential to action and the right to have one's part matter. This is true in the Pentagon, in marriage, in friendship, and in politics.
> (Heilbrun, *Writing a Woman's Life*, 18).

If postmodernism is, as Elizabeth Fox-Genovese suggests, "an assault on power in all forms," (Fox-Genovese 1991, 183) then feminist literary theory after World War II is one of post-modernism's most far-reaching power redistributions. As has been suggested throughout this book, the contemporary feminist movement applies the theory that the "personal is political" to all aspects of life including work, sexuality, family, racial and ethnic identity and spirituality. And, thus, it is logical that even art and the aesthetic would come under this feminist lens. Previously thought of as "too personal" or divorced from "the real world," literature and the literary imagination became, during the postmodernist period, a focal point for feminist inquiry. Many women would ask: Who makes art? How do we decide what is "high" art and what is "low?" How are women and men represented in this art and why? What is the relationship between art and life, art and social equality and political action? *Who* really decides and by what criteria?

Although some of these same issues were addressed by female theorists from Mary Wollstonecraft in the eighteenth century to Virginia Woolf at the beginning of the twentieth, contemporary women authors increasingly demanded political answers to these questions after World War II. In her landmark essay, "When We Dead Awaken: Writing as Revision" (1971),

Adrienne Rich would remark that in the fifties and sixties she began "to feel that politics was not something 'out there' but something 'in here' and of the essence of my condition" (Rich 1979, 44). And for artists like Rich, the "in there" was located squarely in the struggle for control between women and men over the literary imagination and production. The latter half of the twentieth century, therefore, would see a demystification of art as well as a struggle for control over artistic creations.

In her ground-breaking collection of essays entitled *The New Feminist Criticism* (1985), Elaine Showalter defines the female literary terrain by analyzing the stages of feminist theory in the post-World War Two period. In part, I have based the organization of this discussion on Showalter's scheme, but have condensed some of her categories and added a "post-patriarchal" division of my own. In this way, it is possible to see the evolution of feminist literary theory from 1945 to the present as an inquiry into (1) 1945-75: the female struggle for self-definition in a misogynist world (2) 1975-85: the creation of a "gynocentric," woman-centered world of literature, thought and language; (3) 1985 to the present: a post-patriarchal analysis of women and men as "prisoners of gender" and a questioning of gender itself. It should be noted, however, that although it is useful for purposes of analysis to chart such an evolutionary course of contemporary women's literature, it is incorrect to believe that each stage neatly follows in linear fashion. To a greater or lesser extent, *all* of the above stages exist contemporaneously as women seek imaginative autonomy in a patriarchal culture. In addition, there is clear disagreement among women writers as to whether the term "post-patriarchal" should exist since many people feel that society is still male-dominated. Although patriarchal society has not disappeared, I use the term "post-patriarchal" to denote a period of self-consciousness in which gender relations have changed in theory, if not in actual practice.

Women in a Misogynist World (1945-1975)

During the late forties and early fifties, a number of important books written by female philosophers, anthropologists and historians concentrated their analysis on the problematic nature of women in a misogynist, patriarchal society. From Simone de Beauvoir's definition of women as "other" in *The Second Sex* (1949) to Mary Beard's *Woman as Force in History: A Study in Tradition and Realities* (1946) to Margaret Mead's *Male and Female* (1953), women theorists during the early post-war years were setting the stage for the publication of Betty Friedan's *The Feminine Mystique* in 1963. Showalter describes this phase of feminine theory as an attack on the "misogyny of literary practice . . . stereotypes, textual harassment" in all of its cultural manifestations. From this post-war anger comes Kate Millett's *Sexual Politics* (1970), a book that Elaine Showalter calls "the first major book of feminist criticism in this country" (Showalter 1985, 5).

In fact, the late sixties and early seventies are a fertile time for this assault on the "literature of misogyny," an attack admirably launched by Mary Ellman in her discussion of "phallic criticism" in *Thinking About Women* (1968). Other critiques of misogyny are found in Katharine Rogers' *The Troublesome Helpmate: A History of Misogyny in Literature* (1966); Eva Figes' *Patriarchal Attitudes* (1970); Elizabeth Janeway's *Man's World, Woman's Place: A Study in Social Mythology* (1971), Germaine Greer's *The Female Eunuch* (1971); Susan Koppelman Cornillon's edited collection, *Images of Women in Fiction: Feminist Perspectives* (1972); and Mary Allen's *The Necessary Blankness: Women in Major American Fiction of the Sixties* (1976), to name but a few of the many excellent books which, according to Ellen Dubois "establish incontrovertibly the existence and varieties of male bias in traditional academic inquiry."[1]

Complementing this theoretical indictment of misogyny are numerous literary anthologies which focus on "images" of women in literature and gather together literary stereotypes of women created by both male and female authors. These collections, which provide students, teachers and interested readers with an opportunity to analyze the male defined images of women include: Mary Anne Ferguson's *Images of Women in Literature* (1973), Michelle Murray's *A House of Good Proportion* (1973), Pat Rotter's *Bitches and Sad Ladies: An Anthology of Fiction By and About Women* (1975), and Barbara Solomon's *The Experience of the American Woman* (1978). Many of these books raise women's consciousness about their fate in both literature and life; critics begin to answer the question, "Why Are There No Great Women Artists?" asked by art critic Linda Nochlin in an essay included in Vivian Gornick and Barbara Moran's important essay collection from this period, *Woman in Sexist Society: Studies in Power and Powerlessness* (1972).

As politically powerful as this first phase of feminist theorizing was, however, it had its limitations. Despite its best intentions to seek solutions, a literary politics based on male domination and abuse was often negative and reactionary. It saw the male as the norm and the woman as the deviation, the male as the tyrant and the woman as the victim. In order for women writers to define a new literary order, they would have to be proactive instead of defensive, creative instead of protective. What was needed in the mid-seventies, therefore, was a new direction for feminist inquiry. And, it is possible, that the feminist analysis of rape by Susan Brownmiller in 1975 provided just the requisite catalyst for the transition from the first theoretical phase of post-war feminist theory to the second. For it was Brownmiller who began to discuss rape, discrimination and other acts of violence against women as political oppression, not social deviancy in her landmark book *Against Our Will: Men, Women and Rape* (1975).

Importantly, at the same moment, Annette Kolodny was making the link between the political and the aesthetic meaning of rape in her critical work, *The Lay of the Land: Metaphor as Experience and History in American Life and Letters* (1975) which connects male sexual violence and American literature through the violent "land-as-woman symbolization."[2] Kolodny argues that in their quest for domination over people and nature, men "rape" either literally or metaphorically the passive nature around them. The association, therefore, between a peaceful women's and a violent men's culture and language becomes an immensely important concept in the second phase of women's literary theory in the late 70s and early 80s.

In an essay entitled "Rethinking the Seventies: Women Writers and Violence," (1981) Elaine Showalter quotes Brownmiller's assertion that women must go on the offensive in the fight against violence; women, themselves must "redress the imbalance and rid ourselves and men of the ideology of rape."[3] Showalter, Brownmiller and other critics call for an end to the victimization of women by men in literature and life. And, in another of her perceptive essays entitled, "Towards a Feminist Poetics" (1979) Showalter encourages women to reject male cultural violence and the female preoccupation with misogyny and victimization; she hopes that during the eighties, women's imaginations will take them beyond violence to a new positive, life-affirming literature *defined by female*, not male values. Showalter suggests that the female-centered morality of Adrienne Rich may designate her as the "spokeswoman for a new women's writing," a literature "which explores the will to change" (Showalter 1985, 135). And it is in "female-centered aesthetic" that the second phase of women's theory exists from 1975 to the early eighties.

A Woman-Centered World of Literature, Thought and Language: 1975-1985

In 1979, historian Gerder Lerner published an important book on women and history entitled *The Majority Finds Its Past: Placing Women in History*. After analyzing a series of provocative issues on the impact and influence of women's culture, Lerner asks her reader to reflect upon a question of central importance: "What would history be like if it were seen through the eyes of women and ordered by values they define?"[4] The answer to this question is what Elaine Showalter calls "gyno-criticism" and a "woman-centered inquiry" in her essay, "Feminist Criticism in the Wilderness" (Showalter 1985, 260). Gynocriticism and its gynocritics no longer dwell on the sins of male misogyny; rather gynocriticism concentrates its efforts on defining and analyzing the female imagination in literature, language, feeling and ethics. Showalter defines the women's cultural tradition as "a collective experience within the cultural whole, an experience that binds women writers to each other over time and space" (Showalter 1985, 260). Whether literal or metaphorical, male rape is left behind as Showalter and other gynocritics "map the territory of the female imagination and the structures of the female plot" including a more positive and less defensive "female aesthetic" from which feminine philosophies may develop (Showalter 1985, 6).

Although Showalter coined the phrase, "gynocriticism," she was hardly alone in her dedication to "mapping the territory" of women's culture. The seventies and eighties are a powerful moment in women's critical and imaginative writing. Among the influential works of the period are Patricia Spacks' *The Female Imagination* (1975) which analyzes uniquely feminine literary themes; Nina Auerbach's *Communities of Women: An Idea in Fiction* (1978) which compares nineteenth and twentieth century conceptions of women in communities; Ellen Moers' *Literary Women* (1976) which defines a new female heroism distinct from male heroism. Other important books which help to transform women's thinking during this period are: Elaine Showalter's *A Literature of Their Own: British Women Novelists from Bronte to Lessing* (1977); Nina Baym's *Woman's Fiction: A Guide to Novels By and About Women in America, 1820-1870* (1978); Sandra Gilbert and Susan Gubar's definition of a female tradition in *The Madwoman in the Attic: The Woman Writer and the 19th Century Literary Imagination* (1979) and their edited collection, *Shakespeare's Sisters: Feminist Essays on Women Poets* (1979).

At this point, many women writers also turn their attention to the traditional genres of literature including fiction, poetry, drama and autobiography. Their efforts to create a female literary tradition are seen in Dianne Middlebrook and Marilyn Yalom's *Coming to Light: American Women Poets in the Twentieth Century* (1983); Estelle Jelinek's edition on *Women's Autobiography: Essays in Criticism* (1980) and Helene Keyssar's *Feminist Theatre: An Introduction to Plays of Contemporary British and American Women* (1985) all of which provide new female traditions within literary genres.

If some of the early analyses on the "female" literary tradition tend to homogenize the female experience, it did not take long for women from a variety of races, religions and ethnicities to suggest that there are *many* female literary traditions. The late seventies and early eighties witnessed the publication of critical works which mapped the territory of race, religion, class and ethnicity as well as gender. They included Barbara Christian's

Black Women Novelists: The Development of a Tradition, 1892-1976 (1980); Mari Evan's *Black Women Writers, 1950-1980* (1983); bell hooks' *Ain't I a Woman: Black Women and Feminism* (1981); Gloria Hull, Patricia Bell Scott, and Barbara Smith, eds., *All the Women Are White, All the Blacks Are Men, but Some of Us Are Brave* (1982); Trudier Harris' *From Mammies to Militants: Domestics in American Literature* (1982); Hazel V. Carby's *Reconstructing Womanhood: The Emergence of the Afro-American Woman Novelist* (1987), Joanne Braxton and Andrea McLaughlin's anthology *Wild Women in the Whirlwind: Afra-American Culture and the Contemporary Literary Renaissance* (1989) and Toni Morrison's *Playing in the Dark: Blackness and the American Literary Imagination* (1992).

Two important interpreters of the female imagination at this stage are Adrienne Rich and Alice Walker. In her collection of essays, *In Search of Our Mothers' Gardens* (1983) Walker celebrates both "womanist" prose and motherhood as well as the African-American literary tradition. Probably the most important book on motherhood, and one that connects the first "misogynist" phase and the second "female tradition," is Adrienne Rich's *Of Woman Born: Motherhood As Experience and Institution* (1976). Rich's praise of the mother/daughter relationship as a powerful antidote to destructive patriarchal relationships urges women to deflect men's anger and concentrate on loving female relationships of all kinds. This emphasis on motherhood and sisterhood is also reflected in Cathy Davidson and E. M. Broner's edited collection of essays, *The Lost Tradition: Mothers and Daughters in Literature* (1980). Motherhood and the female literary tradition are also discussed in Marianne Hirsch's *The Mother/Daughter Plot* (1989) and Kathryn Allen Rabuzzi's *Motherself: A Mythic Analysis of Motherhood* (1988).

It is also at this point that women's sexual preference becomes another deciding factor in their literary tradition. The topic of lesbianism, often hidden from public acknowledgement by female and male authors alike, finally receives attention as a number of critics begin to construct a lesbian literary tradition. Jane Rule's work *Lesbian Images* (1975) analyzes the various images of female homosexual love in literature. Barbara Grier's *Lesbian Lives* (1976) as well as Lillian Faderman's *Surpassing the*

Love of Men: Friendship and Love Between Women from the Renaissance to the Present (1981) begin to construct a literary canon. Bonnie Zimmerman's "What Has Never Been: An Overview of Lesbian Feminist Literary Criticism" (1981) and an edited collection by Margaret Cruikshank entitled *Lesbian Studies: Present and Future* also provide an excellent starting point.

Responding to the new interest in a women's literary tradition, colleges and academic publishers began to create "women's studies" departments and books series. One of the most important book publications was the *Norton Anthology of Literature By Women: The Tradition in English* (1985) edited by Sandra Gilbert and Susan Gubar which traces the development of women's writing from medieval to contemporary times. Although the Gilbert and Gubar volume signalled the formation of the first "canon" of women's writing, it was certainly not the first publication of its kind. Nine years earlier in 1974, Louise Bernikow compiled *The World Split Open: Four Centuries of Women Poets in England and America, 1552-1950*, her own attempt to rediscover a lost female poetic tradition. An excellent bibliography of early seventies anthologies can be found in Esther Stineman's *Women's Studies: A Recommended Core Bibliography* (1979).

The literature of women from different races, religions, classes, nationalities and sexual preferences was also widely published in the seventies and eighties. Pat Exum's *Keeping the Faith: Writings by Contemporary Black American Women* (1974); Mary Washington's *Black-eyed Susans: Classic Stories By and About Black Women* (1975) and Roseann Bell et al's *Sturdy Black Bridges: Visions of Black Women in Literature* (1979) are followed by multicultural collections like Dexter Fisher's *The Third Woman: Minority Women Writers of the United States*; Cherrie Moraga and Gloria Anzaldua's *This Bridge Called My Back: Writings by Radical Women of Color* (1981). Native American women are represented in Jane Katz' *I Am the Fire of Time: The Voices of Native American Women* (1977); Rayna Green's *That`s What She Said: Contemporary Poetry and Fiction by Native American Women* (1984); Paula Gunn Allen's *The Sacred Hoop: Recovering the Feminine in American Indian Traditions* (1986) and her edited literary anthology, *Spider Woman's Granddaughters: Traditional Tales and*

Contemporary Writing by Native American Women (1989). Paula Gunn Allen has also written an excellent bibliographical article on women of color entitled, "`Border Studies': The Intersection of Gender and Color" for the Modern Language Association's *Introduction to Scholarship in Modern Languages and Literatures* (1992).

During the seventies, the Modern Language Association responded to the interest in "women's studies" by publishing curriculum materials for college and public school teachers who wished to transform their traditional literature courses. The MLA's Commission on the Status of Women collected and produced seven volumes of course syllabi during the seventies, while the Hunter College Women's Studies Collective published its own, *Women's Realities, Women's Choices: An Introduction to Women's Studies* (1983). Other excellent sources for information include A. LaVonne Brown Ruoff & Jerry W. Ward, Jr.'s *Redefining American Literary History* (1990) and Paul Lauter's *Reconstructing American Literature: Courses, Syllabi, Issues* (1983) which also provided introductions to new materials on women. For an extensive listing of American and international women's literature as well as a selection of literary anthologies based on such topics as religion, motherhood, social inequities, see Esther Stineman's *Women's Studies: A Recommended Core Bibliography*, 1980-1985 (1987), edited with Catharine Loeb and Susan Searing. Another excellent source for materials is Virginia Blain, Isobel Grundy and Patricia Clements' exhaustive new dictionary, *The Feminist Companion to Literature in English* (1990) and Elaine Showalter's bibliography in the *New Feminist Criticism* (1985).

Contemporaneously with the creation of a "female literary tradition," another more abstract linguistic movement emerged as well. Inspired by the new psychological research in femininity and motherhood produced by Carol Gilligan, Nancy Chodorow as well as based on some of the French deconstructionist, linguistic theories of Jacques Lacan, Michel Foucault and Jacques Derrida, a new "female aesthetic" in language and thought was conceptualized. While the female literary tradition sought to construct a new or alternative canon of women's writings and to retrieve those female writers "lost to history," the interest in a female writing style or as the French feminist theorists termed it "l'ecriture feminine," sought to create a women's language which would disrupt the Western patriarchal language. If women had their own literary tradition, these writers argued, wouldn't it be logical that they would also have their own linguistic/aesthetic style and value system as well? And wouldn't, therefore, this woman's language be as subversive to male language as any other female enterprise?

The search for the female aesthetic took many forms in the seventies and eighties. In *The Resisting Reader: A Feminist Approach to American Fiction* (1978), Judith Fetterley cautions women to "resist" reading against themselves in male texts while Helene Cixous suggests playful defiance in her famous essay, "The Laugh of the Medusa" (1975). In 1980, many of the French feminist linguistic theories became available in translation when Elaine Marks and Isabell de Courtivron edited *New French Feminisms: An Anthology*.

In addition, the politics of gender "difference" became a focal point for discussion in literature and criticism during this period. Female and male conceptions of psychology and spirituality were analyzed in Shirley Garner's anthology, *The (M)other Tongue: Essays in Feminist Psychoanalytic Interpretation* (1985); Carol Christ's *Diving Deep and Surfacing: Women Writers on Spiritual Quest* (1980) and Elizabeth Abel, Marianne Hirsch and Elizabeth Langland in *The Voyage in: Fictions of Female Development* (1983). Linguistic differences were analyzed in Mary Jacobus' *Women Writing and Writing About Women* (1979) and Gayle Greene and Coppelia Kahn's anthology, *Making a Difference: Feminist Literary Criticism* (1985).

Although debates on gender difference tend to be highly abstract, they are no less political than other forms of feminist inquiry which deconstruct power relations in literature and life. In her essay, "Dancing Through the Minefield: Some Observations on the Theory, Practice and Politics of a Feminist Literary Criticism" (1980), Annette Kolodny invokes a series of military metaphors to characterize her own type of literary criticism as "an acute and impassioned attentiveness to the ways in which primarily male structures of power are inscribed (or encoded) within our literary inheritance."[5] Her goal is clear and her target is precise. Those involved in this literary "guerilla" warfare ultimately desire to "expose" the "minefield" of male bias for what it is—"the male fear of sharing power and significance with women" (Kolodny, 163). Therefore, the oppressive power of patriarchal society, whether it is found in language, literature or the actual lives of real women was under attack in the seventies and early eighties as women and men lined up on different sides of the battlefield of gender difference. By the mid-eighties, many feminist critics would agree with Catherine Belsey and Jane Moore's contention in their book *The Feminist Reader: Essays in Gender and the Politics of Literary Criticism* (1989) that "for the feminist reader there is no innocent or neutral approach to literature: all interpretation is political."[6]

Prisoners of Gender: 1985-present

Although the emphasis on feminine "difference" during the seventies and eighties helped to define the female imagination and its literature and language, some critics and artists worried that it also initiated an unproductive sexual separatism. Several critics suggested that an exclusive focus on female texts might marginalize women's writing further, creating a female "ghetto" for women's literature. Feminist historian Elizabeth Fox-Genovese criticized a woman-centered analysis for placing too much emphasis on biology and not enough on race, class and ethnicity. Other female authors were also concerned that a "woman's culture" might be biologically "essentialist" in nature, once again defining women exclusively in terms of their anatomy. Women of color sometimes viewed this female culture as a "homogenizing" of women's experiences which ignored the social contexts that separate one woman's reality and opportunities from another's.

In an article entitled, "Archimedes and the Paradox of Feminist Criticism" (1981), Myra Jehlen cautions women not to overlook the social and political realities that separate them as well as the spiritual values which unite them. She is also concerned that women not "mystify" male oppression by suggesting that it is the stimulus instead of the impediment to female creativity. Jehlen and other Marxist feminist critics look forward to the day when "women's studies" might encompass both genders and, therefore, become "an investigation, from women's viewpoint, of everything, thereby finding a way to engage the dominant intellectual systems directly and organically."[7]

In her book *Speaking of Gender* (1989), Elaine Showalter also views the early eighties as a time of increasing interest in gender by both female and male critics. Showalter praises the "radical comparativism"[8] of gender critics Myra Jehlen, Coppelia Hahn, Linda Bamber and Eve Kosofsky Sedgwick who read female and male texts in pairs in order to ascertain cultural values and standards. In this way, male texts are no longer read exclusively as examples of misogyny or female victimization. From this new perspective, both women and men are seen as "prisoners of gender" or "inscriptions of gender" (5). Critic Naomi Schor concurs with Showalter and hypothesizes that feminism "gives way" to gender studies around 1985.[9]

This transformation from woman-centered criticism to gender theory is not without its opponents, however. Critics worry that gender studies may lose its political dimension, that it will become a "pallid assimilation of feminist criticism" and, possibly, "a way for both male and female critics to avoid the political commitment of feminism" (Showalter 1989, 10). However, Elaine Showalter and other gender critics reject the contention that gender studies will have a depoliticizing effect on feminism. Instead, Showalter interprets her actions as "a step further towards post-patriarchy. . . . a step worth trying to take together" (Showalter 1989, 11).

In the nineties, female and male gender critics now look forward to a community of egalitarian thinkers who are willing to analyze both genders in order to find answers to inequality in literature and life: sexism, homophobia, domestic violence, racism and religious prejudice. In her essay on "Feminist and Gender Studies"(1992) for the Modern Language Association, Naomi Schor maintains that despite its evolution, feminism is still "a radical and always political form of interdisciplinary or transdisciplinary critique" (Schor, 272).

The feminist response to what Toril Moi first defined in 1987 as "post-patriarchy"[10] has made profound changes in the literary criticism ever since. Eve Kosofsky Sedgwick's *Between Men*:

English Literature and Homosocial Desire (1985) was published in the same year as Sheila Macleod's *Lawrence's Men and Women* and Janet Batsleer's *Rewriting English: Cultural Politics of Gender and Class*. Indicative of the new cross-gendered analysis is Alice Jardine and Paul Smith's anthology, *Men in Feminism* (1987), R. Howard Bloch and Frances Ferguson's collection *Misogyny, Misandry,and Misanthropy* (1989), novelist Terry McMillan's *Breaking Ice: An Anthology of Contemporary African-American Fiction* (1990), as well as Henry Gates' anthologies, *Race, Writing and Difference* (1985) and *Reading Black, Reading Feminist* (1990). An excellent example of the desire on the part of feminist critics to "balance" male and female differences is Joan Tronto's article, "Beyond Gender Differences to a Theory of Care (1987) which argues that a woman's concern with "caring" needs to be balanced by the male preoccupation with "justice" in order to arrive at the optimum morality.[11]

During the nineties, feminist criticism shares many of the same goals with cultural criticism which seeks to evaluate the political and social contexts of "high" art and popular literature. Tania Modleski's *Loving with a Vengeance: Mass-Produced Fantasies for Women* (1982); Janice Radway's *Reading the Romance: Women, Patriarchy, and Popular Literature* (1984) and Mary Poovey's *The Proper Lady and the Woman Writer* (1984) are several excellent examples of feminist interest in popular culture. The multi-gendered approach to serious literature is evident in the work of Gayatri C. Spivak's *In Other Worlds: Essays in Cultural Politics* (1987); Barbara Ehrenreich's *The Hearts of Men: American Dreams and the Flight from Commitment* (1983); Jane Miller's *Women Writing About Men* (1986) as well as Sandra Gilbert and Susan Gubar's multi-volume series *No Man's Land: The Place of the Woman Writer in the Twentieth Century* (1988, 1989) all of which assess the position of women and men within a specific social context or chronological period in literature and culture.

It should not be assumed from this discussion, however, that there is only one form of turn-of-the-century feminism. Despite the movement towards gender criticism, there are still many feminists who insist on either a separation from the violent, hurtful patriarchal world or a complete dismantling of gender demarcations altogether. Two examples of these positions are found in the work of Andrea Dworkin and Linda Alcoff respectively. Essayist, novelist and anti-pornography activist Andrea Dworkin advocates a sexual as well as political separatism from men in her book-length essay *Intercourse* (1987), while post-structuralist Linda Alcoff criticizes feminists who believe that "woman" is an innate rather than a socially constructed quality. Alcoff views gender as just another example of identity beyond the control of any individual, a condition controlled more by language, history or psychology. In fact, Alcoff goes so far as to suggest that "woman" is "a fiction . . . that feminist efforts must be directed toward dismantling . . . Women should refuse to be defined at all and instead work for the de-gendering"[12] of all people.

The Past and the Future: Feminisms and Contemporary Women's Literature

Perhaps the best example of the plurality and multi-visioned perspective that is the trademark of contemporary feminist theory is evident in a 1970 dialogue between two esteemed literary critics, Carolyn Heilbrun and Catharine Stimpson, which was reprinted by Josephine Donovan in 1989.[12] In their "debate" about the ultimate goals of literature, Stimpson takes the role of the politically active feminist, most closely associated with the view that "the personal is political." Heilbrun, however speaks for the woman-centered aesthetic position in contemporary feminist thought which removes itself from the political arena. As a "textual archaeologist,"[13] Stimpson wants to seek out and subvert patterns and stereotypes of patriarchal oppression: "A text is a force, not an artifact," she argues with Heilbrun. "A text may help to invigorate us" (Heilbrun and Stimpson, 66). Stimpson's goal is the equality of power relations, both within and outside the literary text. Displaying both the passion and activism of post-World War Two feminism, Stimpson questions the practical function of literature altogether when she asks Heilbrun: "After we have expressed our anger, and recognized it, and turned it away from ourselves, to what do we turn our attention beyond the amelioration of social inequalities" (64).

Stimpson clearly wishes to "practice" feminism as well as explicate it in a text.

As a feminist critic, Carolyn Heilbrun does not reject Stimpson's position, but rather seeks to provide a philosophical complement to Stimpson's activism. Heilbrun contends that while Stimpson "look[s] for the ways in which women have *not* been represented in literature," she "look[s] for the imaginative world that often lies unseen, at least in much literature" (63). Heilbrun's ideal critic is less political, less concerned with actual power relations, "aloof from the practical view of things," while Stimpson's feminist critic is "capable of simultaneous actions, disinterestedness *and* advocacy" (67).

And yet—despite their differences—both women authors are decidedly political. While Stimpson's feminism seeks to liberate women from restrictive gender roles, Heilbrun concentrates on choice for both sexes: "What we need now is to give *men* the vicarious experience of renunciation and awareness," she argues. "I am ready to use the literature of the world to train men to read themselves, rather than only to train women to notice how unheard or exploited they have been . . . [male] violence and the love of action are learned more easily than awareness or love" (72).

Although this debate is well over twenty years old, it is, in some important respects, still the major dilemma confronting women and literature at the end of the twentieth century. It suggests the strength of the feminist vision since it allows for mutual respect of disparate opinions within the same literary movement. The Heilbrun/Stimpson debate does not end with a final "victory" for either side; instead, Heilbrun, acknowledges the debt that she owes to the work of the scholar/activists who preceded her. "I have built my ideal feminist critic, as men have been wont to do, on the hard work of women," she concedes to Stimpson at the end of the dialogue. "But unlike men, I acknowledge the debt and know that without your feminist criticism there would be no foundation for mine" (73). And, if it is possible to delineate the single most important theory which post-war women's literature and thought have contributed, it would have to be this belief in compromise and the necessity of sharing power among all peoples. If there is a "language of power" in women's literature, it is found in Stimpson and Heilbrun's faith in balance and harmony—a shared vision of a world without winners and losers, a vision genuinely needed in the closing years of the contentious and often violent twentieth century.

Notes

1. Ellen DuBois et al, *Feminist Scholarship: Kindling in the Groves of Academe* (Urbana: University of Illinois Press, 1987), 36.

2. Annette Kolodny, *The Lay of the Land: Metaphor as Experience and History in American Life and Letters* (Chapel Hill: University of North Carolina Press, 1975), ix.

3. Elaine Showalter, "Rethinking the Seventies: Women Writers and Violence," in *Women's Voices*, ed. Pat Hoy et al (New York: McGraw Hill, 1990), 572.

4. Gerda Lerner, *The Majority Finds Its Past: Placing Women in History* in *The New Feminist Criticism*, ed. Elaine Showalter (New York: Pantheon Books, 1985), 260.

5. Annette Kolodny, "Dancing Through the Minefield: Some Observations on the Theory, Practice, and Politics of Feminist Literary Criticism," in *New Feminist Criticism*, ed. Elaine Showalter (New York: Pantheon Books, 1985), 162.

6. Catherine Belsey and Jane Moore, "Introduction," in *The Feminist Reader: Essays in Gender and the Politics of Literary Criticism* (New York: Basil Blackwell, 1989), 1.

7. Myra Jehlen, "Archimedes and the Paradox of Feminist Criticism," in *The Signs Reader: Women, Gender & Scholarship*, ed. Elizabeth and Emily Abel (Chicago: University of Chicago Press, 1983), 71.

8. Elaine Showalter, "Introduction," in *Speaking of Gender*, ed. Elaine Showalter (New York: Routledge, 1989), 5.

9. Naomi Schor, "Feminist and Gender Studies," in *Introduction to Scholarship in Modern Languages and Literatures*, second edition (New York: MLA, 1992), 275.

10. Toril Moi, "Introduction," in French Feminist Thought, ed. Toril Moi (London: Basil Blackwell, 1987), 12.

11. Joan Tronto, "Beyond Gender Differences to a Theory of Care," *Signs* (Summer 1987), 644-63.

12. Linda Alcoff, "Cultural Feminism versus Post-Structuralism: The Identity Crisis in Feminist Theory," in *Feminist Theory in Practice and Process*, ed. Micheline Malson et al. (Chicago: University of Chicago Press, 1986), 307-10.

13. Carolyn Heilbrun and Catharine Stimpson, "Theories of Feminist Criticism: A Dialogue," in *Feminist Literary Criticism: Explorations of Theory,* ed. Josephine Donovan (Lexington: University of Kentucky Press, 1989), 62.

Works Cited

Secondary Sources

Abel, Elizabeth and Emily Abel, eds. *The Signs Reader: Women, Gender & Scholarship*. Chicago: University of Chicago Press, 1983.

Abel, Elizabeth, Marianne Hirsch, and Elizabeth Langland, eds. *The Voyage In: Fictions of Female Development*. Hanover: University Press of New England, 1983.

Allen, Mary. *The Necessary Blankness: Women in Major American Fiction of the Sixties*. Urbana: University of Illinois Press, 1976.

Allen, Paula Gunn. *The Sacred Hoop: Recovering the Feminine in American Traditions*. Boston: Beacon Press, 1986.

Auerbach, Nina. *Communities of Women: An Idea in Fiction*. Cambridge: Harvard University Press, 1978.

Bartkowski, Frances. *Feminist Utopias*. Lincoln, Nebraska: University of Nebraska Press, 1989.

Belsey, Catherine, and Jane Moore, eds. *The Feminist Reader: Essays in Gender and the Politics of Literary Criticism*. New York: Basil Blackwell, 1989.

Benstock, Shari, ed. *Feminist Issues in Literary Scholarship*. Bloomington: Indiana University Press, 1987.

Blain, Virginia, Isobel Grundy and Patricia Clements, eds. *The Feminist Companion to Literature in English*. New Haven: Yale University Press, 1990.

Boneparth, Ellen and Emily Stoper, eds. *Women, Power and Policy: Toward the Year 2000*. Second Edition. New York: Pergamon Books, 1988.

Braxton, Joanne and Andrea McLaughlin, eds. *Wild Women in the Whirlwind: Afra-American Culture and the Contemporary Literature Renaissance*. New Brunswick: Rutgers University Press, 1989.

Brownmiller, Susan. *Against Our Will: Men, Women, and Rape*. New York: Simon and Schuster, 1975.

Brownstein, Rachel. *Becoming a Heroine: Reading About Women in Novels*. New York: Viking Press, 1982.

Carby, Hazel. *Reconstructing Womanhood: The Emergence of the Afro-American Woman Novelist*. New York: Oxford University Press, 1989.

Christ, Carol. *Diving Deep and Surfacing: Women Writers on Spiritual Quest*. Boston: Beacon Press, 1980.

——— and Judith Plaskow, eds. *Womanspirit Rising: A Feminist Reader in Religion*. New York: Harper & Row, 1979.

Christian, Barbara. *Black Women Novelists: The Development of a Tradition, 1892-1976*. Westport: Greenwood, 1980.

Conway, Jill et al. *Learning About Women: Gender, Politics & Power*. Ann Arbor: University of Michigan Press, 1987.

Daly, Mary. *Beyond God the Father: Towards a Philosophy of Women's Liberation*. Boston: Beacon Press, 1973.

Davidson, Cathy, and E. M. Broner, eds. *The Lost Tradition: Mothers and Daughters in Literature*. New York: Frederick Ungar, 1980.

de Beauvoir, Simone. *The Second Sex*. Trans. by H. M. Parshley. New York: Vintage Books, 1952.

Dickstein, Morris. *Gates of Eden: American Culture in the Sixties*. New York: Penguin Books, 1977.

Donovan, Josephine, ed. *Feminist Literary Criticism: Explorations in Theory*. Second Edition. Lexington: University of Kentucky Press, 1989.

———. *Feminist Theory: The Intellectual Traditions of American Feminism*. New York: Frederick Ungar, 1985.

Du Plessis, Rachel Blau. *Writing Beyond the Ending*. Bloomington: Indiana University Press, 1985.

Ehrenreich, Barbara. *The Hearts of Men: American Dreams and the Flight from Commitment*. New York: Anchor Books, 1983.

Eisenstein, Hester. *Contemporary Feminist Thought*. Boston: G. K. Hall, 1983.

Ellmann, Mary. *Thinking About Women*. New York: Harcourt, Brace, Jovanovich, 1968.

Evans, Mari, ed. *Black Women Writers, 1950-80: A Critical Evaluation*. Garden City: Doubleday and Co., 1984.

Faderman, Lillian. *Surpassing the Love of Men: Romantic Friendship and Love Between Women From the Renaissance to the Present*. New York: William Morrow, 1981.

Fetterley, Judith. *The Resisting Reader: A Feminist Approach to American Fiction*. Bloomington: Indiana University Press, 1978.

Figes, Eva. *Patriarchal Attitudes: Women in Society*. New York: Persea Books, 1970.

Fox-Genovese, Elizabeth. *Feminism Without Illusions: A Critique of Individualism*. Chapel Hill: University of North Carolina Press, 1991.

Friedan, Betty. *The Feminine Mystique*. New York: Dell Books, 1963.

———. *The Second Stage*. New York: Summit Books, 1982.

Frye, Joanne. *Living Stories, Telling Lives: Women and the Novel In Contemporary Experience*. Ann Arbor: University of Michigan Press, 1986.

Gates, Henry L. *Reading Black, Reading Feminist: A Critical Anthology*. New York: Penguin Books, 1990.

Giddings, Paula. *When and Where I Enter: The Impact of Black Women on Race and Sex in America*. New York: Bantam Books, 1984.

Gilbert, Sandra M., and Susan Gubar. *The Madwoman in the Attic: The Woman Writer and the Nineteenth-Century Literary Imagination*. New Haven: Yale University Press, 1979.

———. *No Man's Land: The Place of the Woman Writer in the Twentieth Century*. Vols. 1 and 2. New Haven: Yale University Press, 1988 and 1989.

———. "Sex Wars—Not the 'Fun' Kind," *New York Times Book Review*, 27 December 1987, 23.

———. eds. *Shakespeare's Sisters: Feminist Essays on Women Poets*. Bloomington: Indiana University Press, 1979.

Gilligan, Carol. *In a Different Voice: Psychological Theory and Women's Development*. Cambridge: Harvard University Press, 1982.

Gordon, Mary. *Good Boys and Dead Girls and Other Essays*. New York: Random House, 1991.

Greer, Germaine. *The Female Eunuch*. New York: McGraw-Hill, 1971.

Hartmann, Susan. *From Margin to Mainstream: American Women and Politics Since 1960*. New York: Alfred A. Knopf, 1989.

Heilbrun, Carolyn. *Writing A Woman's Life*. New York: W. W. Norton and Company, 1988.

hooks, bell. *Ain't I a Woman? Black Women and Feminism*. Boston: South End Press, 1981.

Hymowitz, Carol and Michele Weissman. *A History of Women in America*. New York: Bantam Books, 1978.

Jacobus, Mary, ed. *Women Writing and Writing About Women*. New York: Barnes & Nobles, 1979.

Janeway, Elizabeth. "Women's Literature." In *Harvard Guide to Contemporary American Writing*, edited by Daniel Hoffman. 342-95. Cambridge: Harvard University Press, 1979.

Jelinek, Estelle, ed. *Women's Autobiography: Essays in Criticism*. Bloomington: Indiana University Press, 1980.

Kaledin, Eugenia. *Mothers and MORE: American Women in the 1950's*. Boston: Twayne Publishers, 1984.

Kolodny, Annette. *The Lay of the Land: Metaphor as Experience and History in American Life and Letters*. Chapel Hill: University of North Carolina Press, 1975.

Lerner, Gerda. *The Majority Finds Its Past: Placing Women in History*. New York: Oxford University Press, 1979.

Loeb, Catherine, Susan Searing and Esther Stineman. *Women's Studies: A Recommended Core Bibliography, 1980-1985*. Littleton, Colorado: Libraries Unlimited, 1987.

Lundberg, Ferdinand and Marynia Farnham. *Modern Woman: The Lost Sex*. New York: Harper & Brothers, 1946.

Middlebrook, Diane and Marilyn Yalom, eds. *Coming to Light: American Poets in the Twentieth Century*. Ann Arbor: University of Michigan Press, 1985.

Miller, Jane. *Women Writing About Men*. New York: Pantheon Books, 1986.

Millett, Kate. *Sexual Politics*. Garden City: Doubleday & Co., 1970.

Moers, Ellen. *Literary Women*. New York: Oxford University Press, 1976.

Morrison, Toni. *Playing in the Dark*: *Blackness and the American Literary Imagination*. Cambridge: Harvard University Press, 1992.

Ozick, Cynthia. *Art and Ardor: Essays*. New York: E.P. Dutton, Inc., 1984.

Pearlman, Mickey and Katherine Henderson. *A Voice of One's Own*: *Conversations with America's Writing Women*. Boston: Houghton Mifflin & Co., 1990.

Plaskow, Judith and Carol Christ, eds. *Weaving the Visions*: *New Patterns in Feminist Spirituality*. New York: Harper Collins, 1989.

Rabuzzi, Kathryn Allen. *Motherself: A Mythic Analysis of Motherhood*. Bloomington: Indiana University Press, 1988.

Rich, Adrienne. *Of Woman Born*: *Motherhood as Experience and Institution*. New York: Bantam Books, 1976.

———. *On Lies, Secrets, and Silence*: *Selected Prose, 1966-1979*. New York: W. W. Norton & Co., 1979.

Rigney, Barbara H. *Madness and Sexual Politics in the Feminist Novel*. Madison: University of Wisconsin Press, 1978.

———. *Lilith's Daughters*: *Women and Religion in Contemporary Fiction*. Madison: University of Wisconsin Press, 1982.

Sedgwick, Eve Kosofsky. *Between Men*: *English Literature and Male Homosocial Desire*. New York: Columbia University Press, 1985.

Showalter, Elaine. *A Literature of Their Own*: *British Women Novelists from Bronte to Lessing*. Princeton: Princeton University Press, 1977.

———. *The New Feminist Criticism*: *Essays in Women, Literature and Theory*. New York: Pantheon Books, 1985.

———, ed. *Speaking of Gender*. New York: Routledge & Co., 1989.

Spacks, Patricia. *The Female Imagination*. New York: Alfred A. Knopf, 1975.

Spretnak, Charlene, ed. *The Politics of Women's Spirituality*. New York: Anchor Books, 1982.

Sternburg, Janet, ed. *The Writer on Her Work*. New York: W. W. Norton & Co., 1980.

Stineman, Esther. *Women's Studies: A Recommended Core Bibliography*. Littleton, Colorado: Libraries Unlimited, 1979.

Tate, Claudia, ed. *Black Women Writers at Work*. New York: Crossroad/Continuum Books, 1983.

Wandersee, Winifred D. *On the Move: American Women in the 1970's*. Boston: Twayne Publishers, 1988.

Primary Works

Adcock, Fleur. Selected *Poems*. Oxford: Oxford University Press, 1983.

——, ed. *The Faber Book of 20th Century Women's Poetry*. Boston: Faber & Faber, 1987.

Allen, Paula Gunn, *Shadow Country*. Los Angeles: University of California Press, 1982.

——. ed. *Spider Woman's Granddaughters: Traditional Tales and Contemporary Writing by Native American Women*. Boston: Beacon Press, 1989.

Angelou, Maya. *I Know Why the Caged Bird Sings*. New York: Random House, 1970.

Arkin, Marian and Barbara Shollar, eds. *Longman Anthology of World Literature by Women, 1875-1975*. New York: Longman, 1989.

Atwood, Margaret. *Cat's Eye*. New York: Doubleday & Co., 1989.

——. *The Handmaid's Tale*. New York: Fawcett Books, 1985.

———. *Surfacing*. New York: Fawcett Books, 1972.

Bambara, Toni Cade. *Gorilla, My Love*. New York: Vintage Books, 1972.

Barnstone, Aliki, and Willis Barnstone, eds. *A Book of Woman Poets, From Antiquity to Now*. New York: Schocken Books, 1991.

Beattie, Ann. *Secrets and Surprises*. New York: Vintage, 1979.

Benedict, Elizabeth. *Slow Dancing*. New York: McGraw Hill, 1985.

Bernays, Anne. *Professor Romeo*. New York: Penguin Books, 1989.

Bishop, Elizabeth. *The Complete Poems*. New York: Farrar, Staus & Giroux, 1969.

Blicksilver, Edith ed. *The Ethnic American Woman: Problems, Protests, Lifestyle*. Dubuque, Iowa: Kendall/Hunt Publishing Company, 1989.

Broner, E. M. *Her Mothers*. New York: Holt, Rinehart, and Winston, 1975.

Brooks, Gwendolyn. *Blacks*. Chicago: Third World Press, 1991.

Brown, Rita Mae. *Rubyfruit Jungle*. New York: Bantam Books, 1973.

Boyle, Kay. *Thirty Stories*. New York: New Directions, 1957.

Cahill, Susan, ed. *New Women, New Fiction: Short Stories Since the Sixties*. New York: New American Library, 1986.

Calisher, Hortense. *The Collected Stories of Hortense Calisher*. New York: Arbor House, 1975.

Canan, Janine, ed. *She Rises Like the Sun*. Freedom, Ca.: The Crossing Press, 1989.

Cervantes, Lorna Dee. *Emplumada*. Pittsburgh: University of Pittsburgh Press, 1981.

Clifton, Lucille. *An Ordinary Woman*. New York: Random House, 1974.

———. *Two-Headed Woman*. Amherst: University of Massachusetts Press, 1980.

Cofer, Judith. *Triple Crown*. Houston: Bilingual Press, 1987.

Doolittle, Hilda. *Tribute to the Angels*. New York: Oxford University Press, 1945.

Drabble, Margaret. *The Millstone*. New York: New American Library, 1965.

Evans, Mari. *I Am a Black Woman*. New York: William Morrow, 1970.

Ferguson, Mary Anne. *Images of Women In Literature*. Fourth Edition. Boston: Houghton Mifflin Company, 1986.

Fisher, Dexter, ed. *The Third Woman: Minority Women Writers of the United States*. Boston: Houghton, Mifflin Company, 1980. French, Marilyn. *The Women's Room*. New York: Ballantine Books, 1977.

Gilbert, Sandra and Susan Gubar, eds. *The Norton Anthology of Literature by Women: The Tradition in English*. New York: W. W. Norton & Co., 1985.

Gilchrist, Ellen. *The Annunciation*. Boston: Little, Brown, & Co., 1983.

———. *Drunk With Love*. Boston: Little, Brown & Co., 1986.

Giovanni, Nikki. *Black Feeling, Black Talk, Black Judgement*. New York: William Morrow, 1968.

Godwin, Gail. *A Mother and Two Daughters*. New York: Viking Press, 1982.

Gordimer, Nadine. *Burger's Daughter*. New York: Viking Press, 1979.

———. *July's People*. New York: Viking Press, 1981.

———. *My Son's Story*. New York: Viking Press, 1990.

Gordon, Mary. *Final Payments*. New York: Random House, 1978.

———. *Men and Angels*. New York: Random House, 1987.

Grahn, Judy. *Queen of Wands*. Freedom, Ca.: The Crossing Press, 1982.

———. *The Work of a Common Woman*. Freedom, Ca.: The Crossing Press, 1978.

Griffin, Susan. *Like the Iris of An Eye*. New York: Harper & Row, 1976.

Hansberry, Lorraine. *A Raisin in the Sun*. New York: Random House, 1959.

Harjo, Joy. *She Had Some Horses*. New York: Thunder's Mouth Press, 1983.

Heilbrun, Carolyn. *Reinventing Womanhood*. New York: W. W. Norton & Co., 1979.

———. *Writing a Woman's Life*. New York: W. W. Norton & Co., 1988.

——— and Catharine Stimpson. "Theories of Feminist Criticism: A Dialogue." In *Feminist Literary Criticism: Explorations of Theory*, ed. Josephine Donovan. Lexington: University of Kentucky Press, 1989.

Henley, Beth. *Crimes of the Heart*. New York: Viking Press, 1982.

Howe, Florence, and Ellen Bass, eds. *No More Masks! An Anthology*. Garden City: Anchor Books, 1973.

Jackson, Shirley. The *Magic of Shirley Jackson*. New York: Farrar, Straus & Giroux, 1966.

Jong, Erica. *Fear of Flying*. New York: Holt, Rinehart and Winston, 1973.

Kingston, Maxine Hong. *The Woman Warrior: Memoirs of a Girlhood Among Ghosts*. New York: Random House, 1976.

Kizer, Carolyn. *Knock Upon Silence*. Seattle: University of Washington Press, 1963.

Kumin, Maxine. *The Retrieval System*. New York: Viking Press, 1978.

Lessing, Doris. *Martha Quest*. New York: Plume, 1952.

———. *The Golden Notebook*. New York: New American Library, 1962.

———. *A Proper Marriage*. New York: Plume Books, 1952.

Levertov, Denise. *Collected Earlier Poems, 1940-60*. New York: New Directions, 1979.

———. *O Taste and See*. New York: New Directions Publishing Co., 1962.

———. *Relearning the Alphabet*. New York: New Directions, 1970.

Livesay, Dorothy. *Collected Poems: The Two Seasons* (Toronto: McGraw-Hill Ryerson, Ltd. 1972.

Lorde, Audre. *Chosen Poems, Old and New*. New York: W. W. Norton & Co., 1982.

———. *Our Dead Behind Us*. New York: W. W. Norton & Co., 1986.

Lurie, Allison. *Foreign Affairs*. New York: Avon Books, 1984.

Marshall, Paule. *Reena and Other Stories*. New York: Feminist Press, 1983.

Martin, Wendy, ed. *We Are the Stories We Tell*. New York: Pantheon Books, 1990.

McCarthy, Mary. *Memories of a Catholic Girlhood*. New York: Penguin Books, 1957.

McCorkle, Jill. *Crash Diet: Stories*. Chapel Hill: Algonquin Books, 1992.

McCullers, Carson. *The Ballad of the Sad Cafe and other Stories*. New York: Bantam Books, 1951.

McMillan, Terry. *Disappearing Acts*. New York: Viking Press, 1989.

———. *Mama*. New York: Washington Square Press, 1987.

———. *Waiting to Exhale*. New York: Viking Press, 1992.

Moody, Anne. *Coming of Age in Mississippi: An Autobiography*. New York: Dell Books, 1970.

Moraga, Cherrie, and Gloria Anzaldua, eds. *This Bridge Called My Back: Writings by Radical Women of Color*. Second Edition. New York: Kitchen Table, Women of Color Press, 1983.

Morrison, Toni. *Beloved*. New York: New American Library, 1988.

———. *The Bluest Eye*. New York: Washington Square Press, 1970.

———. *Jazz*. New York: Alfred A. Knopf, 1992.

———. *Sula*. New York: New American Library, 1973.

Murdock, Iris. *A Severed Head*. New York: Viking Press, 1961.

Murray, Pauli. *Dark Testament and Other Poems*. Norwalk, Conn.,: Silvermine Publishers, 1970.

Naylor, Gloria. *The Women of Brewster Place*. New York: Penguin Books, 1980.

Oates, Joyce Carol. *Marriage and Infidelities*. New York: The Vanguard Press, 1972.

———. *The Wheel of Love and Other Stories*. New York: The Vanguard Press, 1970.

Olds, Sharon. *The Dead and the Living*. New York: Alfred A. Knopf, 1983.

O'Brien, Edna. *A Fanatic Heart: Selected Stories of Edna O'Brien*. New York: Farrar, Straus & Giroux, 1984.

———. *A Rose in the Heart of New York*. New York: Doubleday & Co., 1979.

O'Connor, Flannery. *Mystery and Manners*. New York: Farrar, Straus & Giroux, 1961.

———. *3 by Flannery O'Connor*. New York: New American Library, 1960.

Olsen, Tillie. *Tell Me a Riddle*. New York: Dell, 1976.

Ozick, Cynthia. *The Pagan Rabbi and other Stories*. New York: Alfred P. Knopf, 1971.

Paley, Grace. *Little Disturbances of Man*. New York: Penguin Books, 1985.

Petry, Ann. *The Street*. Boston: Beacon Press, 1946.

Piercy, Marge. *Available Light*. New York: Alfred A. Knopf, 1988.

———. *Circles on the Water: Selected Poems of Marge Piercy*. New York: Alfred A. Knopf, 1982.

———. *Woman on the Edge of Time*. New York: Fawcett Crest, 1976.

Plath, Sylvia. *The Collected Poems*. New York: Harper & Row, 1981.

Rich, Adrienne. *The Dream of a Common Language: Poems, 1974-1977*. New York: W. W. Norton, 1978.

———. *The Fact of a Doorframe: Poems Selected and New: 1950-84*. New York: W. W. Norton, 1984.

Roiphe, Anne. *Lovingkindness*. New York: Summit Books, 1987.

Rossner, Judith. *August*. Boston: Houghton Mifflin Company, 1983.

———. *Looking for Mr. Goodbar*. New York: Pocket Books, 1975.

Rukeyser, Muriel. *The Collected Poems*. New York: McGraw-Hill, 1978.

Russ, Joanna. *The Female Man*. Boston: Beacon Press, 1975.

Sachs, Nellie. *O the Chimneys: Selected Poems*. New York: Farrar, Straus, & Giroux, 1967.

Sanchez, Sonia. *Home Coming*. Chicago: Broadside Press, 1969.

Sarton, May. *Collected Poems: 1930-73*. New York: W. W. Norton & Co., 1974.

Sexton, Anne. *The Collected Poems*. Boston: Houghton Mifflin Company, 1981.

Shange, Ntozake. *for colored girls who have considered suicide/ when the rainbow is enuf: a choreopoem*. New York: Macmillan & Co., 1975.

Silko, Leslie Marmon. *Ceremony*. New York: Penguin Books, 1977.

———. Storyteller. New York: Seaver Books, 1981.

Smith, Stevie. *The Collected Poems of Stevie Smith*. (London: Allen Lane/Penguin Books, 1975.

Song, Cathy. *Chinatown*. New Haven: Yale University Press, 1983. Stafford, Jean. *The Collected Stories of Jean Stafford*. New York: Farrar, Straus & Giroux, 1969.

Stevenson, Anne. *Reversals* (Middletown, Conn.: Wesleyan University Press, 1973.

Swenson, May. *New and Selected Things Taking Place*. Boston: Little, Brown & Co., 1978.

Tan, Amy. *The Joy Luck Club*. New York: Ballantine Books, 1989.

Tyler, Anne. *The Accidental Tourist*. New York: Berkley Books, 1985.

Walker, Alice. *In Love and Trouble: Stories of Black Women*. New York: Harcourt, Brace and Jovanovich, 1973.

———. *Once: Poems*. New York: Harcourt, Brace, Jovanovich, 1968.

———. *The Color Purple*. New York: Washington Square Press, 1985.

———. *In Search of Our Mothers' Gardens: Womanist Prose*. New York: Harcourt Brace Jovanovich, 1983.

———. *Meridian*. New York: Pocket Books, 1976.

———. *Possessing the Secret of Joy*. New York: Harcourt Brace Jovanovich, 1992.

Walker, Margaret. *This is My Century: New and Collected Poems*. Athens: University of Georgia Press, 1989.

Washington, Mary Helen, ed. *Black-Eyed Susans, Midnight Birds: Stories by and About Black Women*. New York: Anchor Books, 1990.

Weldon, Fay. *The Hearts and Lives of Men*. New York: Penguin Books, 1988.

Welty, Eudora. *One Writer's Beginnings*. New York: Warner Books, 1983.

———. *The Optimist's Daughter*. New York: Vintage, 1969.

Whiteman, Roberta Hill. *Star Quilt*. Minneapolis: Holy Cow! Press, 1984.

Woolf, Virginia. *A Room of One's Own*. New York: Harcourt, Brace and Jovanovich, 1929.

Index

Adcock, Fleur, "Against Coupling," 90
Alcoff, Linda, 248
Allen, Mary 78
Allen, Paula Gunn, 13, 159, "Grandmother," 105, "Moonshot," 159-60, *Shadow Country*, 171, *The Voice of the Turtle* 223, *The Woman Who Owned the Shadows*, 226
Angelou, Maya, *I Know Why the Caged Bird Sings*, 41-2, 99-100, 202-3 *Now Sheba Sings the Song*, 170
Ansa, Tina McElroy, *Baby of the Family*, 107
Atkinson, Ti-Grace, 75
Atwood, Margaret, 10, 99, 102, 141-2, *Bodily Harm*, 50, *Cat's Eye*, 51-5, 146, 164-5, *The Handmaid's Tale*, 95-7, 112, 163-4 *Surfacing*, 145

Bambara, Toni Cade, 194, 197, "The Lesson," 210, "My Man Bovanne," 209-110
Bartowski, Frances, 44
Beattie, Ann, *Falling in Place*, 86, *Love Always*, 86, "Tuesday Nights," 86
Benedict, Elizabeth, *Slow Dancing*, 81-2, 85-6
Bernays, Anne, *Professor Romeo*, 113
Bishop, Elizabeth, "Roosters," 130, "Who in One Lifetime," 130-1
Blicksilver, Edith, *The Ethnic American Woman* 174
Boneparth, Ellen and Emily Stoper, 9, 33, 48,

Boyle, Kay, "Winter Night," 61-2
Broner, E. M., *Her Mothers*, 103, *A Weave of Women*, 44
Brookner, Anita, *The Misalliance*, 113
Brooks, Gwendolyn, "Blackstone Rangers," 196, "Bronzeville Woman," 29-30, "The Children of the Poor," 188-9, "Kitchenette, Building," 188, *Maud Martha* 189, "The Mother," 188, "Queen of the Blues," 30
Brown, Helen Gurley, 74
Brown, Rita Mae, *Rubyfruit Jungle*, 110-111
Brownmiller, Susan, 238

Callisher, Hortense, "Point of Departure," 90-1
Campbell, Janet, "On a Catholic Childhood," 158-9
Canan, Janine, *She Rises Like the Sun*, 169-70
Cancian, Francesca, 111
Canfield, Dorothy, "Sex Education," 65
Castillo, Ana, "Our Tongue Was Nahuatl," 158
Cervantes, Lorna Dee, "Poem for the Young White Man," 226, "Refugee Ship," 224
Cheever, Susan, *Looking for Work*, 50
Childress, Alice, *Like One of the Family*, 189
Chodorow, Nancy, 55, 75
Christ, Carol, 123-5, 138, 161-2
Chute, Carolyn, *The Beans of Egypt, Maine*, 106

Christian, Barbara, 184-5, 187, 191, 194
Cixous, Helene, 143, 244
Clifton, Lucille, "anna speaks of mary her daughter," 175, "the astrologer predicts at mary's birth," 175, "The Thirty Eighth Year of My Life," 104
Cofer, Judith Ortiz, "Latin Women Pray," 175
Colwin, Laurie, 115
Combahee River Collective, 214-5

de Beauvoir, Simone, *The Second Sex*, 2-3, 5, 124, 126-7, 183
Daly, Mary, 123, 139, 152, 161
Dickstein, Morris, 64
Doolittle, Hilda, (H.D.), 129-30
Drabble, Margaret, *The Middle Ground*, 50, *The Millstone*, 77, 93-4, *The Realm of Gold*, 50
Du Plessis, Rachel, 56, 61
Dworkin, Andrea, 10, 248

Ehrenreich, Barbara, 111
Erdrich, Louise, "Fleur," 169, *Love Medicine* 168, 227
Evans, Mari, "A Good Assassination Should Be Quiet," 199

Faderman, Lillian, 109
Fiedler, Leslie, 101-2
Figes, Eva, 75-6
Firestone, Shulamith, 75-6
Fisher, Dexter, *The Third Woman*, 222, 224-5
Flax, Jane, 10, 111
Fox-Genovese, Elizabeth, *Feminism Without Illusions*, 1-2, 4, 115, 236, 245
French, Marilyn, *The Women's Room*, 35, 38-9
Friedan, Betty, *The Feminine Mystique*, 1-2, 19, 66, 68, 137, *The Second Stage*, 46-8, 56

Gender Studies, 33-4, 111-4, 246-7
Giddings, Paula 185-6, 200
Gilbert, Sandra and Susan Gubar, 10, 94, 140
Gilchrist, Ellen, *Drunk With Love*, 86-8, 167, *The Annunciation*, 167
Gilligan, Carol, 55
Giovanni, Nikki, *Black, Feeling, Black Talk,/Black Judgement*, 195, "Knoxville, Tennessee," 198, "Nikki Rosa," 197-8
Godwin, Gail, *A Mother and Two Daughters*, 50, 105-6, *The Odd Woman*, 50
Goldenberg, Naomi, 163
Gordimer, Nadine 229-30
Gordon, Barbara, *I'm Dancing as Fast as I Can*, 50
Gordon, Caroline, *Collected Stories*, 134
Gordon, Mary, 166, 176, *The Company of Women*, 106, 165, *Final Payments*, 151-2, *Men and Angels*, 50, 165-6
Grahn, Judy, "The Queen of Wands," 170-1, *The Work of the Common Woman*, 40, 110
Griffin, Susan, "I Like to Think of Harriet Tubman," 49

Hansberry, Lorraine, *Raisin in the Sun*, 30-1
Hanisch, Carol, 4
Harjo, Joy, "The Book of Myths," 172, "Anchorage," 224
Hartmann, Susan, 34
Heilbrun, Carolyn, *Writing A Woman's Life*, 7, 236, *Reinventing Womanhood* 160-1
Heilbrun and Catharine Stimpson, 248-50
Henley, Beth, *Crimes of the Heart* 105
hooks, bell, *Ain't I A Woman*, 29
Humanae Vitae, 126

Hurston, Zora Neale, *Their Eyes Were Watching God*, 187

Jackson, Shirley, *Hangsman*, 31, *Life Among the Savages* 31, "The Lottery," 31, *Raising Demons* 31
Jaffee, Rona, *Class Reunion*, 35
Janeway, Elizabeth, 32
Jehlen, Myra 245-6
Jong, Erica, *Fear of Flying*, 68, 77, 81-3
Jordan, June, *Things That I do in the Dark*, 142

Kaufman, Sue, *Diary of a Mad Housewife*, 81
Kincaid, Jamaica, *Annie John*, 106
Kingston, Maxine Hong, 13, 104-5, 154, 225
Kizer, Carolyn, "Pro Femina," 40, *Mermaids in the Basement*, 170
Kolodny, Annette, 238
Kumin, Maxine, "The Envelope," 103

Levertov, Denise, "About Marriage," 88, "Advent 1966," 148, "The Ache of Marriage," 88, "The Dragon-Fly Mother," 170, "To the Snake," 131-2
Lerner, Gerda, 239
Lesbianism, in literature, 109-111, 241-2
Lessing, Doris, 3, 10, *The Golden Notebook*, 7-8, 35-8, *Martha Quest*, 25-7, 74, 129, *A Proper Marriage*, 69-71
Livesay, Dorothy, "Eve," 147
Lorde, Audre, 216, 230, *The Black Unicorn*, 205, "Call," 171-2, "On a Night of the Full Moon," 110, "Now That I Am Forever with Child," 103-4
Lowell, Robert, "Memories of West Street & Lepke," 1

Lundberg, Ferdinand and Marynia Farnham, 19, 63
Lurie, Allison, *Foreign Affairs*, 50-1

MacDonald, Betty, *The Egg and I*, 31
McCarthy, Mary, *Memories of a Catholic Girlhood*, 135-7, *The Group*, 35
McCorkle, Jill, *Crash Diet*, 113-4
McCullers, Carson, "Madame Zilensky," 27-8, "Ballad of Sad Cafe," 31
McMillan, Terry, 10, 218-9, *Disappearing Acts*, 193, 220-1 *Mama*, 107, 219-20, 221, *Waiting to Exhale*, 193
Marshall, Paule, *Brown Girl, Brownstone*, 191-2, "To Daduh, In Memoriam," 191-2, "Reena," 192-4
Masters, William and Virginia Johnson, 74
Mead, Margaret, 127
Millet, Kate, *Sexual Politics*, 6, 75
Moi, Toril, 246
Moody, Anne, *Coming of Age in Mississippi*, 202
Morrison, Toni, *Beloved*, 107, *The Bluest Eye*, 100-1, 211-2 *Sula*, 206, 212-3
Motherhood, in literature, 88-108, 241
Multicultural, literary anthologies 242-3
Murdoch, Iris, *A Severed Head*, 73
Murray, Pauli, "Ruth" 147-8

National Black Feminist Organization, 214
Naylor, Gloria, *The Women of Brewster Place*, 35, 42-4, 217-8

O'Brien, Edna, "The Call," 90, "A Rose in the Heart of New York," 149
O'Connor, Flannery, "The Displaced Person," 28-9, "A Good Man is Hard to

Find," 134-5, *Mystery and Manners*, 128-9
O'Neill, Nena and George, 74
Oates, Joyce Carol, "The Children," 80, *Do With Me What You Will*, 80, *Expensive People*, 80, *The Goddess and Other Women*, 80, *The Wheel of Love*, 79-80,
Ochs, Carol 162
Olds, Sharon, "Best Friends," 108-9
Olsen, Tillie, 13, "Tell Me A Riddle," 22-3, 132
Ostriker, Alicia, 163
Ozick, Cynthia, *Art and Ardor*, 141, 154-5, "The Pagan Rabbi," 155-6, "The Shawl," 174

Pagels, Elaine, 127, 140
Paley, Grace, "An Interest in Life," 67-8
Peck, Ellen and Judith Senderowitz, *Pronatalism*, 81
Petry, Ann, *The Street*, 190-1
Piercy, Marge, "To Be of Use," 40, "The Token Woman," 48-9, "Wellfleet Sabbath," 171, *Woman on the Edge of Time*, 44
Plaskow, Judith and Carol Christ, 162
Plath, Sylvia, 31, *The Bell Jar*, 23-5, 78-9, "Daddy," 68, 142-3, "Mary's Song," 148 "Nick and the Candlestick," 79
Porter, Katherine Anne, *Ship of Fools*, 132
Prose, Francine, "Malachi," 173-4

Rabuzzi, Kathryn Allen, 103
Raine, Kathleen, "Kore in Hades," 145
Rich, Adrienne, "Aunt Jennifer's Tigers," 21, *Dream of a Common Language*, 146, *Of Woman Born*, 4, 76, 91-3, 241, "Compulsory Heterosexuality" 10, 75, 102 "Living in Sin," 72-3, *Twenty-One Love Poems*, 110, "When We Dead Awaken," 20-1, 123, 138, 236-7, "Snapshots of a Daughter-in-Law," 21-2, 31
Rigney, Barbara Hill, 124, 142, 144
Roiphe, Anne, *Lovingkindness*, 97-9, 174, *The Pursuit of Happiness*, 174
Rose, Wendy, "Vanishing Point: Urban Indian," 223
Rosenberg, David, *Congregation* 173-4
Rossner, Judith, *August*, 50, 111, 145-6, *Looking for Mr. Goodbar*, 81, 84-5, 94
Ruddick, Sara, 106
Ruether, Rosemary, 172-3
Rukeyser, Muriel, "The Birth of Venus," 3, "No More Masks," 144-5
Russ, Joanna, *The Female Man*, 44-6

Sachs, Nellie, "O The Chimneys," 131
Saiving, Valerie, 127-8
Sanchez, Sonia, "to blk/record/buyers," 198-9, "liberation/poem," 203
Sarton, May, *Halfway to Silence*, 109, *The Magnificent Spinster*, 109, "My Sisters, O, My Sisters," 3
Sexton, Anne, "Awful Rowing Towards God," 156-8, "Consorting With Angels," 39, "For My Lover, Returning to His Wife," 89, "Housewife," 39, "The Jesus Papers," 156-7
Shange, Ntozake, *for colored girls*, 150-1, 215-6
Showalter, Elaine, 10, 94, 238-9 "gynocriticism," 236, 239-40, *Speaking of Gender*, 246,

"Towards a Feminist Poetics," 239
Shulman, Alix K., *Memoirs of an Ex-Prom Queen*, 81, 83-4
Silko, Leslie Marmon, 229, *Ceremony*, 161, 228-9 "Lullaby," 227-8
Smith, Barbara, 183-4
Smith, Stevie, "How Cruel is the Story of Eve," 147
Song, Cathy, "Chinatown," 225-6
Spacks, Patricia, 37
Spretnak, Charlene, 144
Stafford, Jean, "Cops and Robbers," 72
Stevenson, Anne, "The Suburb," 80-1
Swensen, May, "The Centaur," 66-7, "Women," 91
Stimpson, Catharine, "Preface," xi-xiii, with Caroline Heilbrun, 248-50

Tan, Amy, *The Joy Luck Club*, 107, 174, 224
Tate, Claudia 184
Tepperman, Jean, "Witch," 91, 143
Tyler, Anne, *The Accidental Tourist*, 107-8, *Dinner at the Homesick Restaurant*, 50, *Searching for Caleb*, 107, *St. Maybe*, 107

Walker, Alice, 10, 13, 101, 149-50, *The Color Purple*, 168, 207-9, "Everyday Use," 150, 206-7, *In Search of Our Mother's Gardens*, 103, 133, 150, 176, 183, 195, 204-5, 215, *Meridian*, 200-02, *Once*, 196, *Possessing the Secret of Joy*, 216, *The Temple of My Familiar*, 175
Walker, Margaret, *For My People* 160, 190, *Prophets for a New Day*, 160, "Since 1619," 133
Weldon, Fay, 10, *The Hearts and Lives of Men*, 112
Welty, Eudora, "Circe," 71-2, *One Writer's Beginnings*, 104
West, Rebecca, 88
Whiteman, Roberta Hill, "Dream of Rebirth," 226-7
Williams, Sherley Anne, *Dessa Rose*, 211
Wittig, Monique, *Les Guerilleres*, 44, 140
Wolitzer, Hilma, "Waiting for Daddy," 94-5
Woloch, Nancy, 64, 74,
Women's Studies, bibliographies and anthologies 243
Woolf, Virginia, *A Room of One's Own*, 5-6, 103
Wright, Judith, "Eve to her Daughters," 146-7
Wright, Richard, *Native Son*, 183

W·R·I·T·I·N·G A·B·O·U·T W·O·M·E·N
Feminist Literary Studies

This is a literary series devoted to feminist studies on past and contemporary women authors, exploring social, psychological, political, economic, and historical insights directed toward an interdisciplinary approach.

The series is dedicated to the memory of Simone de Beauvoir, an early pioneer in feminist literary theory.

Persons wishing to have a manuscript considered for inclusion in the series should submit a letter of inquiry, including the title and a one-page abstract of the manuscript to the general editor:

Professor Esther K. Labovitz
Department of English
Pace University
Pace Plaza
New York, NY 10038
(212) 488-1416